AF505880

Letter to
King Richard II

PHILIPPE DE MEZIERES
Sometime Chancellor of Cyprus

Letter to King Richard II

A plea made in 1395 for peace
between England and France

Original text and English version of
Epistre au Roi Richart introduced and translated by

G. W. COOPLAND
Late Emeritus Professor of Medieval History
University of Liverpool

BARNES & NOBLE BOOKS · NEW YORK
A division of Harper and Row Publishers, Inc.
1976

ne pouure
et simple
epistre dun
vieil solitai
re des celestins de paris a
dieuuant. a tresexcellent et
trespuissant tres debon
naire catholique et tres
devost prince. Richart p
la grace de dieu roy da
gleterre &c. pour autu
ne confirmacion tele qle
de la vraye paix et amo
fraternelle du dit roy
dangleterre. et charles p
la grace de dieu roy
de france
Bone ihu scribe i
cor de meo uul
nera tua preciosissimo
sanguine tuo. ut sem
per cognoscam quid

Published in the U.S.A. 1976 by
HARPER & ROW PUBLISHERS
BARNES & NOBLE IMPORT DIVISION

ISBN 06 494794 7

First published 1976

Frontispiece
The opening page of the
British Library manuscript of
Epistre au Roi Richart
(MS. Royal 20.B vi, fo.2r)

Printed and bound in England by
Hazell Watson and Viney Ltd
Aylesbury, Bucks

PREFACE

I wish to make clear at the outset that my interest in this famous *Letter* is based on its value as a historical document, which helps to illustrate the thought and policy of the late fourteenth century in the West. I have not been concerned with its importance in the history of the French language or in its place in French prose literature. The sanctions invoked by the writer, his assumptions, and his methods of argument are the points which excite our interest and attention.

If we penetrate behind the screen of dream, parable, metaphor, and figure, to the essence of the *Letter*, we may find a certain freshness and nobility, in marked contrast to the meanness of motives in our own age; although this may not achieve the impossible of preventing the modern use of the epithet 'medieval' as a term of reproach and condemnation.

Philippe's view of the evils resulting from the French war, and of the harm done by the Great Schism of the West, his assessment of responsibility for the loss of Christian power in the Near East, are expressed with force and eloquence, and his conception of the Holy Places as being the 'public lands' of all Christendom is notable. To many the section of the *Letter* containing his arguments in favour of Richard's marriage to an infant daughter of Charles VI may appear the least convincing part of his work, although some justification for them may be found in his intense longing for the setting of a seal on a permanent peace between the two great Christian monarchies of the West.

A word may be said on the method of presentation of the manuscript here transcribed. The text itself contains fairly numerous minor errors, resulting apparently from the carelessness of the scribe, working presumably from dictation. None of these is sufficient to obscure meaning, and I have, after deliberation, preferred to leave the text in the form in which it reached Richard II. It may be added that in highly decorated 'Presentation Copies' of works in the period, similar and more frequent errors of transcription are often to be found.

In conclusion, I wish to tender my sincere thanks to the following for the help, advice, and encouragement they have given me in various ways during the preparation of this work: Professor A. S. Atiya, Professor G. Barraclough, Professor C. Brooke, Professor C. R. Cheney, Mrs. Ruth Morgan, Professor A. R. Myers, Dr. J. J. N. Palmer, Mr. P. G. Psaras,

Dr. C. H. Talbot, Professor F. W. Walbank, and Dr. Joan Williamson. I would record, too, my gratitude both to the British Academy for financial assistance towards the cost of preparation of this work, and to the University of Liverpool for a most generous grant towards the inevitable expenses of its publication. I have been fortunate in having the benefit of the expert technical help of the staff of Liverpool University Press. Finally, I have had throughout the advantage of essential aid from Miss Gertrude Winter.

G.W.C.

CONTENTS

INTRODUCTION

The Letter to Richard II, here introduced, was written by Philippe de
Mézières probably in mid May in the year 1395, when the writer was
aged 68 or 69. We propose now to offer such outline of his life as will
serve to illustrate those aspects of his career and character which bear on
the manner and content of the *Letter* itself. In undertaking such a
sketch, we are met at the outset by a peculiar difficulty. In later life,
that is in his fifties and onwards, Philippe was to become a prolific
writer, both in French and Latin. Scattered throughout his writings are
to be found many references to events in his experience, but unfortunately for the historian those references are never dated, or, at least,
dated with any precision.[1] Thus he tells us that he had been left for dead
on a battlefield, that he had been present in Naples at the time of the
assassination of the young King Andrew, that he had escaped from
corsairs at the entrance to the Adriatic, that he had passed some considerable time in Spain and had gazed from the Spanish shore near
Gibraltar across to the African coast, that he had travelled by sea to the
land of the Teutonic knights, that he had journeyed through the desert
of Sinai, and had met and talked with men who had lived in lands
beyond the European horizon. These are some but not all, of the ingredients of his biography, and we are often left to surmise as to where
in his career they are to be placed.

Philippe de Mézières, a junior member of a family of the lesser nobility, was born about 1327 in the Picard village of Mézières. At the age
of 18, following the fashion of the youth of the time, he left his home
and set out for Italy, presumably to seek adventure, and fought for a
short time in the service of Lucchino Visconti. Later in the same year
(1345), we find him at the court of Naples, on friendly terms with the
young King Andrew, and present in the city on the day of the assassination (18 September 1345).

We may be allowed to wonder how this youth of 18 or 19 was able

---

1. For example, *De la Chevallerie de la Passion de Jhesu Crist*, Arsenal MS. 2251,
f. 12v, 'Ardant Desir, lors jeune homme et petitement fondez en prudence et en science,
ne en la pratique du monde, combien qu'il eust este un bon temps soudoyer en Lombardie
pour aprendre le fait d'armes et au service du noble roy de Sicile, Andrieu, frere du
vaillant Loys, roy de Hongrie . . .'

to travel in this way and, although royalty was much more accessible in the fourteenth century than in more democratic times, how he could become so quickly on intimate terms with the young King. However this may be, in the following year Philippe took some part in the minor crusade of Humbert II of Dauphiné in the region of Smyrna, and we may guess that a Cypriot connection may have begun here. The expedition abandoned, Philippe moved on to the Holy Land, where he arrived at Jerusalem in the spring of 1347. Here we come to an experience that is crucial in his career. He tells us himself that he arranged for the celebration of a Mass in the Church of the Holy Sepulchre on behalf of 'an oriental prince' in whose service he was. This prince was almost certainly Peter, heir to the throne of Cyprus. At the same time, he records that, while worshipping in the Church, he had a vision, wherein Jesus Christ gave him the 'Tables of the Law', on which were inscribed the constitution and regulations of that Military Order of the Passion which he hoped to found. After the Mass, he enrolled two noblemen into his Order, one, Albert Pachost, a knight errant from Poland, the other, Etienne de Lucinge.[2] These details are important for the understanding of Philippe's mind and career. We are asked to accept the almost incredible, that this young man of under 20 had already formulated those ideals and aims which were to govern his outlook and direct his actions throughout a long life, and to which he clung so late as 1397, when any prospect of their fulfilment had already been lost in the disunion of the West and the disaster of Nicopolis.

After a short visit to Cyprus at the end of 1347, Philippe set out as representative of Prince Peter of Lusignan to seek support in the West for a crusade. This meant contacts with Pope Clement VI and John, duke of Normandy, future king of France. The mission failed, and now comes a gap in the record of some fourteen years. There is one brief appearance at Avignon in the autumn (?) of 1349, when he considered joining the ill-fated expedition of James II of Majorca to try to recover his kingdom.[3] It seems legitimate to suppose that it was during the earlier part of this interval that he passed a considerable time in Spain, perhaps in the service of Alphonso XI of Castille, or at least in close contact with that monarch. It was in Spain, too, that as *jeune et fol*, he became deeply affected by the astrological practices of the country,

2. Arsenal MS. 2251, f. 13r.
3. G. W. Coopland, *Le Songe du Vieil Pèlerin*, vol. i, p. 618; referred to hereafter as *Songe*.

which he was able to throw off only by long prayer and fasting.[4] The cynic might remark that if *'jeune et fol'* applied to his Spanish experiences, it applied still more to those in the Holy Land.

It also seems possible, if we may judge from various entries in the *Songe du Vieil Pèlerin*, that he was in the French royal service at some time in this period, and this is borne out by the known fact that, under the orders of Marshal Arnoul d'Audrehem, he presided over a trial by battle at Pontorson in September 1354.[5]

Perhaps it was at this time that Philippe made his journey, probably from some port in northern France, through the Kattegat, to visit Prussia and the Teutonic knights. And we are tempted to suppose that perilous voyages in the seas off the coast of Norway belong to these years,[6] voyages made the more perilous by the fact that northern navigators had not as yet adopted the mariner's compass.

We have now to accept an abrupt change of scene and the fact that by the autumn of 1361 Philippe was Chancellor of Cyprus at the age of 34. Peter had now succeeded to the throne of Cyprus and Jerusalem, and the two enthusiasts for the crusade, with the co-operation of the famous Carmelite, Pierre Thomas, Papal Legate in Cyprus, embarked on an intensive campaign of propaganda in the West, seeking support from kings, princes, and great nobles. In Philippe's own words, written at the age of 70, towards the close of a long career,

Il est verite que ledit solitaire en sa jeunesse avoit parfait desir, selon la capacite de son jeune sens et feble entendement, c'est assavoir pour la douleur qu'il avoit que la sainte cite de Jherusalem et la Terre-Sainte estoient en la main des ennemis de la foy, que une guerre se fist par les crestiens contre les Sarrasins pour recouvrer la dicte Terre-Sainte. Cestui grant desir lui fu tellement incorpore ou inspire que c'est la chose qu'il a plus desiree en ce monde, comme le scet Dieu, pour laquelle, c'est assavoir pour le saint passage . . . de par son maistre et seigneur le vaillant roy de Chipre, par XV ans ou environ, continuelment ne fist autre mestier que d'aler d'Orient en Occident, de Midi en Septentrion, a la plus grant partie des princes de la crestiente, a l'empereur de Romme Charle et aux autres roys, princes et communes de la crestiente.[7]

For the most part he was met by assurances of goodwill and little material assistance. The powers of Europe had other preoccupations. To this the footnote must surely be that the Ottoman Turks made their entry into Western Europe in 1356 and captured Adrianople in 1361.

4. *Songe* i, p. 518.   5. *Songe* ii, p. 279.
6. N. Jorga, *Philippe de Mézières, 1327–1405, et la croisade au XIVe siècle*, p. 249.
7. *Epistre Lamentable* in Kervyn de Lettenhove, *Oeuvres de Froissart*, t. 16, p. 507.

However, in 1365 a great expedition was prepared in Cyprus, Alexandria was attacked, captured, and pillaged, and success seemed assured. But with divided counsels and against the strong opposition of the King and Philippe, the Christian army withdrew.[8]

In spite of so decisive a setback, Philippe continued in the following years his attempts to rally the West to further crusading efforts, and this explains his presence in Venice when in January 1369, Peter of Cyprus was assassinated and his friends murdered or imprisoned.

Philippe remained in seclusion in Venice until early in 1372, when he went to Avignon to join the entourage of the newly elected pope, Gregory XI.[9] At the beginning of 1373, aged about 46, he returned to France, perhaps summoned by Charles V, and it was, henceforward, in that monarch, ten years his junior, that he placed his hopes. The keynote, indeed, of the next seven years in Philippe's life, is his close relationship with the French king, explicable only by the coincidence in views and hopes on the part of the two men.

Philippe was made a member of the King's Council, was entrusted with various missions, both charitable and of wider import, was allowed some share in the education of the future Charles VI, and was nominated as a member of the Council of Regency which was to govern after the King's death if need should arise. More important than all this, however, was his everyday intimacy with the King, their long conversations, and the recorded fact that Philippe sat for four hours with the King in his chariot on the way to Melun, listening to his views on the

8. *Songe* i, pp. 2–3, 297–8.

9. It is in this period that Philippe succeeded in introducing to the Western Church the Feast of the Presentation of the Blessed Virgin Mary, to which the date of 21 November had been assigned by the Eastern Church for many centuries. The establishment of the feast seems to have been associated 'cum representatione figurata', and received the official approval of the Church at Avignon under Gregory XI in 1372. A dramatic performance was probably given in that year under Philippe's direction, but apart from that, in one of the most illuminating manuscripts of the age, Bibl. Nat. MS. Lat. 17330, we have the record of the religious drama, written by Philippe himself, which was performed on the occasion of the celebration of the feast at Avignon in 1385. The stage setting is described in minute detail. The *dramatis personae* number 22. Among the chief characters are the small child who plays the part of the Virgin, Joachim and Anna her parents, Ecclesia, Synagoga, Lucifer, and so on. The language used is Latin, but the stage directions are so explicit and every movement and gesture of the principal characters so defined that a non-clerical audience could follow the action of the play. We might emphasize here Philippe's strong sense of theatre and almost Defoesque use of detail, illustrated by the minuteness of his description of the costume of each of his characters, a trait shown later in, for instance, his portraits of Pride, Avarice, and Luxury in the *Songe*, and in the topography of the two gardens in the *Epistre*. For full text and commentary see K. Young, *Drama of the Medieval Church*, pp. 225–45 and 472–9; cf. also Grace Frank, *Medieval French Drama*, pp. 64–65 and 70–73.

great problems of the day.[10] All this must be taken into account when we come to assess Philippe's qualities as the writer of this letter of advice to Richard II in 1395. On the material side, Charles V bestowed on his friend houses adjacent both to that palace of St. Pol which was the King's favourite dwelling-place, and to the newly consecrated Convent of the Celestines,[11] and, further, granted him important pensions.

On the outbreak of the Schism in 1378, Philippe, like official France, at first supported Urban, and then, with what seem sincere motives, accepted Clement.[12]

With the King's death in 1380 the situation changed abruptly. There followed the eight-year period of the minority of Charles VI, and of the rule of the great Princes of the Blood with their individual personal and dynastic preoccupations and their indifference to the public welfare.

Philippe retired to the Convent of the Celestines,[13] where he had already established a footing by substantial donations, including a little chapel, presumably that dedicated to the Virgin Mary in which he laid the opening and closing scenes of his *Songe du Vieil Pèlerin*. He was then able to speak of himself as 'un Celestin abortif', and, 'le vieil solitaire', though with some exaggeration, for it must be said that, although his astonishing energies were mainly employed in literary activity, he maintained contacts, both by interview and correspondence, with the outside world, and his recorded relations with Pierre d'Ailly, Bureau de la Rivière, the King of Armenia, Pierre de Luxembourg, and other notables of the time, do not suggest complete severance from events far removed from the austere life of the Celestines. On the other hand, Jorga's thesis that 'Il n'y a pas de grand événement à cette époque, oú l'on ne puisse retrouver l'influence de Philippe de Mézières', requires some modification.

In December 1388, the King assumed his majority, and there seemed now some justification for the hopes of men of goodwill for peace with

---

10. *Songe* ii, p. 296.

11. Although Philippe always speaks as if residing permanently at the Convent, we may note that a certain Thomassin le Valois, charged with murder in 1389 before the Criminal Court at the Châtelet, included in his statement to the Court the fact that he had worked for a long time at the house of Philippe de Mézières at Verberie (arr. de Senlis, Oise). See Duplès-Agier, *Registre Criminel*, t. i, p. 146.

12. *Songe* i, p. 369.

13. The editors of the *Catalogue of Western MSS in the Old Royal and King's Collections of the British Museum* are in error in describing Philippe as a member of the Order.

England and some measure of reform in the administration of the kingdom of France. Philippe's hopes and fears are now expressed in the lengthy *Songe du Vieil Pèlerin* and the *Oratio Tragedica*. The latter, unfortunately still unpublished, belongs to the second half of 1389 and displays a curious alternation on the author's part between hope and despair, between the brutal disappointments of the past and anticipations of a better future. With the conclusion of the truce with England in the first half of 1389 and the continuation of negotiations directed towards the establishment of permanent peace, the political weather appeared to favour a renewal of effort, and it was in this atmosphere that the *Epistre au Roi Richart* was written.

Now, wise after the events, we know that the disaster of Nicopolis (1396) was to end all hope of united opposition to the Turkish advance, although this was still not accepted by Philippe in his *Epistre Lamentable*,[14] addressed to Philip of Burgundy in 1397, in which he clings with pathetic stubbornness to his lifelong dreams.

Of the remaining years of Philippe's life, until his death in 1405,[15] we have little knowledge. His retirement from affairs was almost complete, his contacts with the court few, except for his friendship with Louis of Orleans, the King's brother, who may have shared his hopes for Christian unity and dreams of advance to the East.

THE RECIPIENT: RICHARD II

The historians have examined the reign of Richard II with considerable thoroughness,[16] and much speculation as to the character, personality and motives of the King has resulted. Further the genius of Shakespeare has presented us with a picture which may or may not portray accurately King Richard of England; fiction and legend are often stronger and more enduring than history. Here we need select for consideration only those features of the reign which may help us to assess the value of Philippe's *Epistre* and the justification or otherwise for its composition.

Although the natural and traditional method is to treat the King and royal power as focal point, there is much to be said in favour of an

---

14. Edited by Kervyn de Lettenhove in *Oeuvres de Froissart*, t. 16, pp. 490–523.

15. See Jorga, op. cit., pp. 511–12 for details of his tomb and epitaphs.

16. For the standard account of the reign see Anthony Steel, *Richard II* (1962). For specialized studies see Gervase Mathew, *The Court of Richard II* (1968); Deryk Brewer, *Chaucer in his Time* (1968); M. V. Clarke, *Fourteenth Century Studies*, ed. L. S. Sutherland and M. McKisack (1937).

approach to the problems of the reign by way of consideration of the so-called magnates, as supplement to this natural and traditional method. With this aspect in view we have surveyed a dozen of the great families whose names occur and recur during the reign.[17] These are the people who, with the King's uncles, during the minority and at important points in the reign, obscured the king and his authority and finally destroyed them. Though in theory none denied royal power, theory and practice were widely divergent. The deposition of Edward II by his barons[18] and the enforced concessions extracted from Edward III, together with the long minority of Richard, had brought about an increased focusing of social and political power in the hands of the magnates, which they were to relinquish slowly and reluctantly. Results of the survey of these families are surprising and bewildering, for we are presented with a kaleidoscope of marriages, alliances, acquisitions, and divisions.[19] Certain general statements may be useful. Thus, nearly all the families under consideration were linked by blood or marriage tie with Henry III and his descendants. The adequate presentation of this ruling section of society offers extreme difficulties and the danger of descent into indigestible catalogues is obvious; but we may epitomize the scene by stressing that genealogical tables are among the most important illustrative documents for the reign.

This society was curiously cosmopolitan,[20] and the fact that Richard's immediate ancestry was English stands out in marked contrast to that of his predecessors. Richard himself, however, was the son-in-law of the Emperor Charles IV and, later, of King Charles VI of France, though, on the whole, as the century moved to its end, his contemporaries were turning more to marriage alliances within the realm.

In contrast to the position in France, where the rulers of Navarre,

17. These include the Arundels, Beauchamps, de Bohuns, de Burghs, Clares, Courtenays, Hollands, Mortimers, Mowbrays, Nevilles, Percies, and Staffords.

18. Many of them the ancestors of the chief actors in Richard's reign.

19. This is not the place in which to enlarge on this theme, but from an examination of the *état civil* of some three hundred or so members of noble families, and allowing for the incompleteness of the evidence, certain lines of inquiry suggest themselves. These include child marriages and the reasons therefor, second and third marriages, numbers of children, child mortality rate, causes of death, especially among males, and so on. And behind all this, we may recognize the innumerable occasions presented by this network of relationships for discussion, gossip, plot, and quarrels, that lay beneath much of the diplomacy of the time. The summit conference of those days, as now, emerged from a tangle of argument and conflict of interests.

20. It includes alliances between great English families and those of Scotland, Ireland, Wales, France, Spain, Portugal, Denmark and Sweden, Gelderland, Hainault, Milan, Bar, Brabant, Navarre, Holland, and Brittany.

Brittany, Foix, Burgundy, and Bourbon threatened the House of Valois, English nobles held widely scattered lands, and tended to group them for administrative purposes rather than to create territorial blocks.[21] Hence we get such apparent incongruities as the duke of Lancaster holding manors in Sussex. At the same time, it must be emphasized that the greater among these magnates managed their possessions in semi-regal fashion,[22] with large staffs of chancellors, stewards, accountants, household servants, justices, and so on, and the breakdown of the military side of the feudal system involved the creation of small private armies of indentured retainers.

It is this vast complex that we have to see as obscuring real exercise of royal authority at various points of the reign, and out of it comes one particular combination which resulted in the ruin and death of Richard II.

Coming to closer quarters with the Richard of 1395, we see a recently widowed king, aged 28, with behind him, first, a minority of comparative insignificance, broken only by the episode of his part in the Peasants' Revolt, which we may accept as an episode and nothing more (except in so far as it may have had effect on his character), and on which it is dangerous to build theories; a period of increasing frustration as he grew older; the revolutionary proceedings, in July 1386, of the establishment of the Committee of Government, which practically took over royal power: one might almost call this a sort of preliminary deposition of the king, a prelude and rehearsal of the final disaster of 1399; Richard's abortive attempt to assert himself by questioning the legality of this Committee, and the subsequent triumph of a group of the magnates, known as the Lords Appellant, marked by the defeat of the King's friends at Radcot Bridge (1387), and followed by the activities of the Merciless Parliament and the execution, imprisonment, or exile of his chief supporters; finally, as bearing on the Richard of 1395, his successful assertion and proclamation in Parliament of his majority in May 1389. To all this must be added his happy marriage to Anne of Bohemia (1382) and her sudden death in June 1394. From 1389 to 1397 there ensued a period of comparative calm and constitutional government, during which we may see the restraining influence of John of Gaunt and William of Wykeham, and the capable administration of faithful subordinates.

21. See G. Mathew, op. cit., p. 112.
22. See G. A. Holmes, *The Estates of the Higher Nobility in Fourteenth Century England.*

Richard, then, in the year 1395, the year in which he received the *Epistre*, was established as King, with his court not unlike, except in scale, those of contemporary princes. Like many of them he loved fashionable clothes (and fashion was influential then as now) and jewellery, was extravagant in building, and appeared to have some interest in letters. During his childhood, in the household of his mother, Joan of Kent, he had had direct or indirect contact with such people as Sir Lewis Clifford, the friend of Deschamps, and Sir John Clanvowe, the author of what has been described as 'the best Chaucerian poem that is not by Chaucer',[23] and, later, in his own court he had as one of his intimates Sir John Montague, later earl of Salisbury, friend and adviser of Christine de Pisan, and writer of poems in French. Anne of Bohemia, Richard's first wife, had grown up in a cultivated atmosphere.[24] Richard himself must have been almost bilingual, like many of his contemporaries, in French and English, and, perhaps, had some knowledge of Latin.[25]

It was the year 1386, probably, when Chaucer had been deprived of his offices by the duke of Gloucester, that saw the beginning of his work on the *Canterbury Tales*, and it is of the greatest significance that these *Tales*, the real foundation of one of the greatest European literatures, were written in English[26] and were probably read and heard at the royal court.[27] It may be suggested that England on the literary side, was

23. *The Book of Cupid, or, the Cuckoo and the Nightingale.* He was also the author of a religious treatise (now in the Bodleian Library), which is a forthright condemnation of the accepted chivalric ideals of the age as personified in the Black Prince and Chandos, and of the splendours of court life.

24. See G. Mathew, op. cit., pp. 16–17.

25. Froissart (Kervyn de Lettenhove, op. cit., t. 15, pp. 140–2) tells us that he brought to Richard from France a book of poems, which, after some delay, he presented to the King at Eltham. The King took it and, after admiring the handsome binding and inquiring what the poems were about, opened the book and read some passages aloud.

26. For study of the use of spoken and written English, French, and Latin in England, see D. Brewer, op. cit., pp. 15–17, 134–5 and 193–5.

27. It seems fairly safe to assume that entertainment at the court, besides readings by poets of their works, included the presentation from time to time of 'Interludes' or 'Entremés' of the kind, though on a much less elaborate scale, as that studied by Mrs. Loomis in her article in *Speculum*, vol. xxxiii, pp. 242–55, Secular dramatics in the Royal Palace, 1378, 1389, and Chaucer's *tregetoures*. The first of these was presented during the feast given by Charles V in honour of the Emperor Charles IV on the occasion of his visit to Paris in 1378. It portrayed the siege and capture of Jerusalem by Godfrey de Bouillon, and Mrs. Loomis ascribes its composition and stage management to Philippe de Mézières. This seems possible though, of course, it remains an assumption. Philippe certainly was at great pains in the *Songe* to describe the stage setting at the various consistories held by Queen Truth and her attendants in their journey round the world. Cf. also Brewer, op. cit., p. 182.

Though not strictly relevant to our main theme, we may note in connection with

beginning to emerge from Europe. Further, we may add that the description of Chaucer's Squire,

> He could make songs and poems and recite,
> Knew how to joust and dance, to draw and write.

may be applied in some degree to Richard the King as well as to other young nobles of his day. It is true that Richard did not distinguish himself in combat in the lists, the popular spectacle of the day, nor did he choose, as his cousin Bolingbroke and John Montague did, to make the laborious journey to Lithuania to take some part in the crusades of the Teutonic knights. This journey was in itself a sort of joust, and we need not credit Bolingbroke and others with any burning zeal for the conversion of the heathen Lithuanians to Christianity.

We have next to consider Richard's attitude towards the question of peace with France. Froissart may be taken as representing opinion, prevalent both in Richard's immediate entourage and abroad, that the time had come to end a war which had lasted intermittently for half a century.[28] Richard, immediately after assuming royal power, started a series of embassies and conversations, mainly at Leulinghen, and, at the time of the receipt of the *Epistre*, a truce, an extension of earlier ones, was in full force. The story of truce-making in the period is a complicated one and it will suffice to say that this truce may be taken to represent a general but not universal desire for peace on both sides of the Channel. It is a period of innumerable meetings and negotiations and postponements, for hawks[29] as well as doves were involved, as is well illustrated in the *Songe*. Towards the end of their journey, Queen Truth and her companions, Mercy, Peace, and Justice, arrive in London, and hold a Consistory in 'the great Church'. Although 'les bourgois' and 'le commun' are present, it is to the King's uncles, the chivalry, the King, and the clergy that the Queen and her companions address themselves. From a mass of somewhat confused and incongruous metaphor

---

Philippe's strong sense of 'theatre', Karl Young's discovery of the text and stage directions of the liturgical play on the Presentation of the Virgin Mary at the Temple, which has its place in the history of the French theatre. See n. 9, p. xii above; and for Philippe's possible connection with the play *L'Estoire de Griseldis*, see n. 53, p. xxix below.

28. Echoing Philippe's words, Froissart attributes to Richard the conviction that the war had lasted too long, that too many brave men had been slain, too many evil deeds perpetrated and too many Christians sent to perdition. See Kervyn de Lettenhove, op. cit., t. 15, p. 155.

29. The attitude of Gloucester on various occasions affords sufficient testimony to this.

and allegory, certain points may be noted. The King's uncles, his father, and grandfather are described as Black Boars, which have for years ravaged the vineyards of France, but one of them has miraculously begotten a White Boar: Richard II. But the Black Boars have not only put restraint on the exercise of his royal powers, they have also impeded his efforts to achieve the peace with France which he ardently desires. Philippe's account of the ending of the consistory is important. As the visitors prepared for departure, there was a great murmuring among the audience. The older soldiers, veterans of the war, and the archers, showed their disagreement, but there were some among the knights, along with the merchants, who would have shown their dislike of the war but for fear of the Black Boars and, in particular, of the earl of Arundel.[30]

In any assessment of the situation, we have to realize that there were many to whom the war had been a career, and a profitable one, for the intervals between the landmarks of Crécy, Poitiers, and Bretigny have to be filled in by a state of continuous border warfare and plunder. There was a business side to the chivalry of the age and the capture of a wealthy opponent meant a large sum in the way of ransom.[31] Genius epitomizes all this in a few words: Ancient Pistol, in whose knowledge of the French language there appear to have been gaps, says to his French opponent at Agincourt, 'What is your name?' The Frenchman cries out, 'O, Seigneur Dieu!' on which Pistol comments, 'Signeur Dew should be a gentleman.'[32] There was also ransom in a minor, though wider, sense as applied to the universal habit of marauding soldiery of forcing the peasant to buy back from them his own property.[33] Another factor in the attitude of those opposing peace with France was that, despite immense courage and hardihood, there was clearly to be seen in the character of a Bertrand du Guesclin or a Black Prince a certain brutality which would scarcely tend to include them

30. See *Songe* i, pp. 395–403.

31. For an example of what could be gained in the way of plunder, see Duplès-Agier, op. cit., t. ii, pp. 177–213, the trial of Merigot Marchès; and for an illustration of the means by which ransom might be assessed, see the same work, t. i, pp. 379–93, the trial of Hennequin du Bos, who while a prisoner of the English at Carlisle gave information concerning the finances of other prisoners.

32. For the profit and loss side of war see also *Coriolanus*, Act I, Sc. v, Enter certain Romans, with spoils.

First Roman. This will I carry to Rome.

Second Roman. And I this.

Third Roman. A murrain on't! I took this for silver.

33. See G. W. Coopland, *Tree of Battles*, pp. 56–57 and notes.

among the doves. To the merchant and the peasant their better qualities were not so obvious.

Closely connected with the possibilities of peace with France was the question of the royal marriage between Richard and Isabel, the little daughter of the French king, which was to put, as it were, the seal on such a treaty of peace. Dr. J. J. N. Palmer has recently examined very closely and with great skill the background to this marriage.[34] For our purpose it is sufficient to note that possibilities of an alliance other than that with the House of Valois were receiving some consideration at the time (how seriously it is difficult now to say), for example with the house of Aragon, with that of Bar, with Alençon, and also with the Harcourt family. But it seems clear that French pressure was strong for a French marriage alliance, and we are told that Richard himself found the prospect very pleasing.[35] The net result was that Richard's marriage, on 4 November 1396, to a girl of 7 or 8 years was to be the final 'confirmation' of peace between England and France. The way was now to lie open, at least in theory, for the combined strength of England and France to rally the forces of Christian Europe for great enterprises in the Near East. But events did not favour the programme, and within a matter of weeks came news from Nicopolis,[36] the answer to many questions.

CHARLES VI, KING OF FRANCE

The views, hopes, and plans set forth in the *Epistre* are those of Philippe de Mézières and are expressed by him in his own personal fashion. It seems clear, however, that they were the views also of Charles VI. It is, indeed, round the persons of the two monarchs, of England and France respectively, that all projects for peace revolve.

34. See *Bulletin of the Institute of Historical Research*, vol. xliv (May 1971) for the background to Richard II's marriage to Isabel of France (1396).

35. Froissart, after mentioning the possibilities of alliances with Burgundy, Hainault, etc., goes on to say that Richard was much drawn to the idea of a French marriage, and to those who objected on the grounds of the Princess's youth, he appears to have replied with the same arguments put forward by Philippe in the *Epistre*, '. . . on luy a dit que la fille du roy de France est trop jeune et que encoires dedens cinq ou six ans il ne s'en pourroit aidier; mais il a respondu et dit ainsi que Dieu y ait part, et qu'elle croistra en eage, et trop plus chier pour le present il l'a joeune que aagie. Et a ce il baille raison selon sa plaisance et ymagination, et dit ainsi, que se il le (*sic*) a joeune, il la duira et ordonnera a sa voulente et la mettera et enclinera a la maniere d'Angleterre, et que il est encoires jeune asses pour attendre tant que la dame soit en eage competant.' Kervyn de Lettenhove, op. cit., t. 15, pp. 155–6.

36. The battle was fought 28 September 1396, and the news reached the French court on Christmas Day. For detailed account of the battle see A. S. Atiya, *The Crusade of Nicopolis* (1934).

Charles VI, 'the Well-Beloved', was born on 3 December 1368, and was thus two years junior to his future son-in-law, Richard II. His father, Charles the Wise, of far from robust constitution, died on 16 September 1380, at the age of 43, after having achieved considerable success both in the English war, 'sitting in his chair',[37] and in bringing comparative order into the administration of his domains. The controlling hand removed, effective power fell to the King's uncles, and it is their ambitions and interests that prevail over good government in the following years. They were lords of great territories and showed little sense of what we may call 'national' interests. Louis of Anjou (1339–84) went off on the Sicilian adventure (1382); John, duke of Berry (1340–1416) by his lack of co-operation, caused the abandonment of a serious project for the invasion of England, and later became notorious for his maladministration of Languedoc; Philippe, duke of Burgundy (1342–1404), the youngest of the King's uncles, by his marriage in 1369 to Marguerite, daughter of Louis de Male, count of Flanders, had begun the long progress of the house of Burgundy towards the possible revival of the Middle Kingdom; Louis II, duke of Bourbon (1337–1410), the King's maternal uncle, perhaps the worthiest and least influential of them all, turned his attention to other spheres of activity and undertook, with Genoese patronage, the African expedition of 1390.

Charles's childhood and youth were passed in the fashion of the time. That most unbiased source, the Royal Accounts, include sums paid towards the cost of games of dice, his activities in the 'jeu de paume', in the practice of archery, for 'vessies de beuf . . . pour l'esbatement du roy', for playing pitch and toss, and for buying musical instruments, for falconry, and for purchasing collars for his greyhounds. There were sums paid out for rewarding those who had entertained the King, such as his fool, minstrels, Marie d'Arraz, a singer, and a diver. The purchase of ink and parchment to make 'copybooks' for the King and his brother Louis is also noted. One item which deserves to be rescued from the obscurity of these accounts is the sum of money he gave to the carpenters on the occasion of his visit of inspection to what was to be one of the world's most famous buildings, the Bastille of St. Anthony, then at the modest beginnings of its four hundred years of history.[38] The significance of one event in the King's youth is difficult to estimate. In

37. *Songe* i, p. 552.
38. See L. C. Douët-d'Arcq, *Comptes de l'Hôtel des rois de France aux XIVe et XVe siècles*, pp. 176, 178, 185, 208, 211, 212, 213, 234, 235 ff.

November 1382, shortly before his fourteenth birthday, probably at his own insistance, he was allowed to accompany the French army to Rosebecq, and, although perhaps kept away from the main battle, must have witnessed some of the horrors of hand-to-hand fighting.

In 1385 the King married Isabel of Bavaria, and in December 1388 he declared his majority and there followed a short period of hope for men of goodwill, whom Philippe de Mézières may be taken to represent. But this was tragically ended by the King's attack of frenzy in August 1392. The remedies suggested by his physicians were the obvious ones of rest and quiet, and these seem to have been for a while effective. Then came the almost incredible events of the night of 31 January 1393, when the King and some friends took part in a sort of masque, the so-called Bal des Sauvages. Five of them were burnt to death when their clothes caught fire, and the King himself was only saved through the presence of mind of the duchess of Berry. A second bad attack of frenzy resulted. This brain sickness, whatever its cause and nature, was to recur at increasingly frequent intervals throughout the remaining thirty years of his unhappy reign, and the results both for high policy and administration need not be elaborated.

Finally, to add a little to our picture of the Charles VI of the *Epistre*, we may turn to those chapters of the *Songe*,[39] in which Philippe is offering counsel for the King's behaviour, significant for the manners of the time and the King's own way of life. Two main facts emerge from study of these most illuminating passages: the first is that the King kept such late nights as to render him incapable of effective participation in the work of his councils, for he might sit there yawning and half asleep while important decisions were being taken; secondly, that at this stage in his life, Charles was feverishly addicted to violent sport and exercise. This, then, was the young man from whom, six or seven years later, such great enterprises were expected and demanded by the writer of the *Epistre*.

THE MESSENGER: ROBERT THE HERMIT[40]

In the *Epistre*, Philippe anticipates the criticism of those who might urge that his knowledge of Richard II was not first-hand, but purely

39. *Songe* ii, pp. 206–8, 212–14.
40. The following account is based mainly on Léon Puiseux, *Robert l'Ermite*, Mém. de la Soc. des Antiq. de Normandie, vol. xxiv (1859).

hearsay. To this objection he replies that he has been fully informed of the King's personal attractiveness by the messengers sent, both openly and secretly, to the King of England by his beloved brother, King Charles, and, in particular, by that worthy man of God, Robert the Hermit, the special messenger, under God, between the two kings, who has, further, assured him of Richard's desire to support the project for the deliverance of the Holy Land. In passing, it is noteworthy that Philippe, whose journeys extended from Alexandria to Lithuania, to the Norwegian seas, and to the Straits of Gibraltar, had never travelled the short distance that separated him from England. There is a passage in the *Epistre*, however, which shows a fairly close, albeit indirect, personal contact between the author and King Richard. He expressly states that he had recently handed to the King's half-brother, John Holland, the earl of Huntingdon, a copy of his work, *La Sustance Abregie*,[41] concerning his Order of the Passion, which the latter was to present to the King.

Robert le Mennot, to be known later as Robert the Hermit, was born at Dieppe about 1343, of noble family, related to Guillaume de Martel, Sire de Basqueville, a member of the King's household. Like many youths of his station in life in this restless age, and indeed like Philippe himself earlier, he sought adventure with armies in Greece and Syria, in the countries of the Turks and the Tartars, and in the Holy Land. We are told that late in 1392 he took passage at Beirut in a Genoese vessel bound for Europe. At the height of a violent storm near the island of Rhodes, while praying for the safety of the ship and those on board, Robert heard, coming from a great brilliance which enveloped him, a voice, telling him that his prayer would be answered and that all would be saved, and, further, that he was commanded by God to go to the King of France and bid him make peace with his enemy of England. When the two sides had met to discuss terms, he was to take a bold part in the meeting and speak out in favour of peace. Those unwilling to listen to his message would pay dearly for their refusal. In due time Robert landed in safety at Genoa and made his way thence to the papal court at Avignon. From Avignon he journeyed to Paris, preaching the need for peace as he went, and earning the title of 'the Hermit' by his eloquence, simplicity, and austere way of life.

41. *La Sustance de la Chevalerie de la Passion de Jhesu Crist*, Bodleian Library, Ashmole 813, ed. A. H. Hamdy, in *Bulletin of the Faculty of Arts* (Alexandria University, Egypt), vol. xviii (1964).

The negotiations for peace were in progress between English and French representatives at Leulinghen, and King Charles was actually nearby at Abbeville, where Robert, arriving at Eastertime, in April 1393, was introduced to him by his kinsman Guillaume de Martel. Charles listened to his plans with great interest and seemed to conceive a strong liking for the Hermit. From a somewhat confused story told by those present at the conference at Leulinghen, it is clear that Robert, with the approval of Burgundy and the Chancellor, Arnaud de Corbie, was allowed to take an important part in the discussions. It is notable that among his arguments in favour of peace he laid strong emphasis on the pressing danger presented by Turkish advance into the Eastern Empire. His eloquence made a considerable impression on the English delegates, including John of Gaunt, but with the notable exception of the earl of Arundel and the duke of Gloucester, the former of whom, it may be remembered was singled out by Philippe for special condemnation in the *Songe*.[42] We may assume that it is from this point that Robert's mission as 'special messenger under God' began. We do know that in the spring of 1395 he arrived in England bearing letters to Richard and his uncles from Charles, dated 15 May, including perhaps the *Epistre*.[43] He met the King at Eltham, where he was warmly received, and, during a month's stay, there was ample opportunity for discussion of the questions of the day, including peace, a royal alliance, the healing of the Schism, and the possibilities of a joint Crusade.

The rest of Robert's career does not directly concern us here. He continued to play a part in the long negotiations for the ending of the Schism, and was still active as late as 1407.

It may be noted that there is a serious gap in the evidence needed for making an accurate assessment of the influence exerted by such worthies as Robert (and, indeed, Philippe himself) on opinion and events of their age. We know, roughly, what they did and something of what they said. What we do not know is the secret of the impression they made on their contemporaries. There was, evidently, some overflow and expression of deep inner conviction, what we vaguely call personality, which had a profound, if often transient, effect on their hearers. Enthusiasm may not lead to action and much of human history reflects the transition of spirit into letter.

---

42. *Songe* i, p. 403.   43. See J. J. N. Palmer, op. cit.

GENERAL SURVEY OF THE *EPISTRE*

The *Epistre* may be taken as the definitive expression of a policy of reconciliation between the crowns of England and France, which had been endangered by counter-proposals involving a possible Aragonese alliance.[44] It may be said to break through and defeat a project, perhaps favoured by Richard himself, by offering a richer prize. We are inclined to compare the *Epistre* with the summit conference of which we hear so much in our day, for it followed the exchange of letters and embassies of a tentative sort, and there can be little doubt that the letter of 15 May 1395, reproduced by Lettenhove,[45] bears the same relationship to the *Epistre* that Philippe's *Sustance abregie de la Chevalerie* bears to his larger exposition, *De la Chevallerie de la Passion de Jhesu Crist.*[46]

The *Epistre* is not in any strict sense of the word a letter, but rather the medium employed by Philippe to set forth his views and pleadings on the great issues of the day. These are, first, the establishment and confirmation of a lasting peace between England and France, and the solution of this is to be the key to the settlement of the vital question of the division of Christendom resulting from the Great Schism of the West, and second, the creation of the new Order of the Passion, which, in turn, is to make possible the journey of the two kings to the Holy Land. The seal to be set upon the peace which may lead to these desired objectives is a marriage alliance between the royal families of France and England, in the persons of Isabel, infant daughter of Charles VI, and Richard II of England.

As an observation preliminary to any analysis of the *Epistre*, it is to be noted that in spite of incongruities of presentation, the unacceptable metaphors, the repetitions and apparent naïveties, the people concerned were living in their own modern times, and that the issues raised represent the burning questions of the day, and were just as real as any which trouble our own age, though perhaps not so universal.

There are three factors in the Old Solitary's presentation of his case which may conveniently be mentioned here as applying to the whole tenor of the treatise. There is first the question of sanctions, and here the answer may be given without qualification that these are to be found

44. See J. J. N. Palmer, op. cit.
45. Kervyn de Lettenhove, op. cit., t. 15, pp. 388–90.
46. Arsenal MS. 2251.

in the Scriptures, and, particularly, in the Christian doctrine as set forth in the New Testament. Such sanctions were recognized even in the pleadings before the Parlement of Paris, and it may be added that there is no suggestion that Christian teaching should be modified to suit the manners of contemporary society. It is, rather, society which has to be changed to accord with divine teaching.

Next, any argument based on possible economic advantage resulting from the Anglo-French alliance is lacking, although Philippe, in the narrower sphere of his plans for Crusade, was quite prepared for detailed examination of the cost of the expedition.[47]

Finally, there is the curious feature that Philippe at no point makes any reference to the fact that the unfortunate Charles VI, whose views he claimed to represent, was at intervals by no means in his perfect mind. It is true, however, that in the letter of 15 May, ostensibly from Charles to Richard, but almost certainly the work of Philippe, the French King does assure Richard that at the moment of writing he is *en bon point*.

Examination of our document reveals two major aspects: (*a*) as a phase in the Hundred Years' War, of which we know the consequences; (*b*) as a view of thought and methods of argument of a past age. The first can be dismissed fairly briefly. The effects of the movement represented by the *Epistre* were, as we know, transitory. Nicopolis, the deposition and death of Richard II, the civil war in France, and the renewed English invasion were history's reply to Philippe's pleadings.

It must be confessed that some effort is required from the twentieth-century reader before he can penetrate through this strange jumble of allegory, parable, and figurative writing, to the real concern of the author with the problems of his time and his concrete suggestions for their solution. The document, however, remains of considerable value as illustrating the approach and methods of an intelligent man, of very wide experience, who, although he speaks of himself as an Old Solitary, was a Solitary who had spent much time at the courts of popes and kings[48] and was still, in old age, in contact with those in authority.

We proceed now to outline briefly the salient features of the *Epistre*, noting in analysing his treatment by allegory and parable that the underlying theme throughout is peace between England and France

47. See especially *Nova Religio Passionis*, Mazarine MS. 1943, and cf. *Songe* ii, pp. 435–40.

48. *Epistre*, f. 38v.

and the ending of the shedding of Christian blood by Christians. The work opens with a Prologue, in which the writer announces his intention of dealing with his subject under nine different headings or 'matters', 'in sacred memory of the nine orders of angels'.

His first chapter introduces the central allegory of Charles VI of France as personified by the sacred balm, potent for the healing of wounds, and Richard II of England as the lodestone with its power of attraction. With an abrupt and not easily acceptable change of metaphor, the balm becomes a shining carbuncle, or ruby, and the lodestone a precious diamond.[49]

Next comes his solution for the healing of the Schism. The Church is the wounded and divided Mother, and her wound must be healed by the joint action of the two kings, who are called upon to emulate the sacrifice of Curtius in his leap into the stinking gulf.

The wounds which symbolize the French war and the Schism are grievous ones, but there is one more grievous still, which casts shame on all Christendom, namely the downfall of Christian power in the Holy Land. In his third chapter Philippe uses with great skill the parable of the kings Malavisé and Vigilant,[50] to analyse with considerable accuracy the situation in this regard, showing clearly the internal reasons for the defeat of Christianity in the Orient, the lack of both unity and good administration, and at the same time debiting their share of the blame to the princes of the West, who had failed to respond to a call for help from their brethren in the Holy Land.[51] The twentieth-century reader may be tempted to reflect on the causes for the advance of heathendom westward in his own age. The remedy proposed by Philippe, the adoption of which he had been urging for forty years, consists of the famous

49. All that Philippe says concerning precious stones and their properties is to be found in the *Mineralium* of Albertus Magnus (*Opera Omnia*, vol. v, lib. i [Paris, 1890]). This includes his statements on the carbuncle, p. 32; the lodestone (magnes), p. 40; the emerald (smaragdus), p. 45; and the diamond (adamas), p. 30; always with the proviso that Philippe's remarks are not necessarily based on first-hand reading.

50. At first sight this seems to be a straightforward reference to a work well-known to Philippe and his contemporaries. Long research, however, and a series of inquiries in many quarters have failed to furnish a clue to the work or to the very well-told story of Malavisé and Vigilant. After many years spent in Philippe's company, I find it hard to believe that he has invented both the name of the work and the parable extracted from it. He is certainly capable of borrowing from other sources without acknowledgement, in the manner of his age, but I have not found examples of actual invention of both source and quotation. For the time being, *faute de mieux*, I must leave the problem as one awaiting solution.

51. For the background to the dwindling of Christian power in the Holy Land, see Robin Fedden, *Syria and Lebanon*, ch. 7, 'Crusader castles', especially pp. 180–2.

Order of the Passion, by the creation of which the energy of the chivalry of the West was to be diverted from the shedding of Christian blood to the explusion of the Infidel from the Holy Places. It must be admitted that Philippe shows little concern over the shedding of the blood of the followers of Mohammed. A special feature of the proposed New Order was that it was to act as a sort of vanguard, which would seize such ports and strong places as would enable the two kings, of France and England, to disembark in safety and lead the committed Christian armies to complete victory.

In his fourth chapter, or matter, the writer may be said to be preparing the groundwork for his later strong pleadings in favour of a marriage alliance between the royal houses of France and England. It is noteworthy that it is here that we have plain evidence that other marriage projects were not without powerful advocates in certain quarters in England, rumours of which had reached France. The method employed is an interesting comparison between medicines which were pleasant to taste because of their sugar coating, which hid inner bitterness, and medicines of gentler but more lasting benefit.[52] A long dis-

52. Philippe's observations throughout the *Letter* throw much light on medical practice in his day, as regards both diagnosis and treatment. The patient's horoscope was accepted as guide to his constitution, and the position of the planets ruling at the onset of his illness was taken into serious account as indication of the required treatment. In 1363, Guy de Chauliac, physician to Pope Urban V (1362–70), issued his treatise entitled *Cyrurgia*, and Philippe may well have been acquainted both with him and his work. Other handbooks for treatment were in common use and often included diagrams illustrating the planetary influences affecting various parts of the body. One might almost call them medical ready-reckoners.

As regards specific remedies mentioned by Philippe, balm, or balsam, was one of the most widely used unguents, and its properties were deemed to be those claimed by him; popilion was an ointment derived from the berries of the poplar tree, mixed with other herbs and plants; *unguentum apostolorum* was so named because it contained twelve ingredients, and it was also called *gracia Dei* in some English leech books of the period. Scammony, digridium (juice of scammony), and aloes were used as purgatives, though the dangers of their over-violent action were recognized. Cassia fistula and manna were other purgatives of gentler nature, which were considered to be more in accord with the human constitution. Catholicon was the universal remedy of the time.

In contrast to the above, we note the following passage which occurs in *De la Chevallerie de la Passion de Jhesu Crist* (Arsenal MS. 2251, f. 27v), 'Vous devez savoir . . . que le fin triacle est composez du plus fort venin que on puet recouvrer des bestes plus venimeuses, sicomme serpens, dragons, regles, tarantes, aregnies, escorpions et autres bestes venimeuses. De tout cestuy venim perilleux, foule et bien batu en un mortier, le maistre qui ne redoubte point ledit venin en fait et compose le fin triacle qui guerist les personnes envenimees, qui est un grant miracle en nature, c'estassavoir que venin doye estre enchassie par venin, qui est contre la regle de medecine qui dit le contraire se cure par son contraire.'

Philippe's idea that poison could be cured, as it were, by poison, may have derived from his contacts with Arabs, either in Cyprus or in Palestine, to whom this principle, opposed to Western theory and practice, appears to have been known.

sertation on marriage leads to wide use of examples, mainly from the Scriptures but also extending to famous men of the ancient and medieval world. In a final warning to Richard, he begs him to remember the disastrous results of his great-grandfather's marriage, which led to the infliction of that wound which Richard has been called upon to heal, and goes on to express the hope that he may be granted a wife such as that Griselda of whom Petrarch wrote.[53]

The next chapter of the treatise may be described as a sort of post-script to and elaboration of the theme introduced at the conclusion of the previous section. By the grotesque story of the harpy and a detailed account of the failure of Moses and Aaron to sanctify God at the Waters of Strife, by which they forfeited their right to lead the Israelites into the Promised Land, Richard and Charles are warned against the terrible possibilities of the renewal of the war.

I am indebted for the substance of the above note, and for that on *boucon* (n. 4, p. 19, below) to Dr. C. H. Talbot of the Wellcome Institute of the History of Medicine. Cf. also, 'Ecrits contemporains sur la Peste', *Histoire Littéraire de la France*, vol. 38 (1938), pp. 325–90, and *Le Livre de seyntz medecines of Henry, Duke of Lancaster*, ed. E. J. Arnould (1967).

53. At this point it is appropriate to consider Philippe's connection with the story of Griselda here mentioned. At some date between 1384 and 1389, Philippe wrote a book entitled *Le Livre de la vertu du sacrement de mariage et du reconfort des dames mariees*. This work was assumed by Jorga, writing in 1896, to be no longer in existence. In 1933, E. Golenistcheff-Koutouzoff, dealing with the Griselda story, showed that among the seventeen surviving examples of the French prose translations of Petrarch's story, two, Bibl. Nat. f. fr. 24.398 and f. fr. 1175, contain a prologue, which identifies these transla-tions as being chapters 4–7 of 'le tierch livre' of Philippe's *Le Livre de la vertu, etc.* Further, the prologue shows clearly that Philippe had translated into French this story, which he had found among the writings of Petrarch, 'jadis son especial ami'. In examin-ing the prologue, Dr. E. Golenistcheff-Koutouzoff quoted from MS. f. fr. 24.389, which contains *Le Livre du Chevalier de la Tour Landry pour l'enseignement de ses filles*, into which is incorporated the story of Griselda. I am indebted for these facts to Dr. Joan Williamson, who further informs me that MS. f. fr. 1175 is actually the complete manu-script of Philippe's work *Le Livre de la vertu, etc.*, which she is in course of editing.

So far we have noted established facts. We pass now into the region of surmise and possibilities. Grace Frank (*Medieval French Drama*), Barbara Craig (*L'Estoire de Griseldis*), Laura H. Loomis (*Speculum*, xxxiii), and Mario Roques (*L'Estoire de Griseldis*), assume with varying degrees of certainty that Philippe was also responsible for the drama of *L'Estoire de Griseldis en rimes et par personnages*, known to us in a single illustrated manuscript (Bibl. Nat. f. fr. 2203) of 1395. Chaucer's *Clerk's Tale* is not brought into the discussion by any of these scholars. My own feeling in the matter, after my long association with Philippe, is that he was not responsible for this rhymed version. It may be noted that nowhere else, as far as we know, does he use a verse medium, with the exception of one passage in the *Songe* (i, pp. 207–8), almost certainly borrowed. Also, although Philippe wrote easily, perhaps too easily, in French, there is the danger that we may overload him with too many attributions; the *Epistre au Roi Richart* belongs to the first half of 1395, the Arsenal MS. *De la Chevallerie, etc.*, bears the date 1396, the play with which we are concerned here, quite alien to these works in subject and style, belongs also to 1395, when Philippe was 68 years of age.

The sixth chapter is eloquent, confused, and borders on the mystical. Much use is made of the metaphor of the vineyards of Engadi[54] and of the wine produced in a certain vineyard of the same name in Cyprus which takes three years to mature. These three years are taken to signify various stages of reconciliation between France and England. At the end of this time the two kings are to sit together at the table described in the Book of Proverbs, and in great humility and brotherly love, become immersed in the wine of Engadi, which represents true peace, love, and justice. The writer ends by praying for condemnation of all who would stand in the way of peace.

The following 'matter' is, in some respects, the most interesting of the entire treatise. It is, in effect, an observer's commentary on the contemporary scene and a view of what may be termed the economic and constitutional results of war. The King, economically speaking, may fall into servitude to all his subjects who are involved in the maintenance of the war. In the actual course of operations, if the King himself is victorious he is often unable to call a halt to his conquests, but if,

54. Philippe's reference to the vineyard of Engadi finds its origin in a verse in *Canticum Canticorum* (Vulgate 1: 13), which reads, 'Botrus cypri dilectus meus mihi, in vineis En-gaddi', which is translated in the King James's Bible (Song of Solomon, 1: 14) as: 'My beloved is unto me as a cluster of camphire (margin, or cyprus) in the vineyards of En-gedi.' Camphire, or cyprus, would appear to be some kind of aromatic tree, possibly used as a support for the vines, and the vineyard of Engadi referred to here is that near the Dead Sea in Palestine, the fruitfulness of which was praised by Josephus, Eusebius, and St. Jerome. The two latter also mention the balsam growing there, which may account for Philippe's somewhat obscure statement (55v), '. . . par aucuns docteurs, parlant moralment, les dictes vignes d'Engadi soient entendues par les arbreciaux qui distillent le fin balme . . .'.

Philippe knew his Scriptures and his Cyprus. It is unlikely that he really believed the 'cypri' in the text referred to the island of Cyprus, but he chose to make an arbitrary interpretation of the word for his own literary purpose.

Mr. Psaras of Limassol has kindly furnished me with the following extract from a translation of the *Excerpta Cypria* of Ludolf von Sudheim, who visited Cyprus in 1340, describing one of the Templars' main vineyards, named after the vineyard of Engadi in the Song of Solomon: 'In the diocese of Paphos lies the vineyard of Engadi, which has not its equal in the whole world. This vineyard lies on a very high mountain, and it is two miles long. Right round it is a steep slope, like a wall. The vineyard itself is completely level, and can be approached from one side only, by a very narrow path. In this vineyard grow many kinds of vines and grapes . . . The vineyard was once the Templars' but belongs now to the Hospitallers of St. John at Rhodes. In the days of the Templars, there were always a hundred slaves, i.e. Saracen prisoners, daily at work in it . . .' This corresponds fairly closely with Philippe's description of the vineyard and its produce; the vineyard was, at least until a few years ago, still in existence.

As regards the name 'marouant' given by Philippe to the wine, Mr. Psaras suggests a connection with the Greek 'mavro', meaning 'black'. One of the oldest varieties of grapes existing in Cyprus today is the 'mavro' or black grape, and Mr. Psaras quotes another traveller, Jacob von Bern, who visited Cyprus in 1346, as saying, 'Again, in the island country of Cyprus, there is to be found wine called Maraa.'

on the other hand victory is obtained by one or other of his commanders, that commander may insist on a place in the King's counsels both
unmerited and dangerous. In contrast to the mystical heights of the
previous chapter, we come down to earth with the homely reference to
the King's valet, who grumbles because he has to get up earlier than
usual because of the war. Throughout we have the continual reminder
of the dangers to the King's immortal soul and his responsibility for
the death of so many unshriven Christians.

With the eighth chapter we are back in the world of allegory and
parable and the kings of France and England are presented with the
detailed picture of two orchards or gardens, the one delectable, standing
for peace, and the other perilous, representing war. In the first of these
we have Philippe's Utopia, in which those conditions prevail which
were noticeably absent in the living world about him. It has the pathos
of all such attempts at depicting the ideal society, while neglecting to
take into account the nature of man. Its walls, its gates, its central fountain, its streams, and its inhabitants are described with his usual passion
for symbolism and detail. The general effect is a sort of bovine serenity
of mind and effortless comfort. Two statements have special interest.
The first is that the king of this Utopia stood for authority and the
common good and was respected as the father of his people. The second is
that no citizen of the garden could say of anything 'This is my own': which
to the twentieth-century citizen may have a curiously familiar ring.

The garden perilous with its symbolic walls, gates, fountain, etc., is
by contrast a place of hazards and discomfort, preyed upon by leeches
and locusts, where cold winds blow and no fruits ripen. The only songs
to be heard were of lamentation and woe, and the wearied citizens might
hear at any moment the trumpets sounding the alarm.

It is between these two gardens that Richard and Charles have to
choose, the way of peace or the way of war.

Philippe, at his most eloquent, next presents, still in the same chapter,
the parable of two ships, commanded by the kings, making the passage
between Scylla and Charybdis, representing the chivalry of France and
England respectively. It is of prime necessity that the two kings should
steer a middle course, disregarding the arguments put forward by either
side against the signing of a peace treaty. Perseverance by the kings in
following a straight course will result in the end in a rallying to their
cause by the chivalry of the West, and bring the royal ships to safe
harbour in the Orient as divinely ordained.

The main proposition set forth in the ninth and final chapter of the letter is for a union by marriage between the two royal houses of France and England. Before coming to the plain declaration of his plan, however, the writer feels it fitting to indulge in a series of deductions from the actual spelling of the name 'Richart', which we may presume appealed to his contemporaries, though to us it appears somewhat puerile.

Although Philippe five or six years earlier had in the *Songe du Vieil Pèlerin* written in strong condemnation of child marriages,[55] we are obliged to accept the case he now presents in favour of the marriage of an infant daughter of Charles VI to Richard II as skilful and eloquent. His treatment has its incongruities. He uses ponderous examples from the animal kingdom, of horses, elephants, and camels, to show the importance of early training. He then proceeds to demonstrate that the proposed marriage will give the English king the opportunity to educate and train his wife in her conjugal duties and her lofty state as queen, so that he may eventually say of her, 'This is my wife, this is my daughter.' Philippe also reminds Richard that a few years of waiting are of little import in comparison with the greatness of the prize to be won. To us the picture is displeasing, when we remember that it is the fate of a girl of about 8 years of age that is in question. A marriage had been the origin of sixty years of war between France and England, but now the two kings would be as closely knit as David and Jonathan, Roland and Oliver, Charlemagne and Arthur, and as brothers, descendants of St. Louis, could set out on the long journey to the conquest of Turkey, Egypt, and Syria, arriving with God's help at the earthly city of Jerusalem, and finally, after long and deserving life, reach the city of God, the New Jerusalem.

In the concluding passage of the letter, dictated, as he emphasizes, at the command of Charles VI of France, Philippe asks forgiveness for his advocacy of the use of strong medicines for the healing of the great wounds of the time, stresses the danger of placebos, and, finally, prays that God may send down from Heaven upon the two kings, that very sovereign remedy, the Grace of God.

55. *Songe* ii, p. 347.

THE NEW ORDER OF THE PASSION OF
JESUS CHRIST CRUCIFIED

Even the briefest introduction to the *Epistre* must include some account of the project for the foundation of the famous Order of the Passion, for the end of hostilities between England and France and the healing of the Schism are in Philippe's mind but necessary preliminaries to his great plan for the re-establishment of Christian power in the Holy Land. A complete study of Philippe's writings on the matter has yet to be made, but the salient facts may be resumed here. The first written exposition of Philippe's ideas is, apparently, to be found in the Mazarine Latin MS. 1943, which contains, in somewhat confusing form, two separate summaries, outlining the organization and administration of the Order, drawn up in 1368 and 1384 respectively. From then onwards, pleas for the foundation of the Order are to be found in the *Songe du Vieil Pèlerin* (1388–9), in *La Sustance Abregie de la Chevalerie* (Ashmole MS. 813), of date some time between 1389 and 1394, in the *Epistre* here presented, in *De la Chevallerie de la Passion de Jhesu Crist* (Arsenal MS. 2251) of 1396, which includes another version of *La Sustance Abregie*, and finally, in the *Epistre Lamentable* of 1397, written, be it noted, after the disaster of the battle of Nicopolis. There may be references in other works, for example, the *Oratio Tragedica*, which as yet remain unpublished.

The chronology of Philippe's transitions from hope to despair, and from despair to hope are made plain by the succession of patrons on whom he relied: Hugh and Peter of Lusignan, Charles V and Charles VI of France, Charles VI, perhaps, in combination with Richard II of England, and, finally, after Nicopolis, Philippe, duke of Burgundy.

The aims of this Order were of the loftiest, and the documents we have cited show an extraordinary combination of the visionary and the practical. The lessons of former failure are to be understood and taken to heart. What is now projected is a permanent Christian settlement in Palestine with highly organized administration. It is as if Philippe envisages the transfer to the Near East of a system which is a strange blend of French royal household management and strict conventual life, with the military organization demanded by the environment. The period of service in the Order was to be for a minimum three years, but for many it was to be a life career, with provision made for their wives and children in the event of their death.

This well-disciplined Order, recruited from all the nations of Europe, is expected to react on the spiritual state of Western society as a whole, and then to pursue a grandiose plan of campaign. Thus, the Spanish princes are to attack Granada, pass into Africa, and, incredibly, to advance to Alexandria. France and England, Scotland and neighbouring powers will rendezvous at Venice and sail direct to the Near East, and so cause the Turks to halt their European advance and retire to rescue their homeland. High and Low Germany, with Prussia, Hungary, and Scandinavia are to march to Constantinople. All these hosts are to make their final meeting in Jerusalem.[56] Philippe was very fond in his writings of using the medium of a dream, but here we really are in dreamland, and, at the age of 70, he can scarcely be credited with clear vision of the Europe of his day.

In the Arsenal manuscript, on the other hand, we have clear testimony to a vigorous and systematic propaganda campaign in favour of the Order. Philippe calls Robert the Hermit, Jehan de Blezi, Loys de Gyach, and Othe de Granson, '*chevalier d'onneur du roy d'Engleterre*', his four evangelists, who between 1390 and 1395 preached the new Gospel of the Order of the Passion. Their mission had important results. Candidates for admission to the Order to the number of 61 came from France (24), Spain (2), Aragon (2), Gascony (3), Navarre (5), Germany (1), England (22), and Scotland (2); while assistance, falling short of membership, was offered by another 27, in France (18), Lombardy (1), the Church (5), and England (3).

It seems likely that the aforesaid messengers carried with them the *Sustance Abregie*, and one may suppose that copies of it may still survive unrecognized in the archives of English and European noble houses.

The sad conclusion of the matter and of forty years' striving is well summed by Philippe in the *Epistre Lamentable* when, much troubled in spirit he says,

le povre homme lors laissa cheoir sa penne et par grant tristesse mist sa vielle teste entre ses deux mains sur l'establie sur laquelle il escripsoit, et a grant soupirs, par maniere de Lamentation, en recongnoissant et reffrignant ses pechies et les pechies de la crestiente catholique, parloit a Dieu en lui priant mercy pour la crestiente . . .[57]

56. See *Epistre Lamentable* in Kervyn de Lettenhove, op. cit., t. 16, pp. 491–8.
57. Kervyn de Lettenhove, op. cit., t. 16, p. 514.

Letter to
King Richard II
1395

PHILIPPE DE MEZIERES

Letter to King Richard II

[2r] A poor and simple letter, addressed by an Old Solitary, dwelling in the Convent of the Celestines of Paris, to that most excellent, most puissant, worthy, Catholic and devout[1] prince, Richard, by the grace of God, King of England, *etc.*, with the hope of confirming true peace and fraternal love between the said King of England and Charles, by the grace of God, King of France.

O bone Jhesu, scribe in corde meo vulnera tua preciosissimo sanguine tuo; ut semper cognoscam quid [2v] desit michi, legam, scenciam, et intelligam dolorem et amorem tuum, bone Jhesu. *Amen.*

Here begins the Prologue to the letter

Most gracious Prince,

That I may obtain, through the goodness of God, a kindly and patient hearing from your royal majesty, humbly and devotedly I beg that it may please you to call to mind how the King of kings, sweet Jesus, being very tired after much journeying on foot and a long fast, stopped to rest at the well of Sicar, and not only listened kindly to the sinful woman of Samaria, but spoke to her at length for the saving of her soul and, so, for the salvation of the people of Samaria. All this is more clearly written in the holy Gospel.

Most devout King, although because of my sins and because, like Moses, I do but stammer, I am not worthy to speak or write to your royal wisdom, yet, trusting in Him who caused the ass of Balaam the prophet to speak, I will raise my voice with King David, the most holy prophet, and direct my words to the Holy [3r] Spirit, praying Him devoutly that He may so govern what I write thus clumsily, that it shall be to His praise and for the peace of Christendom, and comfort of your royal Majesty. And in all this I call on the help of the blessed Virgin Mary, who brought forth and presented to us the God of peace, called the Way, the infallible Truth, and everlasting Life. So I submit this feeble work, so rudely composed, to the correction of your

---

1. It is to be observed that among the forms of address to be found in the *Letter,* the adjective *redoubté* is absent. For Philippe's views on this title see *Songe* ii, pp. 163-5.

royal wisdom and indulgence, which is renowned throughout the world.

Most excellent Prince, Joel the prophet wrote in the Holy Scriptures that young children should see visions and old men dream dreams. Joseph, husband of the Virgin Mary, learned in a dream that Herod sought the death of the sweet child Jesus, and to save Him from death he took Him into Egypt. Daniel the prophet as a young man saw in a dream the vision of the statue of King Nebuchadnezzar, and according to his interpretation of the dream, the King for his pride was deprived of his senses and condemned to eat with beasts of the field for seven years, [3v] and then through Daniel's prayers was restored to his right mind and his royal majesty. Consider what God did in the case of Joseph, son of Jacob the holy patriarch. He, following the dreams of Pharaoh and his interpretation of them, was made a Prince of Egypt, and preserved the people from famine for seven years. And although all dreams do not come true, and although in general Catholic Christians should not put their trust in them, at the same time, experience shows that sometimes they are fulfilled, in whole or in part. This is borne out by the dream of the three kings of Cologne, who, to escape the malice of Herod, wisely returned to the East by another route. It is further confirmed by the evidence of the old chronicles, as may be seen in the book of dreams of that very valiant prince, Scipio Africanus,[2] and in several other reliable chronicles.

Now in this feeble letter, nine different matters are to be treated, in sacred memory of the nine orders of angels.

The first establishes a concordance as between certain precious stones and medicines and the high persons of the kings of France and England. This is done by way of a dream, [4r] in which are figured peace and love between the two kings, in which, also, are recalled the evils which have come from the wars between their ancestors and which will come again should the war re-open, and the lesson drawn that there should be peace between the two kings and in all Christendom.

My second subject is the schism in the Church and its evil results in the past and present, and the remedy, that is, true peace between the two kings.

The third matter deals with the holy journey overseas; and, as preparation for that passage, the Old Solitary offers to the King of England

---

2. *Somnium Scipionis*, preserved in Macrobius. For an English version see *Collectanea Hermetica*, W. Wynn Westcott (ed.), vol. v (1894).

a new Order of Chivalry, essential for the said passage and for the reform of all Christendom.

The fourth matter treats of a marriage which has been proposed for the King of England, by which holy peace between the two kings could be hindered; and treats, too, of the remedy for such hindrance.

In the fifth chapter, certain plain examples are given, serving to condemn the shedding of Christian blood.

[4v] In my sixth chapter, I show that to confirm and strengthen peace between our two kings, the carbuncle and the diamond, figuratively speaking, must be immersed in, and watered, and imbued with the precious wine from the vineyards of Engadi.

The remaining three matters ennumerate various examples which may help towards the establishment of that real peace so much desired by all good men and all Christendom.

Most gracious Prince, this present writer, old and solitary, while in contemplation had a dream—a dream whose fulfilment interpreted according to the letter, many would find impossible of belief. But if, following the doctrine of St. Paul, it is interpreted according to the spirit, the dream will be found to be true.

In this dream, the pure balm, which, on account of the great strength and heat of the southern sun, was hitherto to be found only in one place in all the world, that is, Cairo in Babylon, now, through the bounty of the Author of Nature, grows in the cold and often frozen regions of the West, that is to say, in the kingdom of France.

Another marvel is revealed in this dream. The precious stone called the lodestone, not the one [5r] found in northern and transmontane lands that attracts to itself iron, but the one that is mined only in the high regions of Greater India, this too is now to be found in the cold lands of the West, that is, in the kingdom of England.

And a third wonder is that the vineyards of Engadi, specially mentioned in the Scriptures, flourish now in these two kingdoms, in such wise that, according to the hopes of many good men, they will produce wine that may gently intoxicate the two kings and many of their valiant knights.

All this will be explained more fully in what follows, and may God, by His grace, keep the aforementioned balm and lodestone, and preserve the vineyards from frost. Here ends the prologue.

Here begins the letter

Now let us pass on, in God's name, to consider the virtue of our fine balm, [5v] moralising broadly thereon, so as to arrive at the concordance of our aforesaid dream; and by this concordance it will be found, by God's grace, that the said dream is no vision of the night, engendered by over much wine, that is forgotten in the morning.

Balm is a precious liquid which flows drop by drop from a little shrub, nourished by the dew of heaven. Among its virtues, three may be mentioned which bear on our theme. Others we leave aside for the sake of brevity.

The first virtue of this balm is that as soon as it is applied to a wound, it removes pain and cleanses the wound in such a way that neither decay nor dead flesh can long remain, and restores the nerves, if they have received injury, to their former vigour.

Its second virtue is that in a marvellously short time it brings together the edges of the wound, and this much more quickly than any other medicine.

Its third virtue is that it heals and removes all traces of the scar [6r] left by a wound, so that it seems as if there had never been one. Moreover, if any flesh is wanting, our balm will make it grow again in its former shape, removing any disfigurement.

Let all this be said in figure, concerning the virtues of pure balm as medicine, as a reminder of the great wounds which have been so poorly healed in the last forty or sixty years.

To come, then, to the exposition of the said dream and of the figure of the balm imagined by the Old Solitary: In order to arrive at the concordance with that peace desired by all good men, it should be remembered, speaking figuratively and subject to the correction of your royal majesty, most devout Catholic King, that for the last sixty years and more there has existed an open and mortal wound, so full of poison that it has infected the whole of Christendom, and especially the western parts thereof, which could be healed neither by the teachings of Galen, Hippocrates nor Avicenna, nor by all the physicians of Salerno, for lack of pure balm.

By the said wound can be clearly understood that fatal war, started [6v] and pursued by your grandfather, the valiant King Edward, and your father, the valiant Prince of Wales, on whom may God have mercy, against their brothers in Christ and brothers by descent, the three kings of France, Philip, John and Charles, whom may God absolve.

Lamentation

O evil, perilous and mortal wound, by whose poison so many kings, dukes, counts and barons, and the ancient and valiant chivalry, both of France and England, and elsewhere, have been brought so tragically to destruction of body and soul: Alas, alas, how many churches by the venom of the said wound have been destroyed! How many widows and orphans created, to die of hunger and ill-treatment! And what is still worse, the holy Catholic faith, in large measure, forgotten and destroyed! All this through pride, greed and envy, and for the sake of transitory and wordly possessions, which no king can hold for sixty years together, which is but a moment of time [7r] for the soul, which is eternal and which will possess for ever those things, good or bad, for which it has laboured in this world.

O wound accursed of God, sent for the punishment of sin, whose poison, fatal to so many Christian people, passes description. May the day on which it was first inflicted be wiped from the calendar of the days of the year. The tongue of man cannot fully tell of the malice of this wound, yet good men should, with tears, offer their prayers to God for its healing; for it has brought more danger and done more harm than all the plagues of Egypt, which destroyed Pharaoh and his idolatrous people. This plague has brought death to Catholic kings and Christian people, members of the Church of God and of our true head, Jesus Christ.

It is laid down in divine, civil and moral law that the son who receives his father's possessions, is bound to pay his debts and right the wrongs done by him. But how can the heirs compensate for so many great ills inflicted by their fathers? In truth, they will be in great need of much fine balm to [7v] heal this wound, which is not yet closed or made clean. Here ends this brief lamentation over the aforesaid wound.

It is natural that every sick man who has suffered long should wish to find a good doctor, so that he may seek from him a particular medicine suited to his ailment. Because this Old Solitary, for his sins, has sometimes been stricken and infected by the poison of the aforesaid wound, he feels pity now for those who have died by reason of it and still more concern and compassion for his Christian brethren who are now alive, lest they should, in time to come, be infected by the poison of this wound which has not yet been healed. After consulting many physicians, he has betaken himself to that great Physician, the One who gives their virtue and power to words, stones and herbs, begging Him often, though with insufficient fervour, that it might please Him to soften His wrath and send down from Heaven such medicine [8r] as may cleanse and heal that oft mentioned wound.

After many tears shed before God, the sovereign Physician, by the good men of the two kingdoms of France and England, praying for the complete healing of the wound, there came to the Old Solitary, abortive, useless and unworthy to be named, through great and ardent longing, a dream, in which it was revealed that God, through His grace and the prayers of the Virgin Mary, had sent into France the pure balm spoken of above, which, as he thinks, in effect will be transformed into a shining carbuncle. And to England He has sent from the East, that is from Heaven, the lodestone, and if its virtue is lifted up and exalted and strengthened by the fine balm, the Old Solitary believes it will draw unto itself, by its great compassion, a large part of the great sickness which spreads from the wound, so long as the said balm and lodestone are mingled in due proportion, and in spirit imbued with the wine from the vineyards of Engadi.

Now let us pass on to establish a moral in the figures I have proposed, [8v] in order to arrive, once for all, at the cure for the wound, so often described and so dreaded by all good men, that is to say, true peace between the two Western monarchs of France and England. And although at present this wound does not openly spill out its venom, because of the truce which has been agreed, at the same time, in the opinion of some, in substance today it may be compared with a tumour, which does not show on the surface, but grows within the body, undermining and rotting the surrounding flesh; or with a fire, covered with ash, which is ready to blaze up and consume all around it when the ash is disturbed; and the poison may be intensified, something much to be feared, unless the God of peace and charity, in His great mercy, should provide a remedy in the form of the pure balm and the precious lodestone.

If the wise men of France and England would, under God, weigh carefully in the balance of their judgement the virtues of the balm described above, and apply them to a particular person, it may be stated plainly that in the kingdom of France there is no [9r] royal person to whom these virtues can be more justly and properly attributed than that very exalted, noble and gracious creature, King Charles VI, as will appear by the seemliness of the comparison of the fine balm with the said King Charles.

With regard to the first quality of fine balm, namely, that it removes the pain of the wound and cleanses it, diminishing and driving out the poison, all men, both English and French, know that since the beginning of the reign of the young King Charles, by the grace of God, in his kingdom of France the suffering from the wound, that is, the accursed war, has been more reduced and it has thrown out less poison in the way of battle and the shedding of blood, than in all the past thirty or forty years. This is, as it were, what is called in medicine the crisis which indicates convalescence or end of the sickness.

Let us thank God and render tribute to the Author of Nature, Who has bestowed on our fine balm this special grace, denied to his predecessors fifty years past.

Here ends this brief comparison of the fine balm with the person of [9v] King Charles, in respect of power to remove pain.

As to the second quality of the balm, that is, that it draws together the two edges of a wound in such wise that there remains no trace of it, let us identify the two parts of this mortal wound, so often mentioned. Surely, in the main, they represent the two kings, of France and England. The wider the wound, the more poison and dead flesh and decay are present in the parts bordering the wound. But by God's mercy, our fine balm, Charles, by his virtue and goodness and by his royal and singular grace, will play his part in bringing together the two edges, that it to say, himself and his beloved brother Richard, King of England, in a true union of love and friendship, in such way, in my view, that the poisons of pride, envy and anger, of complaints, and memories of old wrongs and enmities between the two kings will no longer [10r] remain; and all this through the influence of the pure balm and the precious lodestone.

And so, with the dew of Heaven falling upon the two sides of the wound, it will, by the goodness of God, be found to be healed, and the two edges, so long apart and divided, will be rejoined in love, so that in brief space the fatal poison, which in our time has flowed in great streams, may be halted and the wound healed. And may God by His grace grant us this gift.

Here ends the concordance of the fine balm with the person of King Charles in respect of the joining of the two edges of the wound.

Now let us proceed to the third virtue of fine balm. We have said that pure balm removes all trace of scars, which are the ugly outward signs left by a wound after it has been healed; and also by its virtue, balm removes all misshapenness. Indeed it does more, for, if flesh is wanting, it causes it to grow again, so that the wounded part is brought to the natural level of the rest of the limb affected.

All these qualities [10v] and virtues of balm can, speaking figuratively, clearly be applied to the person of Charles, King of France, if he is aided and strengthened by the wisdom and goodness of his brother Richard, King of England.

It is true that the scars and outward signs of our wound, that is, the war, after the achievement of peace and the closing of the wound, cannot in fact and literally be wiped out or recompensed, that is, the destruction of churches, cities, castles and towns, nor can the bodies and souls, killed and damned by the poison, be resurrected, nevertheless, in their effect on the enduring spirit of man, infused with the goodness of God and the grace of the two kings, these scars, that is, the hatreds, rancours and malevolence which exist between the subjects of the two kingdoms, who through the poison of the wound, have, at times, been in opposition, will be totally erased.

We must quietly hope that such great power will proceed from the balm and the lodestone and so much mutual love, [11r] that, by the grace of God, they will be like unto a polished mirror, in which all their subjects, and especially those who have been accustomed to excite and increase the venom, and also all foreigners, whether friendly or hostile to peace, will view themselves, and will feel compelled, under God, to follow the example of their natural leaders, lords and kings. What is more, if need be, they, the kings, will see to it that the missing flesh grows again in the wound and the cavities are filled up, which otherwise might disfigure the healed wound. Each side must do its share, so that, by the mercy of Jesus, both sides will be satisfied and divisions removed and brought to nought. Then shall be fulfilled the words of the Scriptures, The old and evil times are passed and the earth is renewed in goodness and joy. And may God, by His grace, grant us these things.

Here ends the rather long concordance of the third virtue of the fine balm, compared in general with the very gracious and beloved person of Charles, King of France, and his royal majesty, that is, [11v] as regards the removal of the deformity left by the wound.

The power of the lodestone compared in figure with the King of England

It is now time, with God's help, to give some brief account of the state and particular virtues of the precious lodestone, as they apply to the most high, noble and gracious royal person, Richard, by the grace of God King of England.

As introduction, without invoking apocryphal histories, it is a fact that Albert of Cologne, the learned philosopher and doctor, one of the wisest since Aristotle, in his book on precious stones, says in set terms that in the uttermost parts of Greater India there is to be found, with great difficulty, the fine lodestone, which has such qualities that, not only does it attract iron, as does the lodestone of the West, but in addition, wonderfully and with great affection, draws to itself the very body of man. In support of his claims for this precious oriental lodestone, the said doctor relates in his book the following story of one of its remarkable qualities.

[12r] If this lodestone is placed beneath the head of a woman sleeping with her husband, without her knowing anything about it, as soon as she falls asleep, if she has been unfaithful to her husband and broken her marriage sacrament, because of the power of the said stone, she will have such troubled sleep and such horrible dreams, that she can no longer stay in her bed, but must fall from it to the ground while still sleeping. On the other hand, if a woman has been chaste and kept her marriage sacrament, she will straight away, on falling asleep, be constrained to kiss and embrace her husband in true conjugal love—entirely different from the other, who falls from her bed.

This lodestone has very great power, according to the said philosopher, the great Albert. The man who would use and get full advantage from the virtues of precious stones must wear them with a heart free from mortal sin. This is shown by the way in which the beautiful emerald, guardian of chastity, in the presence of luxury is split and [12v] shattered. The story of the lodestone told above demonstrates to us its power to attract the flesh of man, provided that it is borne worthily and without sin, as in the case of the good woman who by the virtue of the lodestone was drawn in love to the body of her lord and husband.

Further, this lodestone has another quality, very important, although quite well known, especially to seamen in the Adriatic and Mediterranean seas. This is that an iron needle, rubbed against the lodestone, always points to the Polar or North Star. Thus, by the help of this needle, rubbed against the lodestone, sailors in those seas can look always towards the said star, find their way through the sea, and so arrive safely in port.[3]

Again, some say that the lodestone serves to stay the flow of blood.

Here ends our account of the three virtues of that most precious stone, the lodestone.

If one wishes [13r] to draw a moral from these three virtues of the lodestone, then, as I think and hope, there is no one in the kingdom of England to whom they can be more fittingly applied than to the worthy and royal person of Richard, by the grace of God, King of England.

Now, let us proceed in God's name to the gracious and happy comparison, so often and so joyfully noted, of the lodestone with the person of the King, beginning with the virtue of attracting the body of man, that is, the whole man, to his love, under God.

Everyone, both French and English, knows that, as was said about the balm, since the consecration and rule of the young King Richard, the evil wound, so often referred to, has spilled out less poison than at any time during the last sixty years. This is not surprising, for God, abominating the effusion of Christian blood, which has been so cruelly shed by the princes and people of England, has multiplied His mercy and by [13v] special grace has made the rose to bloom in England among the thorns, which, by its fragrance, that is, the virtue of the lodestone, has drawn to itself in love, and each day continues to do so, not only the hearts of the King's subjects, but also those of strangers.

This gracious red rose, the noble King Richard, renewing the memory of the precious blood of Jesus Christ, and enflamed by the love of God and of his neighbour, by the virtue of the lodestone, which loves peace and unity, has in his heart hated the shedding of human blood, and by grace has become the son of God by adoption and love, according to

---

3. Cf. G. W. Coopland, 'A glimpse of late fourteenth century ships and shipping', *Mariner's Mirror*, vol. 48, no. 3 (1948), pp. 189, 191; also *Songe* i, pp. 558–9. Through a misreading of a somewhat obscure reference in Jorga, op. cit., I mistakenly attributed here details of Philippe's adventures in northern seas to the *Oratio tragedica* instead of the *Soliloquium peccatoris* (Arsenal MS. 408). The latter I have not yet read.

the saying of St. John the Evangelist in his Gospel, *In principio erat verbum*.

The great virtue of the above-mentioned lodestone, that is, the virtue of the precious stone spoken of by St. Paul the Apostle, having descended on our lodestone of England, that is, on the person of the very worthy young King, Richard, has not only drawn to him in love the hearts of his subjects and other men of standing who meet and have speech with him, but, what is more, has attracted his enemies, accepted [14r] by long habit as natural enemies, namely, the good men of France and, indeed, our much loved King Charles himself, by the grace of God, etc., and also his uncles, none of whom he has ever met.

Now, may God grant that the fine lodestone of the East be placed beneath the heads of kings and princes, on the one side and the other, so that, under God, they may be constrained to embrace one another and so bring to pass that love and peace so much desired by all good men.

Some enemies of peace might say that this Old Solitary while praising the gracious lodestone, does not sufficiently control his pen, and that the blind man is no judge of colours; to whom I reply that, of the four evangelists, two only, that is, St. John and St. Matthew, were eye-witnesses of the works of the blessed Jesus Christ. The other two, St. Mark and St. Luke, were witnesses by hearsay, whose example this Old Solitary follows in his over-brief praise of the lodestone, having been fully informed of the attractive power of the said young King Richard by all the messengers, open and secret, sent to the King of England by [14v] his beloved brother, King Charles, and, in particular, by that worthy man of God, Robert the Hermit, the special messenger, under God, between the two Kings.

O glorious King of England, figured as the lodestone! Let me follow the example of my great master, St. Jerome, Doctor of the Church, when he wrote to Monseigneur St. Augustine, and say, Let me praise your genius and the virtue of the fine lodestone which God has implanted in your soul. A virtue that is praised grows continually in the heart of a magnanimous man, but in the heart of the presumptuous and vainglorious, this virtue is turned into pride and vanity. May God defend you, noble King, friend of peace, from this vice.

Further in the matter of the power of attraction of the glorious lodestone, this power under God is so great that, if it be strengthened and bedewed by the fine balm, which it has miraculously attracted to itself, there will be a conjunction of love between the two powers, each of whom is of the seventh generation, the one through his father and the other through his mother, from the great Louis, King of [15r] France, that is the two brothers, descendants of the said St. Louis, Charles, King of France, and Richard, King of England. And there is nothing lacking to establish, God willing, this conjunction, save a face-to-face meeting between the two brothers, already attracted to each other. And let that man be cursed, like Cain and Lamech, who puts obstacles in the way of such a meeting.

Here ends the brief account of the power of attraction of our virtuous and gracious lodestone, here set forth in figure.

Turning to the second virtue of the lodestone, namely, that it attracts iron, and that an iron needle rubbed against it will point steadily to the North star, that is the lodestar, which guides ships into safe harbourage, let us pass on to the concordance, speaking in figure, of this second virtue and similitude of the fine lodestone with King Richard, for whom the lodestone stands.

We have said above that our lodestone draws to himself the heart and flesh of men in God-fearing love. Now let us see how he attracts iron to himself and how he communicates his virtue to the iron needle. It may be said, sadly enough, that the valiant chivalry of England [15v] while obeying the divine order to punish sin for about sixty years, has been changed and made into an iron needle, or goad, so sharp that it has forced souls without number to burn in Hell; and the Black Boars, pitiless towards their Christian brothers, under pretence of prowess and worldly valour and some asserted right, have sharpened their tusks against the chief cities of Spain, France and elsewhere, so fufilling the prophecy made by Merlin in his book. All the same, it may be said that for all the dread cruelty of the said needle, and after wonderful victories and worldly and passing triumphs, little lasting profit has remained to the Black Boars. This is not to be wondered at, for God allowed them to go into these kingdoms for the correction of the kings, princes and people of the kingdoms, to punish iniquity and not in order to obtain full lordship, for, as the proverb says, Lombardy will belong to the Lombards, Spain to the Spaniards, France to the French and England to the English. Let this be said, so that, as this old, solitary writer believes, [16r] the valiant knights of England and France may henceforward abandon the task of the iron goad which, as already said, has pierced so deeply their Christian brothers, and by the command of God and the two Kings turn their weapons against the enemies of the Faith, to make recompense in the sight of God for the great evils which they have wrought.

Let us return, then, to the comparison of the virtues here mentioned with our figured lodestone. It may be gladly said that today, by God's grace, our lodestone has wonderfully drawn to itself the iron, that is, the chivalry, of both England and France, represented by the goad and its cruel work; and, moreover, this needle, or goad, brought close to our lodestone, Richard, has changed its course through this contact, and looks, as do the sailors, to the North Star. By this North Star, speaking with deference, I mean nothing other than the very sweet Virgin Mary, called the Star of the Sea, who brings back straying mariners to their right course, according to Monseigneur [16v] St. Benedict. If in all danger the example of the sailor, who stands over the compass-box when out of sight of land, is followed, and she is steadfastly and unceasingly kept in sight by the goad, that is, the chivalry, and especially by our lodestone, who has his gaze ever fixed on this Star, she will show the right way to withdraw from the above described work of the goad, so displeasing to God; and will revive true peace and love between the two Kings and their knights; and, finally, this loving Star will bring them, after numberless victories against the enemies of the Faith, into safe harbour. And may God bring these things to pass to the comfort of my old age.

Here ends the brief and imperfect comparison made in respect of the second virtue of the fine lodestone, in attracting iron to itself.

As for the third virtue of the fine lodestone, that is to say its power to staunch the flow of blood, it can be said, speaking figuratively, that in the past sixty years no king or prince of the kingdom of England has done so much to prevent the shedding of blood [17r] as has King Richard, figured as the fine lodestone. The lapidaries state that the onyx, coral, the beautiful pearl and the fine emerald by its coldness, all have great power to stay the flow of blood, but none so much as our lodestone. His subjects, the English, have been accustomed to shed the blood of their Christian brethren in Spain, Britanny, Scotland, Normandy, France, Guienne, Champagne and Picardy, in such wise that the greater part of our Christendom has been stained with blood by the sword of the English, to the horror of the Catholic world. But today, by the goodness and grace of God, and by the power of the lodestone, this blood has ceased to flow, and God grant that from henceforward it will flow no more, so that the prophecy of Isaiah may be accomplished and the swords and spears be beaten into ploughshares, and that through the mutual peace and love of the balm and lodestone may be fulfilled the words of David the prophet, Mercy and truth are met together and justice and peace have kissed each other. And may God grant us [17v] these things.

We, both French and English, must devoutly believe that this power to prevent the flow of blood has descended on our gracious lodestone from the aforesaid sweet Star, on whom his gaze has ever been fixed, that is, the Pole Star, the Virgin, who carried in her body that ruby, Who poured out His blood upon the tree of the true Cross to redeem the world, in satisfaction for all the blood which has been shed, from the time when Abel the Just was killed by his brother Cain, until the day of His holy Passion, and to restrain the spilling of blood from the time of His resurrection until the end of the world. This precious blood, shed for the human race, and especially for Christian people, should, out of love and reverence for our Redeemer, suffice without the further bloodshed of which we have spoken. Because King Richard and King Charles have fixed their eyes and their devotion on the precious Star, that is, the Virgin Mary, she has prayed that they should be granted power to restrain the shedding of the blood of their Christian brothers and kin. [18r] Our two kings and their chivalry must be on their guard, lest through evil counsel they fall again into that sickness, for, as the proverb says, relapse may be worse than the illness itself.

O noble King, figured as the lodestone, may it please you to call to mind a noble and pious saying of the valiant and wise Theodosius, Emperor of Rome. Certain of his barons and peers reported to him that one of his knights had, as it were, blasphemously spoken ill of him, and they said that this man was deserving of death and the emperor ought to inflict this punishment. Then this valiant, Catholic emperor raised his eyes and hands to Heaven, and said, Would to God that I could bring the dead back to life, rather than put to death those still living! This holy emperor had, indeed, his eyes fixed on the Star of the Sea, and held in great horror the spilling of human blood and the putting of men to death.

Again, noble Prince and gracious King, remember Titus, son of Vespasian, Emperor of [18v] Rome, and himself later Emperor, at the siege of Jerusalem, in which eleven times one hundred thousand souls died by starvation and the sword, except for eighty and seven thousand who were sold at the rate of thirty for one denier, in quittance and remembrance of the thirty pieces of silver for which they sold the blessed Son of God. When the valiant and worthy Titus saw the great mortality of those who were his enemies and the enemies of his religion —for the Romans were idolators and those in the city were Jews—and saw, too, how the Jews of Jerusalem cast their dead, who could not be numbered, over the city walls into the ditches, the good Titus, seeing all this, was so overcome by pity that, raising his eyes and hands to Heaven, with tears cried to God, Lord God, thou seest how much I grieve for these people, for had they been willing to submit to Rome and recognise her as they had done in times past, not a single man would have died.

This is the same Titus, Roman emperor, who one day in the evening said to his knights, Alas, I have wasted this day. This was because it so happened that on that day [19r] he had bestowed no gift or favour on his knights and subjects. This pagan and idolatrous emperor was, indeed, magnanimous and pitiful, having great compassion for those who died. And as the king and people of Nineveh will condemn the Jews in the Day of Judgement, as the Gospel tells us, so it is much to be feared that this worthy pagan, Titus, will condemn Christian kings, who have not repented of their sins as did the king and people of Nineveh, but have persisted, with little excuse, in slaying their fellow Christians.

Hence, take warning, O devout King, figured as the lodestone, and your brother, also, King Charles, figured as the balm, and beware lest, through following the advice of your knights, nurtured in bloodshed, blood should be seen dripping from your fingers when you appear before the sovereign Judge, to whom you must render account for all your sins, down to the tiniest thought and the smallest degree.

Here ends the concordance, such as it is, of the third virtue of the lodestone with the person of the gracious King Richard, figured as the lodestone, to serve as a moral and warning against the shedding [19v] of Christian blood henceforward, and a plea for compassion for the slain.

All that has been said so far, though rough, wordy and ungraceful, has for its aim nothing other than the accomplishment of true peace and unfeigned love between the two Kings figured as the balm and lodestone. For the final ratification of such love, you should remember that at the beginning of this poor letter it was stated that the balm would be changed into a glowing carbuncle and the lodestone into a precious diamond.

Now let us deal first with the balm. It may be said that the name Charles, that is in Latin *Karolus*, is equivalent to *Kara lus*, that is, beloved light. O for how long and with what tears and prayers to God has this dear light been looked for in France, by which light the darkness of ignorance and the accursed war, which have so long endured, may, by the grace of God, be transfigured and that both French and English may see each other as Christian brothers and cousins, forgetting, in true love, past offences.

Speaking in figure, among precious [20r] stones, the carbuncle is the most brilliant, and at night a fine large stone sheds a bright light around itself. Our precious carbuncle, having been anointed with fine balm, that is heavenly oil, at his consecration, aided by the goodness of God and the power of the lodestone, will, to my mind, send out such rays that God's Temple in Jerusalem will once again shine with light, and the holy sepulchre of Jesus and Mount Calvary will be restored to the glory of the Catholic Faith.

This light may be compared with the flame found in the Temple by Nehemiah and Ezra, which had long been obscured, but which, uncovered, lit up once more the Temple, rededicated and restored to its ancient glory, and the Holy City, rebuilt in its former power.

O how precious is that light proceeding from the carbuncle and from the lodestone transformed into the diamond, united by true love, peace and charity in God! The hearts and souls of these precious stones will be changed into one will in God, and by their light all Catholic peoples, who [20v] until now through war and division have wandered in darkness, will see clearly the straight way leading to Jerusalem. Happy will be the man who approaches the brightness of that light, that is, the presence of the two Kings, and in the circle of that light strives towards the goal of peace in the service of God. And accursed be those, as we have said, who on fictitious grounds, or for worldly gain, or for vain glory, labour to extinguish the rays of that light. It were better for them had they never been born.

Here ends our consideration of the transformation and concordance of the fine balm.

Now let us deal, in God's name, with the conversion of the lodestone into the diamond. The diamond, next to the carbuncle, that is the ruby, is the most valued and highly prized of precious stones, and the one most frequently worn on solemn occasions by the great princes of this world. If any man should wish to moralise on all its virtues, he would need a large book in which to do so. But for the sake of brevity, [21r] for our theme two only of its properties need be discussed. The first of these is that, according to the lapidaries, the diamond is very potent against poison. The second is that it preserves love between him who gives it and him who receives it. Now, let us come to the significance of our lodestone changed in its nature to the diamond. As regards its power over poison: The chief poison and the most dangerous to body and soul, and the one which can do most harm to the royal majesty of Richard, the noble and puissant King of England, is the war, with its slaughter of Christian men of both France and England, by which countless numbers of God's baptised creatures have been killed and slain, and the souls of many condemned to Hell for ever. This mortal poison is worse than the one called *boucon*[4] in Italy and Syria, for the latter kills only the man who takes it, but our aforesaid poison some-times causes the death of hundreds and thousands in a single day. It may be said that, through God's grace, unto the present day, our lodestone, changed [21v] into the diamond, has possessed such virtue, that the said poison, that is the war, has had little power, and this is also true of the virtue of the carbuncle. And although this poison has been offered more than once in the form of an electuary to our diamond, yet, by the virtue received by him from the Author of Nature, he has been preserved from it. O how wonderful it is that, even as the flower of the vine drives away serpents, so, in the presence of our diamond, the said poison can find no place nor take effect.

Here ends the concordance of the lodestone with the diamond in respect of its power over poison, from which poison may God defend us.

As regards the ability of the diamond to engender and preserve love between the giver and him who receives, providing that it is given and received with goodwill, free from envy, greed and corruption, those people who were privy to the first signs of friendship, links of affection and cordial peace between the balm and carbuncle and the lodestone, now the diamond, know that the [22r] first movements towards friend-ship as between the two kings were made by the diamond. The very gracious and loving King Richard, following the vocation to which he had been called and predestined by Jesus, the gentle Author of peace,

4. This appears to be a general term for poison, from the Italian *boccone*, and not a specific drug.

was, so to say, transmuted from the nature of the Black Boars from whom he sprang, into the precious lodestone, with its miraculous power of attraction, as we have explained earlier, and afterwards into the rich diamond. And he was transported by fraternal love towards his brother, King Charles, and the transport was so strong and great that, by the goodness of God, in a brief moment the glowing carbuncle was also transmuted figuratively speaking by the virtue and love of the diamond, and carried into the heart and soul of our diamond in such a way that the love of the two precious stones, by the grace of God, became merged into one whole, to the satisfaction of this Old Solitary and all good men.

Let the diamond and shining carbuncle beware [22v] lest by adverse counsel, or by the servants of Mars or Mercury, the great virtue described above should be in any way crushed, divided or sullied. For should this happen, which God forbid, it would be proof that the said stones did not derive their origin from that rich mine, whence the stone was taken from the mountain and fashioned without hands, according to Daniel the prophet. May our gracious diamond persevere and fulfil his calling in all respects, so that this love shall be lasting, and the dreaded poison, of which we have so often spoken, be banished from the hearts of our two kings, from the cities and from the frontiers, so that the Kings, through God's grace, may be found worthy to hear the same blessed song of the angels as the shepherds heard, that is to say that in our days glory may be to God on high and on earth peace to men of good will.

Here ends the concordance of the fine diamond and of the manner in which it preserves peace between the two Kings.

God knows that if this Old Solitary [23r] had been able to find any thing or any jewel of greater price or value in this world than the balm and the precious stones described in this letter, with its rough and ready moralising, to help in bringing about the longed for peace and friendship between these two descendants of the good king, St. Louis, he would gladly have done so. And it is to be believed that God will extend His grace to our royal persons, chosen by Him from among the rulers of Christendom, and that they will bear in mind the virtues of the precious stones that I have ascribed to them, and apply their efforts to the joint task of building up and sustaining the welfare of Catholic kingdoms. May it please God to grant us this.

*The second subject in this present letter is concerned with
the mortal schism in the Church, and the remedy therefor by
way of peace between the Kings*

According to the art of medicine, if the ointment called popilion is
continuously applied to a wound which is wide and festering, the
wound will never close, but will, rather, become worse. It is better
[23v] on serious wounds to make frequent and immediate use of the
ointment which is called *unguentum apostolorum*, that is the Apostles'
ointment, which to begin with is corrosive and then, afterwards, soothing. O excellent King of Great Britain, there is an open wound in
Christendom today, and this wound has spread its poison throughout
the Christian world. Hitherto this has been treated with the ointment
popilion, that is to say, by flatterers, who, under pretence of healing,
keep the wound open. This accursed wound, leaving aside all parables
and figures, is the mortal schism in Holy Church, the mother of these
two sons of St. Louis. She lies in her bed, sick, wounded, in fragments,
divided in two. And, what is worse, each of our two Kings has taken
to himself one half of his said mother, claiming to heal her sickness,
while abandoning the other to be devoured by dogs and birds of prey.
Unless this is changed, she will never be cured of her wound.

It is written in the Holy Scriptures, [24r] Honour thy father and thy
mother, that thy days may be long in the land. Again, it is written,
Whoso curseth his father or his mother, shall die the death. O divine
words, menacing and perillous to all who do not pay due honour to
their father and mother. Now let us turn to the concordance and exposition of the said wound, using the harsh ointment of the Apostles,
always with love and reverence towards our two sons of St. Louis, who
have for so long allowed to languish the mother who bore them and
who gave them a new birth in the sacrament of baptism and the other
sacraments, so that they might reign in Paradise.

Tell me, I pray you, O gracious, royal children, what reply will you
make to the slain Lamb when, as God and man, He comes to judgement, and accuses you of great negligence and cruelty, in that you have
left His bride, for whose marriage He shed His blood upon the tree, for
so long to languish and remain torn in two. Because of this wound and
horrible sickness, much blood has been spilt, and the unity of the
Church and [24v] Christian charity have been for so long, and still are,

disturbed and divided by great hatred, and, worse still, sects and here-sies in the Faith are everywhere increased and Catholic Christians, making a double-headed monster of their mother, say to one another, not in love but in wrath, I am for Paul, I am for Apollo, that is, I am for Boniface, I am for Benedict.

Surely, both Kings should be greatly fearful of this judgement threatened by God. Of what avail is a great host of brave knights and your royal power, which vanishes like a shadow in the sun's rays, when your mother, sick and torn apart, languishes in captivity, waiting help from her children, the Catholic kings whom she has consecrated and anointed with her holy oil of mercy, and fed from her breasts; and long-ing especially for help from those Kings, whose power and dignity, as firstborn of the Church, are renowned throughout Christendom?

And if the prelates of the Church have been negligent, and through ambition and greed [25r] have caused the said wound and have cared little for its healing, because each of them has said, *Qui tenet, teneat*, that is, He who has, let him hold, and they have feared, and, perhaps, still fear, lest they should be diverted from their simony and disorderly way of life if they had over them a saintly Pope in Rome, sole Vicar of Christ our Creator; if such is the case, it behoves the Kings to restore the Church, as the very holy King David did, when he restored the Synagogue and increased its ceremonies and the number of its divine services, which was the mere foreshadowing, from which you Kings emerged into the sunlight.

O gracious and worthy princes, if you are well informed by the lay-men and clerks of your great Council concerning this wound, which I have bewailed so often, and the daily increasing ills which have sprung therefrom, you will find that this mortal schism is nothing other than a deep cleft, caused by ignorance and malediction.

[25v] How great is the number of lambs and goats and sheep in Christendom, who think that they are being led to good pastures by true shepherds, when all the time, in God's eyes, these are not rightful shepherds, but mercenaries. The proof: they see the wolves about to devour their flock and flee, for, according to the Gospel, they are but hirelings. This cleft and abyss of ignorance today is, alas, so deep as to be beyond fathoming.

O noble princes, you will remember the deep and horrible gulf which appeared suddenly in the city of Rome, which gave forth so mortal a stench that all who breathed it died forthwith. And the plague was so deadly that no one could find a remedy. Finally, the Romans consulted their gods to find an answer, and were told that for the cure of the plague and the safety of the State, it was needful that the noblest and finest [26r] Roman of them all, on horseback and fully armed, should leap into the gulf, and at once the plague would be ended. To shorten the story, after long consultation with intent to find someone among them who was willing to offer himself to death for the deliverance of the city, there appeared among the princes and nobles of Rome, one, Curtius, who, of his own free will, and with much honour and glory, fully armed and on horseback, before all the assembled people of Rome, leapt into the abyss, and at once the opening closed and the epidemic ended, to the everlasting and glorious memory among the Romans of the very noble Curtius, as is set forth more fully in Roman histories.

On the question before us, we may say that this abyss of the schism is more dangerous than that of Rome, for the latter threatened only the city, but this one in the Church swallows and devours not only the citizens of Rome, but countless people throughout Christendom.

Some may say, in sorrow, that in this breach, the depth of which [26v] no man so far has measured, expedient though the knowledge might be, the cardinals, after the death of Gregory XI, intervened to deepen it with the spade of ambition for their personal gain, to the prejudice of the unity of their mother, the Church. Hence, it has become expedient that our Kings should find a remedy, so that the breach should be closed and no longer bring death.

Now let us consider calmly where in the city of Rome, that is, in Christendom, we may find the finest and noblest among its princes, who may put an end to this mortal sickness of body and soul, this accursed chasm, this fatal, gaping wound. For this we must find two people, who are, as described above, the best and the noblest. It is very possible that in an assembly of worthy members of Christendom, their choice would fall first on our glowing carbuncle, accompanied by the virtuous diamond.

O noble Kings, in the performance of this cure, for which all men long, do not await the summons of the world, for [27r] God has long chosen you for this work and has especially entrusted you with it. Grasp the reins and, fully armoured with virtue and great humility, seated on your horse, that is, on your royal power, one after the other leap triumphantly into the gulf, and so redeem Christian folk from death and bring real healing, without fear or favour, to the great evil which rises continually from it, and this without lending an ear to those

Churchmen who wish to rule and whose rule, in the words of the prophet, is not of God.

And be sure that if you undertake this divinely ordained mission with devotion and diligence, for the salvation of Mother Church, God will be gracious to you and close up our schism, to the healing of the Christian world and to a greater and more lasting glory than that of Curtius.

Most noble King of Cornwall and Prince of Wales, crowned with the royal majesty of England, this holy enterprise and divine mission of bringing back life to the Church, entrusted to you and your beloved brother, the King of Gaul, [27v] cannot be truly achieved in the opinion of some, and of this old writer among them, unless, through God's help, that flame which has been more or less hidden for so long, be uncovered and allowed to burn freely, that is to say, that peace and love between you and your beloved brother, King Charles, be openly displayed. For this reason, with great respect, moved by zeal for the general good, I, an old man, venture to say that supposing, which God forbid, the war between France and England were today as fierce and rigorous as in the days of the divine chastisement, when King Edward and King John were reigning, in such case, you ought, without long discussion, either to make peace or a truce of one hundred years and a day, so that together you might bring healing to that accursed wound, of which we have said so much, and which is so menacing to the souls of men.

And while today there is mutual love between you through the shared virtues of the diamond, and you are not at war, what excuse can you make to God? In truth, I greatly fear that if you prove negligent, God will show His wrath, you will be unpleasing in His sight and will feel His rod of correction. May God spare us this negligence [28r] and grant you His grace to resist adverse counsels.

Enough has now been said in general lamentation, concerning the sickness of our mother, Holy Church, and the remedy therefor, so much desired by all good Catholics.

*The third subject to be discussed is the Holy Passage,
which should be made by our two young Kings, of France
and England*

It is written in the Book of Moralities, in form of a parable, that there was once a powerful King, whose name was Malavisé, who was at war with a neighbouring King, called Vigilant. This King, Malavisé, put his trust more in human strength than in the justice of his cause, in diligence, or in the help of God. And so, little by little, he came to neglect both justice and knightly discipline, in such wise that at the end of the war he lost, first, his capital city and, finally, his kingdom. He was forced to retire to a strange and distant part of his dominions, which he still held, a region which was often cold [28v] and frozen.

King Vigilant, being in the capital city of his enemy, which he had conquered, made three solemn ordinances in confirmation of his victory. First he caused to be burnt and publicly destroyed all the banners, coats-of-arms and emblems belonging to King Malavisé. Secondly, to the sound of the royal trumpets, he banished from the kingdom the King his enemy. Thirdly, he kept the people of the country in subjection.

After a while, King Malavisé came to recognise his bad government, and saw clearly that it was through his own failings that he had lost his kingdom, without hope of soon regaining it because of the great strength of his enemy. In spite of this, so that he might keep fresh the memory of the wrongs done to him by King Vigilant by the three ordinances aforesaid, he issued a decree in his royal court to the effect that a certain old and poor knight, who had lost all his possessions, at all the great festivals and royal assemblies, when the King was seated at table [29r] surrounded by his knights, this old knight, poorly clad, should come into the hall, and advance to the King's table, sounding, loud and clear, a great hunting horn, and in a strong voice say to him, O Sire, formerly King Malavisé, remember the great wrongs, harm and villany that King Vigilant has inflicted on you and all your line. Remember, too, that it was for lack of good government and justice that you lost your kingdom and that your loyal subjects were forsaken. Having said this, and with no more words, and without doing reverence, the old knight was to leave the court and return to his humble dwelling. This parable, if studied with goodwill, should demonstrate clearly its intention and meaning.

Most excellent and devout Prince and worthy King of England, by gracious leave of your Royal Highness, this present old and poor Solitary, speaking through the old and poor knight aforesaid, always with due respect toward your Majesty, your brother, King Charles, and all other Christian princes, will make plain and interpret and apply to his theme this parable.

[29v] Now, as regards the interpretation of the story, by King Mala-

visé may be understood a Christian king, representing in his person the Emperor of Rome and all other Christian kings, and by King Vigilant, the Sultan of Babylon, as appears from the actions of the two kings in the parable.

Now let us pass, in the name of God, to the exposition of King Malavisé, that is, of the Christian kings who have long been ill-advised, and still are. Through lack of good government, and, above all, through lack of justice, which includes the Faith of Jesus Christ and His holy works, and lack, also, of knightly discipline, first the capital city of all Christendom, that is the holy city of Jerusalem, the foundation stone of the Catholic Faith, and then the whole kingdom, the Promised land, have been lost, and conquered by King Vigilant, the Sultan of Babylon, who has held it [30r] for one or two hundred years, to the great shame and disgrace of Christian kings, alas, so ill-advised.

If, by chance, any Christian king attempts to exonerate himself for this evil counsel and the loss of the Holy Land, by saying that it was not by him or his predecessors that this loss came about, but by the King of Jerusalem who was reigning at that time, the plain reply may be made that if Guy of Lusignan, at that time through his wife King of Jerusalem, had had succour from his brothers and cousins, the kings of Christendom, it is very likely that the holy city of Jerusalem, which was lost in his day, would not have been lost. And later, if Henry of Lusignan had had help, likewise he would not have lost the city of Acre and what remained of the kingdom of Jerusalem and the Holy Land. The said city of Jerusalem, and the kingdom thereof, the origin and foundation of the Faith, this very special kingdom, surrounded on all sides by enemies, these public lands of Christendom belonging on grounds of Faith and honour, not only to all Christian peoples [30v] but also to their kings and princes, this city should never have been withdrawn from the common guard and safe-keeping of these Christian kings, for the honour of the faith; but, for the sake of good government we could not have four, five or six kings all dwelling in the kingdom at the same time to ensure its protection. It should have sufficed that a single Christian king, in the name of himself and all the others, should have the rule, always with the provision that should necessity arise, he could call on the help of all Christian kings. And because the aforesaid Kings of Jerusalem, and those ruling elsewhere in the said kingdom and in the coastal towns, did not receive the help of which I have spoken, all was lost, to the great shame and disgrace of the

Christian rulers, justly named Malavisé. It has been said earlier that King Malavisé lost his kingdom through lack of justice and neglect of knightly discipline. The same is exactly true of the said Kings of Jerusalem since the loss of the Holy City. This failing was evident to the Emperor, the Roman Pope, [31r] and all the kings of the Christian world, who, for the sake of the Faith of Jesus Christ, were responsible for remedying these failings, in what was the common concern of all Christians. For this reason, which can easily be supported by divine, civil and moral laws, one might say that all the emperors, popes, and kings, on account of their negligence, were parties to the loss of the Holy Land, though this by no means excuses the aforesaid Kings of Jerusalem. And, further, because they have so long delayed the recovery of the Holy Land while occupied in shedding the blood of one another, in the sense of the parable they may truly be called *roys malavisé*, which is a great dishonour to the fame of their royal lines; for according to the laws, sons are bound to redress the mistakes of their fathers, that is to say, those that can be redressed.

Again, in accordance with the parable, King Vigilant, that is, the Sultan of Babylon, to the discomfiture of the Christians as they slept, set fire to and destroyed the banners, emblems and arms of King Malavisé, that is to say, the Crucifix and all [31v] other precious signs of the Christian Faith. Further, publicly, to the sound of trumpets, he proclaimed the banishment of King Malavisé, representing all Christian kings, from the kingdom of Jerusalem. And, in fine, with great contempt and in defiance of all Christendom, he held, and still holds, in subjection all the Christian people of the kingdom, which throws no little shame on the power and pride of Christian kings.

Again, the parable states that King Malavisé, having lost his kingdom without hope of recovering it, withdrew to a distant province which still remained to him, a region where extreme cold was frequent. Here, under the image of King Malavisé, are clearly portrayed the great kings of Christendom, who, along with their predecessors, have withdrawn to the West, cut off by cold from the power and love of God, kings who ought to dwell in Jerusalem and Eastern parts for the increase of the Faith. Among these Western kings, according to the imaginings and longings of the Old Solitary, in his dream [32r] dreamed in contemplation, there are two, who, through God's grace, have confessed that it is not without justice that they and their ancestors have been called in this Letter *roys malavisé*.

So that, by the grace of God, the name Malavisé may be changed in spirit to Bien-avisé, they have accepted the ordinance concerning the poor, old knight, to remind them continually of the wrongs which King Vigilant, that is the Sultan of Babylon, and his predessors have inflicted and are still inflicting on the blessed Son of God and their royal majesties. These are the two kings who have been figured in this Letter as the carbuncle and the diamond, who from two faraway and different countries, mortal enemies the one of the other, by the gentle love and inspiration of the Holy Spirit, have been united in heart and mind in peace and love the one to the other, with the aim of taking upon themselves the task of avenging the wrongs done to the Crucified One, and the ancient shame born by all Christian kings, whom we have named Malaviséz.

This Old Solitary is strengthened in mind by the courage and magnanimity [32v] of our two kings and princes, Charles and Richard, the Kings of France and England, and by their high-minded and blessed intention. Encouraged also by the words of the holy prophet, David, which show clearly that the time is come for pardon and the restoration of the holy city of Jerusalem, the said Solitary, in all humility, will assume the part of the poor, old knight, who has lost his heritage, that is, the Christian kingdom of Jerusalem; and he will come, in spirit, into the hall, before the said Kings, and, at this present time before the royal majesty of the gracious and devout King of England, sounding his great hunting horn, which for forty years he has never ceased to sound before emperors, kings and princes throughout Christendom, to summon to God's great hunt the greyhounds and the coursing dogs to capture the rich prize, so that the name Malavisé may be changed. And the Old Solitary, with a loud voice and fervent heart will speak now as he has spoken in the past and recently to the very valiant and worthy King Charles and to those of his noble house, saying,

O great and good King of Great Britain, prince of [33r] Wales and North Wales, Lord of Ireland, and King of Cornwall, remember with grief the ancient wrong wrought by King Vigilant, that is, the Sultan, against our Lord, sweet Jesus the Crucified. Remember Mount Calvary, the holy sepulchre, and the sacred places, watered by the precious blood of the Lamb, which are befouled every day by the false followers of Mohammed, condemned in the sight of God. Remember, and not as in a dream, that your arms, emblems and banners, which bear witness to your power to discomfort and put to flight the enemies of human nature, the enemies from Hell, have long been held in contempt, and still are, in Jerusalem, your spiritual heritage here on earth. These enemies have burnt, destroyed and reviled to the utmost the sanctuary of your Faith, the Cross and holy relics of the Passion of your Redeemer and Saviour, Jesus Christ. O most excellent and puissant King, remember that you and your ancestors have been shamefully banished from your [33v] spiritual kingdom and inheritance, that holy land purchased for you by Jesus at the price of His precious blood and death.

O devout King, bear in mind how your subjects who enter or live in that kingdom are held in serfdom by King Vigilant, beaten and ill-treated, and how they pay great tributes and aids, to the shame and dishonour of all Christian kings, and, in particular, of your beloved brother, Charles, King of France, and of you, the devout and good King of England. Remember too, with a sigh, that the holy Catholic Faith, for which so many of your ancestors, the blessed Kings of England, suffered martyrdom, today in Jerusalem and Syria, in Egypt and in Turkey, and throughout the East, is trodden under foot, dishonoured, destroyed, deserted and abandoned, God's temples in these places lie profaned, ruined and emptied, and the divine sacrifice and Office forgotten and held in abomination. What man is there, baptised in the name of the blessed Jesus, whose heart is so [34r] steeled that he can hear tell of these wrongs and not be moved to compassion, and so to offer in devotion to God his body, his goods and all that lies in his power, to remedy the great evils and this dishonour of Christendom, here briefly recited? It is much to be feared that those Christians who are not thus touched by compassion for these wrongs, will be deprived of a share in Jerusalem triumphant, spoken of by St. Paul the Apostle.

This brief account will suffice concerning the mission of the Old Solitary, and its significance, both in spirit and in written word, as interpretation of the poor, old knight of the parable, touching the righting of the wrongs done by the Sultan of Babylon to all Christian kings, and especially to your very devout and puissant Majesty.

O excellent Prince and worthy Lord, it can easily be believed that, through your steadfast Catholic faith, following the example and virtues of your holy predecessors, and, in particular, of the saintly King Edmund, and of the valiant King of France, St. Louis, you will be well aware that the wrongs I have recounted, done by King Vigilant to you and all your [34v] Christian brother kings, may be called a great wound, greater even than the other accursed wound I have pictured in this Letter. And no wonder, for the more widely spread the damage, the more it is to be feared, and the harder it is to heal. This injury lies chiefly in the destruction of the Faith and reaches directly to the soul of all Christians, both Catholic and schismatic, and so to all kings. And greater shame comes from the damage and injury to the immortal soul and the encroachment on its inheritance, than from the shame incurred by the mortal body and the despoiling and corrupting of its temporal possessions. Therefore cursed was the day on which the open wound between the Kings of England and France came into being, and happy and blessed the day on which the spread of its poison was halted; and we may joyfully say today that the aforesaid wound is nearly healed. God grant that you two Kings may do all that remains to be done, to the consolation of all good people.

[35r] Here the Old Solitary offers to the King of England a new Order of Chivalry of the Crucified One, which is to be sent overseas ahead of the two kings, who, by God's grace, will undertake the holy voyage

O mighty King of Great Britain, St. John Chrysostom records the opinion that for a great lord to suffer his own personal injuries with patience is a matter for praise, but to accept injuries to his God, when he is able to remedy them, is a thing unworthy and full of iniquity. This old writer is well informed as to the great and burning desire that your loved brother, Charles, King of France, has to right the wrongs done to his God, the blessed Son of God, sweet Jesus Christ, by King Vigilant, that is, the Sultan of Babylon. Further, for some years past the said Old Solitary has been kept well informed by that messenger of God, Robert the Hermit, concerning your own lofty purpose and like valour. Thus you two kings, as true champions of the Faith, are now prepared to present yourselves before your God [35v] ready to avenge His wrongs.

And since for the complete cure of the disease, recently described, which is so universal and so harmful alike to the common good of Christendom and the Catholic Faith, strong and well considered medicines are necessary, as well as wise and learned physicians, who are not above employing for the cure of their patients some simple remedy, mixed by the apothecary's humble assistants: assuming this suggested humility on the part of the great physicians and their strong desire for the cure of the universal sickness, O worthy Prince, this Old Solitary, for the moment acting as doctor, is emboldened to offer to your much loved brother, the King of France, and herewith, with great deference, to your royal and devout Majesty of England, a small remedy for the said illness, as a preliminary to the greater medicine, which is essential for the cure of the aforesaid universal malady.

Speaking figuratively, by the greater medicine is meant the holy passage *d'outremer*, which I hope, by God's grace, will be undertaken by the [36r] lofty courage of your brother and yourself, to the glory of God and the exaltation of the Catholic Faith. For the holy voyage of these mighty Kings, there must be great, long and mature preparations, and among these, this Old Abortive, your most unworthy spokesman, in spirit and in writing, most worthy and devout King, offers you a simple preparatory medicine, not only as an aid to the healing of the aforesaid sickness, but for the reform and cure, under God, of the general disorders and sufferings now prevailing throughout Christendom.

This simple medicine, preparatory to the great journey which is to be undertaken by you, true lodestone figured as the fine diamond, and by your beloved brother, the carbuncle called *clere lumiere*, is none other than the blessed new Order of the Chivalry of the Passion of Jesus Christ, conceived forty years ago, under God's inspiration as may be humbly believed, and now to be submitted to the devotion of your royal Majesties. This medicine, then, by God's goodness and by your Majesties, must be established, completed and created from the beginning from among the valiant knighthood and men-[36v]at-arms of the seven languages of Christendom, always according to your ordinances, and this for four main reasons; first for the recall of the soldiery, sullied and foully nourished by the blood of their slaughtered Christian brothers, to knightly repentance and to God's battle; next, it must be created to be the harbinger of your royal Majesties, to go before you into the land of the enemies of the Faith, to seize the ports and strongholds, ready for your reception when you come to make the journey, so that you may land in safety, without risk of enemy attack; the third object is the conquest of the Holy Land, by the grace of God and the favour, help and blessing of your royal Majesties; fourthly and lastly, to further the increase of the Catholic Faith in all parts of the Orient.

And since on the matter of the power and aims of this holy Order, and the plain reasons for which it is now so vital to Christendom, and especially to the needs both of your royal Majesty and of [37r] your brother the King of France, and of the benefits which reasonably can be hoped for from this Order for the honour and reform of all Christendom, your worthy and devout Majesty may already have been made acquainted by your very loyal servant and spokesman, the aforesaid Robert the Hermit, and more recently by the book called *La sustance abregie* of the said Order of Chivalry, which the Old Solitary, humbly and devotedly, handed to your beloved brother, the Count of Huntingdon, to give to you so that you might know the blessings which could result from the establishment of this Order; and, further, because you can be informed thereon by your beloved uncle, the Duke of York and by Sir John Harlestone, and others of your loyal subjects, for these reasons the Old Solitary passes over the full exposition in this letter, and simply commends the creation of the said Order and all its proposed duties to your devotion, most Catholic Prince, and to Jesus, the lord and master [37v] of this, His own Order; and may it please Jesus in His compassion to inspire in you the desire to establish and exalt this Order, to your glory and His holy service. And may God grant this plea.

O noble and Catholic King, speaking always with due respect, and trusting in your devotion and humility, I find that there are three plain reasons which, under God, should spur you to embrace with the arms of love and charity this gracious new Order of Chivalry, which takes its title from the Passion of the blessed Son of God. The first of these reasons lies in the strong desire that you have for the salvation of the souls of your Christian brethren, who, following the example set by this holy Chivalry, will be impelled to forsake their way of sin, to serve God, and amend their lives. This desire for the safety of their souls you have shown clearly by your earnest wish to make peace with your brothers, the French, and, hence, with all Christians. The second reason which should influence you, [38r] most devout Prince, is that the debts incurred by your beloved fathers, on whom God have mercy, who in my own times have twice prevented the voyage overseas by their accursed war, might, to some degree, be paid by your sending ahead of you, as has been proposed, this holy chivalry, for the salvation of the souls of your aforesaid forefathers and of your own; and also so that in return for this first offering to God, He will grant you grace to achieve your aims, namely, to make true peace with your Christian brothers, and not be diverted by sin from carrying out, in person, the holy passage, in the company of your beloved brother, the King of France.

The third reason which should move you, wise King, is that by the lead and influence of this Order of Chivalry, your royal Majesty, making the journey as described, in respect of expenses, which will be by no means small, will expend a million florins less than you would if the said Order did not exist, and the same is true for your brother Charles. All this would be, and will be if God wills, to the great benefit of the [38v] whole host of Christendom. This is not surprising, for the less you spend now, the more you will have to meet the cost of the actual journey and your holy enterprise. Your Highness may be informed of the truth of this third reason by the aforesaid Robert the Hermit, and those noble knights who are, under God, prepared to take part in such an Order of Chivalry. And enough has now been said concerning this new Order of the Chivalry of the blessed Crucified One and of the great blessings it would bring to Christendom, to the glory of God and of all who favour this Order.

Here begins the fourth subject of this present letter, that is to say, certain marriages affecting the King of England, by which the achievement of the long hoped for peace might be hindered, and the remedy therefor

Most excellent Prince and worthy King of most Christian England, speaking with all the respect due to your royal dignity, this Old Solitary, frequenting, however unworthily, even into his old age, the courts of popes and kings, enjoyed greatly asking many and diverse questions of the wise physicians of these rulers [39r] touching astrology and medicine, so as to learn and retain certain medical principles which he might employ in case of illness. For this reason, in pursuing his dream, the Old Solitary, trusting in Jesus the sovereign physician, is emboldened in this poor letter to address your royal Majesty in terms of medicine, and of wounds and their cure, although he has no degree in medicine, and submits himself to the correction of your benevolence.

The position, gracious King, is that rumours are widespread in the kingdom of Gaul that certain physicians, great and small, of your kingdom and elsewhere, moved to all appearance by hope of consolation, offspring, remedy for future ills and for the strengthening of one side of the great wound of the West, set forth at length in this letter, and acting, as they think, for the best, have offered you, and continue to offer, an electuary sufficient to heal the ills set out above. You must know, worthy Prince, that, according to the authorities on medicine [39v] there are certain electuaries which seem pleasant to the patient because of the sugar which hides their bitterness, the bitterness of such things as scammony, digridium and aloes, which are strong, bitter and burning. There is danger in such medicines unless some preliminary medicine has been taken and precautions against contrary after-effects planned and carried out. Again, it may happen that, despite great care, these medicines, scammony and the like, are so strong in themselves that nature can neither absorb nor digest them, and they may cause the patient to relapse into an illness worse than his first. Let this warning be given so that all men may take care, as far as they can, not to take any of these strong medicines, because of the great dangers which may result. Perhaps it would be better for the preservation of health to make use of safe and gentle medicines, such as cassia fistula, manna, and that kindly electuary, catholicon, and so allow Nature, which never sleeps, to work, little by little, [40r] and to cleanse and restore good health. And this may suffice as a little prologue to the electuary already proposed.

Most wise and humble King, by this recommended electuary, along with its prescribed directions, offered to you by those physicians, your loyal subjects and others, speaking figuratively and in the spirit of the dream set forth above, may be understood a certain marriage alliance advised for your royal Majesty, which is a very pleasant electuary, so long as it is properly made up; but from this same electuary improperly composed, the very wise King Solomon got little profit, that is to say, from the very bitter scammony coated with sugar, harsh and violent in its effect, in the person of the daughter of the King of Egypt.

Now it is clear, O noble Prince, that according to divine, civil and moral law, there are four main reasons for which kings should marry, namely, to obtain succession, to make honourable alliances, to achieve or preserve peace in their kingdoms, and, in the fourth place, to avoid fornication and live honestly and chastely according to the sacrament of marriage. And wise men may say that all [40v] kings who are both worthy and friends of God, should weigh carefully in this matter of marriage these four conditions, which are pleasing to God and to the good men of their kingdoms. And if one or two of these conditions are lacking, a king, before such a marriage is carried out and consummated in the sight of God, should hesitate, commend himself to God, and reconsider like a wise man, following the precepts of the law, and not lightly allow himself to be thrown into this dangerous pit, for it is too late to repent when the wheel is turning and already started on its course.

Most worthy Prince, this Old Solitary and hesitant writer does not intend by what he has said above to assail the holy sacrament of marriage, which God the Father ordained and commanded by his own word, and His blessed Son, Jesus Christ, confirmed at the marriage feast of Archedeclin, but he calls to mind while contemplating on the matter, the three states that Jesus spoke of in his Gospel, namely, the state of matrimony, the state of chastity or widowhood, and the sovereign [41r] state of virginity. According to the Scriptures, those of the first state will be rewarded in the glory of Paradise with the thirtieth crown, the chaste and widows with the sixtieth crown, but to the virgins will be given the one hundredth crown and they will be in the presence of the Lamb wherever He goes.

O King, renowned for virtue and wisdom, the man who loves his lord with a pure love and without desire for worldly gain, hopes with all his heart that his said lord, by the grace of God, may be virtuous in action and adorned with all such high qualities as may be acquired in this world. Jesus knows that this Old Solitary, admiring the virtues that God has emplanted in you, according to public renown, and also being made well aware of them by the report of the poor hermit, Robert; and, at the same time, loving in your royal person sweet Jesus, King of true peace, Who has inspired in your heart the good fruit of the peace of Christendom; this Old Solitary, then, considering that of the three estates aforesaid you are deprived, though without sin, of the chief, [41v] that is, of virginity, for this reason is emboldened at this moment, for what it is worth, to recommend the state of chastity, because in the sight of God it ranks next to that of virginity, but in no way by this means to slight the state of marriage.

Anyone who calls to mind the good men of this world spoken of in the Old and New Testaments and in the ancient chronicles from the beginning of the world, will find that those who have lived virtuously in chastity and continence, according to the opinion of the world and for the salvation of their souls, have enjoyed among the worthy special eminence and renown. What shall be said of the firstborn of our father, Adam, Abel the Just, who died virgin and, therefore, chaste, and left no issue? And Elijah the prophet, now joyful in Paradise, abstained from having children by human procreation, although he was the father of countless people by his teaching and example. Daniel the prophet, elect of God, and, according to the Scriptures, chaste, by his holy continence merited the rank of governor of King Nebuchadnezzar and of the empire [42r] of the Assyrians. And the holy patriarch, Joseph, for his steadfast chastity became a prince in Egypt and was endowed with wisdom to interpret the dreams of Pharaoh. And what is to be said of that very holy widow, Judith, who through the power of her chastity beheaded Holofernes and saved the people of Israel from destruction?

Who can reckon the number of kings and princes of Christendom who have lived in chastity, of whom the memory in Heaven and earth is more glorious than of a thousand others who married? As, for example, the most noble Godfrey de Bouillon, who through the strength of his chastity cut through the Saracen host at the battle of Antioch; and also the Emperor Henry I and his wife, the Empress Radegond, who remained virgin; and it was he, also, who righteously dismissed from his court all heralds and minstrels, and gave the money, that was usually paid to them, to the poor. What a number of kings there have been in England, in France, and in other kingdoms, who have lived chastely, and some of whom have been martyred, whose memory is sweeter than that of a hundred others who married. And let this be said to the glory of God concerning the estate of [42v] chastity, of which it is written, Let him who is able, choose it. And to encourage the life of chastity, the Apostle St. Paul said to all those whom he had converted, Would that you might all be as I am, chaste and virgin, for the outward show of this world dies and passes into nothingness.

Now let us pass on to the first of the above stated reasons why kings and all good Christians should marry, that is, to have succession, and we shall find that it is not in the power of man to ensure issue, at least such issue as he would wish, for God reserves this to Himself alone, and grants or witholds issue according to His will, His favour, or divine decree for the merit or demerit of the kings or people concerned. It is written that for the sins of the people, God allows the hypocrite to reign, that is, according to the gloss, the tyrant.

How many valiant men in this world had no heirs of their body to succeed them! Melchizedek, great King of Salem, that is Jerusalem, is described by the doctors of the Church and in Holy Writ as without father and without mother, [43r] signifying Jesus Christ, who had no earthly father, for he was incarnate of the Holy Spirit, and was without mother after the fashion of other mothers, for he was born of the Virgin Mary, yet the Scripture makes no mention of any descendant of Melchizedek.

Who is more famous than King Alexander? Yet he left no child to reign after him. Who was more valiant and powerful in their time than Julius Caesar and his nephew Octavian, Emperor of Rome, who were monarchs of the world, and yet died without heirs of their body to succeed them? How many valiant men have there been of the New Covenant, emperors, kings and princes, confessors and martyrs, who have passed from this world without leaving direct issue, and yet whose memory is more renowned than that of a thousand others who have left successors.

It is a natural and comely thing that a husband should desire children, and if these are worthy, the father will be very happy, but all the days of his life he will remain in fear lest he should lose them; and if [43v] this does happen, he will never again rejoice. This may be held to be true of your grandfather, the noble King Edward, whose joy over the great victories that God granted and bestowed on your beloved father, his valiant and conquering eldest son, the noble Prince of Wales, was small in comparison with the bitter grief he suffered at his death. On the other hand, if, as often happens, a king or prince should have unworthy offspring, of bad habits, if he is wise he will never be happy and will wish a thousand times that he had never married.

It is well known that although princes and others who marry may be worthy people, yet for the reasons given above they may beget children who do not resemble their fathers in goodness, as is shown in the Scriptures and elsewhere in the case of Cain, who killed his brother Abel. Hezekiah the most holy king of Jerusalem begat Manasseh, who caused Isaiah the prophet to be cut in two with a wooden sickle, and in addition made the streets of Jerusalem run with the blood of the prophets of God, and finally lost his kingdom and was carried [44r] captive into Babylon. Who was more saintly or a better king of the people of Israel than David? And yet he begat Absalom, who drove his own father out of the kingdom. And Solomon begat Rehoboam, who through his wickedness lost ten kingdoms out of twelve in a single day. Jehoiakim, the good king concerning whom Jeremiah the prophet uttered such great lamentation, begat Jeconiah, a very evil king, who lost his kingdom and was led captive in the transmigration to Babylon. What shall be said of Constantius, brother of the Emperor Constantine, who begat Julian the Apostate? And your ancestor Henry begat Henry, who rose against him. Louis, the worthy son of the great Charlemagne, Emperor of Rome and King of France, begat Lothaire, who held his father, the said Louis, Emperor and King of France, prisoner in the city of Soissons. He who would wish to number the wicked sons begotten of great kings, princes and other valiant and worthy people, would find the task impossible. These considerations and the risk of having bad children because of the iniquities of mankind should not be ignored by wise kings.

[44v] If any man wishes to argue that it is as likely that a good and valiant king, in true marriage, will engender a good and worthy son as he will a bad one, it can be answered that this is true. Nowadays, speaking in figure, when the wise farmer thinks of sowing wheat in a certain field, he examines carefully, first of all, the nature of the soil, for some land is so good that if barley is sown, it comes up wheat. Alas, this does not happen in the West, for there it is too cold. The land in these parts, O worthy Prince, however well it has been tilled, is likely to produce nothing but prickly thorns, as has long been the case in France and England. Hence, he, who, by God's grace, has wheat of the kind that Joseph stored in Egypt to meet the famine, that is, the Bread of Life, come down from Heaven, shall be more safely sustained than if he sowed anew the field of Aceldema, the field of blood, always [45r] full of sharp thorns, which have sent so many French and English men to Hell. Therefore it is expedient, most worthy Prince, that with God's grace, you should examine carefully the field in which you are to sow your wheat, so as to ensure a holy and blessed issue, which shall not partake of the thorny nature of his mother's land. Be not surprised, for in these days, alas, there is no field so fine, or so fruitful, or so well cultivated, or of such good repute, that it does not sometimes, for the sins of father or mother, bring forth prickly thorns only, which choke the red roses and white lilies; and it is a great sin against Nature that such beautiful flowers should lose their sweet scent through the invasion of the thorns.

As to two further reasons why kings should marry, that is to say, for the sake of making honourable alliances, leading to the acquisition of territory, and to foster peace in their kingdoms, something very pleasing to God, what shall we say concerning this argument, [45v] which, according to the opinion of some wise and Godfearing men, is not so well founded as it might seem. God grant that in the scales of your royal wisdom, and in the fear of God, the matter may be well weighed, and that haste, induced by immediate hope of increasing and expanding temporal possessions and adding to your lordships, should not influence you to the prejudice of Christendom; for such possessions and alliances, suspect in the eyes of many, might lead to fresh growth of those deadly thorns, already condemned in this letter, and the opening and infecting once again of the deep wound, greatly lamented in this treatise, and now, to your credit, almost healed. And don't forget, most devout King, that the physicians who prescribe this most soothing electuary, which would give you increase in territory and worldly power, will not be the ones who have to render account for your precious soul, when it stands before the sovereign Judge, before whom you will have to acquit yourself for the souls which have been damned by your conduct, that is, through this marriage and the menace of the [46r] thorns, so often spoken of. From all this may God in His mercy preserve you, and keep you from shedding the blood of your Christian brethren.

Further, worthy Prince, friend of God, while you ponder on these things, call to mind, and sadly, the marriage, then thought a fortunate one, of the mother of the valiant King Edward, your much loved ancestor, from which marriage you are descended, and of the deadly and penetrating thorns resulting from that union, which have been active for sixty years in such a cursed way that the beautiful lilies, from whom you spring, have been horribly trampled under foot and have largely become withered and spoiled, and the greater part of Christendom has been disturbed and led astray, and without much lasting profit to you from so much evil. And although, by divine decree and permission, your predecessors by virtue of the power of these thorns have obtained and won notable victories over their Christian brothers, nevertheless it must be sadly avowed that these thorns have given greater victories to the Enemy of the human race, taking into account the souls without number, from the one side and the other, who have been doomed to suffer everlasting damnation.

[46v] St. Gregory says that from what has happened one can to some

extent judge what will happen and so be prepared for future dangers. This Old Solitary, most gracious King, who longs with all his strength for the accomplishment of that true peace with which God has infused the hearts of you and your beloved brother, King Charles, as if the two were one heart and one soul, has a lively hope that God will preserve you from accepting any such electuary, whose hidden bitterness will in time to come engender fresh thorns, like unto the former oft mentioned and dangerous ones, dreaded by all good men.

Mighty Prince, as to the fourth reason for which a king should marry, namely, to pass his youth and live soberly and chastely in the sacrament of matrimony, you must understand that, although a life of chaste widowhood and virtuous continence has been shown above to be, in some degree, next in perfection in the eyes of God to the state of virginity, if it should please you to prefer this state of abstinence in order to gain the aureole, that is, the thirtieth crown, you may say, for your comfort, with [47r] the Apostle, St. Paul, All things are lawful unto me, but all things are not expedient for the salvation of my soul, which means, in substance, it is lawful for you to marry, but if you wish to gain the greater virtue, it is not expedient, for the good of the soul passes in importance that of the body and things temporal. However, although the great dangers and hazards which often follow from the marriage of great princes and others have been clearly shown above by many examples, in order to demonstrate the greater values of chastity, nevertheless, the same St. Paul wrote that the man who could not be continent, should marry in the name of Jesus Christ, which, in our case, in order to assuage your subjects, and especially those who have offered to you that oft mentioned electuary, means the recommendation to your royal Majesty by those same physicians, or the free choice made by you yourself, of another electuary, which might not be so attractive, but is not so likely to lead to bloodshed, and is without an inner bitterness hidden by a sugar coating, as described above. And so by the goodness of God, in great love of both God and your fellow men, may there be sought and found a wholesome [47v] electuary for our young King of Great Britain, containing neither scammony, digridium, nor aloes, but, both within and without, composed of and derived from the precious balm, much moralised upon in this present writing.[5] And let this electuary be made of manna from Heaven, which can do no hurt,

---

5. A somewhat confused sentence in the French text, the intention of which is, I think, covered by my translation.

so that, by the goodness of God, it may be so fertile that from it may spring fine fruit, to the glory of God, the preservation of peace, and the consolation of your royal fatherhood, of your loyal subjects and especially of your beloved brother, Charles, King of France, and all your faithful friends. May God grant that this be so.

Those physicians who concerned themselves deeply, as already related, in the making of the first suggested electuary, might ask of the Old Solitary, Where is to be found this second electuary, so pure and so agreeable and which contains no trace of bitterness? To which he can reply, in the words of the familiar proverb, To have a good wife who brings with her all blessings, is a special gift from God. If these physicians were as much concerned with the welfare of their patients' souls [48r] as they are with their bodies, the patients would soon be cured. But because often, and today very often, we, wise in the things of this world, neglect the spirit and put the cart before the horse, for this reason, the field brings forth thorns.

St. Anthony, in his Lives of the Fathers, said to another abbot, Do everything that thou doest under the guidance of Holy Writ. No man in Christendom can give a better guide to a king touching his marriage than the Scriptures. No wonder, for in the Scriptures it is the Holy Spirit who speaks, the true doctor, who teaches loyal Christians how they should act. Worthy King, friend of God, you will find in the Bible that great kings and good men pay less heed, in the matter of marriage, to power, riches, or high descent, than to virtue in their wives. The great King of the Assyrians, Ahasuerus, took as queen and wife a humble and worthy woman, niece of Mordecai the Jew, the good and beautiful Esther, who, through that same goodness delivered from death the people of Israel. David, the holy King, took for wife [48v] Abigail the wise, after the death of her husband, she who had turned aside the threat of the thorns, which were ready to spring up between David and Nabal the Carmelite. And Ruth, for her prudence and great humility, was found worthy to be the wife of Boaz, the grandfather of Jesse, from whom sweet Jesus descended in direct line.

Now let us turn to the New Covenant. Constantin, Emperor of Rome and father of the great Constantine, took to wife Helen, at that time an inn-keeper, a very wise woman and of great virtue. Many thought that she was the daughter of the King of England, but Constantin married her for her goodness and as a poor woman, and not as a king's daughter. This same St. Helen, through grace, was judged worthy to find in Jerusalem the true Cross, thus strengthening the Roman Empire, which became Christian. Further, most gracious King, the noble Prince of Wales, your beloved father, took to wife a princess who was not a king's daughter, from which union much good has flowed, so that by you, his offspring, the peace of Christendom, the union of the Church, and the holy passage overseas, with the help of your brother the King of France, by the grace of God, might be brought to pass, for the illumination of the Faith and of all [49r] Christendom. Then shall both Englishmen and Frenchmen, with one voice, say unto you, most noble King Richard, Blessed is the womb which bore thee and the paps which gave thee suck. And may God grant this.

May it please God, worthy Prince, for the furtherance of peace in Christendom and the comfort of your royal person, to grant you a wife such as Griselda, the wife of the Marquis of Saluzzo, who was but the daughter of a poor working man, yet, according to the authentic chronicle of the said Marquis of Saluzzo and Griselda his wife, written by that learned doctor and sovereign poet, Master Francis Petrarch, there is no record, from the beginning of the world until today, apart from the saints, of a woman of such great virtue, nor so loving towards her husband, nor of such marvellous patience, as this same Lady Griselda; and this you have read, or may come to read, in the said chronicle.

May it please you, noble and worthy Prince, to give some attention and study to the humble writing [49v] of a poor old man, of imperfect mind, concerned with the question of the marriage of your royal Majesty, and pray to God that He will instruct you through His angel, as He did Tobias by the angel Raphael, who delivered Tobias from the seven wicked angels, and afterwards taught him how to praise God and order his life. Pray also to God that, through bad advice, you be not numbered among those who excused themselves from attendance at the great king's feast, because they had newly married a wife, for fleshly desire or avarice, and not according to the will of God, Who sanctifies marriages. And now I have said enough in this small and feeble treatise and always with due respect on the subject of marriage, as it concerns your royal Majesty, and on the obstacles which might stand in the way of the longed-for peace and the general welfare of Christendom.

The fifth subject of this present letter, in the form of an example, showing that kings should greatly fear to shed the blood of their Christian brothers; and another example taken from Moses and Aaron

Most excellent Prince and gracious Lord, the main object of this poor letter is the perpetual union and alliance, under God, true peace and [50r] comely, brotherly love between the two sons of St. Louis, King of France, that is, between Charles and Richard, by the grace of God, worthy Kings of France and England, and among all their subjects, and, hence, the peace and unity of the Church and all Christian people. This hoped for love and peace may be sought from Heaven, through the mercy of Jesus, if your royal Majesty, most gracious King, and your brother also, put into effect, boldly and actively, the principles of this feeble letter, and, neither by a doubtful marriage nor by outwardly attractive suggestions and exhortations, made by the enemies of peace, be deceived and turned from the task to which God has elected and called you. From this, may God preserve you both; which He will do, by His holy grace, and defend you, if in your inner heart you have true compassion and bitter grief for the blood of Christian men, shed by your predecessors, and if you shrink from and hold in horror in God's sight the spilling of blood which would ensue if the War were renewed; and may God in His grace keep the Christians of England and France safe from this fate.

[50v] Many doctors of the Church affirm that the hearts of men are more moved by example than by precept, for which reason it seems fitting to the Old Solitary that he should offer to your royal devotion, and to your knights, long nurtured in bloodshed, an appropriate example, so that, henceforth, the shedding of Christian blood might be held in abomination, and also so that it might clearly show the great inhumanity of those who take pleasure in spilling the blood of their fellows.

It is related in a famous book, called the Dictionary, how in the desert of India, in a region called Stragopales, which is near the sea, there exists a great bird called the harpy, cruel beyond belief, which has the face of a man and is a bird of prey. This cruel bird kills at sight the first man it meets. By chance, after a while, it may come to a stretch of water, in which it sees the reflection of its face, which is like to a man's.

This brings back to its mind the memory of the man it has killed, and, at once, it attacks its own image so violently that sometimes its own death results; and if it does not die, it remains for the rest of its days, [51r] stricken with grief for the killing of the man.

This bird, the cruel harpy, speaking figuratively and bearing in mind the purpose of this letter, passes judgement on Christian men, who are even more cruel, and especially on the English and French, although one can say that the French acted thus in defence of their country. How great is that cruelty, since by shedding the blood of our fellow creatures, English and French alike, once more we have killed sweet Jesus Christ, Who died for us and suffered harsh death for our sins. And yet we, both English and French, see Jesus, Whom we have killed, every day in the bitter waters of His Holy Passion, according to the saints, and look on Him, also, in the mirror of Holy Writ. We see Him, Who has the face of man, and like unto us in body, very God and very man, Who came to us in the desert of this world, for us and for our salvation, and we know Him not as we should, but are more cruel than that bird, the harpy. It would be seemly, in seeking mutual peace and love, if we followed [51v] the example of the harpy, showing a new pity for the death of our gentle Redeemer, Jesus Christ, and heart-felt horror at the effusion of Christian blood, so that, speaking with all reverence, the harpy need not, in the Day of Judgement, condemn kings and knights for being more cruel than itself. And may God in His goodness and through the prayers of the sweet Virgin Mary keep from such cruelty the two innocent Kings and their chivalry.

Most Catholic and worthy Prince, ruler of Great Britain, so that you may obtain and preserve true love and peace between the carbuncle and the fine diamond, and lest you should lose the blessed fruit of that peace, call quietly to mind the two brothers of Holy Writ, captains of six hundred thousand fighting men, to which two brothers God spoke, saying, You shall lead the children of Israel into the Promised Land, which I swore to your fathers I would give them. This was said to Moses and Aaron, captains of the people of Israel.

Nevertheless, notwithstanding that God had promised and sworn to the two brothers, Moses and Aaron, that they should lead and guide [52r] God's people into Jerusalem and the Promised Land, yet, because they did not sanctify God as they should at the Waters of Strife, for this were they deprived of that great honour. And God said unto them, that is, to Moses and Aaron, Because you sanctified me not before my people at the Waters of Strife and Rebellion, you shall not lead them into the land that I shall give them, but you shall die in this wilderness. All this is told more clearly in the Bible.

Now, in God's name, let us consider a certain concordance between the two brothers, chiefs of the people of Israel, and our two kings. The Scriptures tell us that the brothers, Moses and Aaron, were of the tribe of Levi, dedicated to God. Moses, the friend of God, was the most perfect of men, and Aaron the most diligent in the government of the Israelites. Whoever might wish to moralise on a concordance between the two brothers, Moses and Aaron, and the two royal brothers, Charles and Richard, leaders of God's people of France and England, could certainly find ample material bearing on the matter. But because [52v] this letter is already overlong, and lest your Majesty should weary of too much writing, the Old Solitary will cut short the figure. It may be noted as regards concordance that the brother Kings, Charles and Richard, both spring from the line of Levi, that is, the blessed St. Louis and the other holy Kings of France and England, specially set apart for the service of God and the preservation and increase of the holy Catholic faith. And it may be said that King Charles is the best of men and King Richard, his brother, the most diligent in the government of his people.

O most excellent Princes, Richard and Charles, brothers, and sons of the holy saints, you should often call to mind that the blessed Jesus has made you leaders together of His people of Israel, that is, of Western Christendom, to take them into the Promised Land; and for this end He has sent you His special messenger, the humble Robert the Hermit, who obeys the command of the blessed apostle, St. James; and in confirmation of the aforesaid message, you are conscious that ever since you heard it, true [53r] love and peace have taken root and grown in your hearts.

It has been revealed to you two Kings that by you peace will be established, the Church made one, and Syria conquered. Take good care that at the Waters of Strife you do not follow the example of Moses and Aaron, but there let God be solemnly glorified in the presence of the people of Israel, committed to you for guidance into the Promised Land. By these Waters of Strife, or rebellion against God, for our purpose, speaking in figure, may be understood all those who hinder the establishment of the longed for peace, on one side or the other, continually demanding from Moses and Aaron, that is, from Charles and

Richard, an abundance of earthly water for themselves, for their households, for their flocks, that is, gold and silver, lands and wealth, demands by which God is offended afresh and war against Him renewed.

Such murmurers against God and against peace should have great fear of the terrible judgement meted out to those that murmured against Moses and [53v] Aaron in the wilderness, as appears in the case of Dathan and Abiram, who, with their wives and children, servants, tents and herds, were engulfed in the depths of the earth and damned for ever and ever. And Miriam, sister of Moses and Aaron, for her complainings was suddenly struck down with a terrible white leprosy, and cast out from the host of God, to her utter confounding. Who can number the countless examples of God's vengeance upon those who have murmured against and disturbed Christian peace.

Now let us pass on to the way, brief and devout, in which, among all the contradictions which the Enemy of mankind furnishes daily, your royal and worthy magnificence, most devout King, and your brother, King Charles, too, can glorify and magnify God, before the rock be twice stricken by the rod of Moses.

Your sanctification of God, most worthy King, consists in conforming to the will of God, Who has made you lord of peace and not of war, concerning which St. Paul the Apostle said that the will of God is your sanctification that is, true peace, which through His precious blood He offered to the world. And to this true peace [54r] wars and dissensions among Christians are opposed in the highest degree. On which, the same apostle said, God is not the God of dissension, but of true peace; to which also St. John the Evangelist bears witness and gives ample support. How can you sanctify God in this world better than in the manner of the angels and saints, who sing without ceasing, Holy, holy, holy, etc. In like way, as Catholic Princes may you have peace on earth and good will towards your Christian brothers. The Holy Spirit, author of peace, according to the word of the prophet, cannot rest except on him who is humble and at rest, that is, in true peace with his neighbour.

Now take great heed, O fortunate Princes, lest the aforesaid peace, offered you by the sovereign God of Heaven, escape from your hands, and by failure in the sanctification, oft-mentioned, Moses and Aaron be deprived of the high office of leadership, and die in the wilderness, without completing the task assigned to them, and that by their own fault, which God forbid, God must choose other valiant princes, Joshua and

Caleb, from His host, finally to lead [54v] His people into the Promised Land. And now enough has been said, by means of the example of the harpy, to stress the abomination of the shedding of Christian blood, and the risk of being deprived of so many blessings through failure to sanctify God, from Whom true peace and all blessings offered to your Majesties flow, as from an everlasting fountain, in which fountain you may discern through grace that true peace and light which shall never fail. May God grant you these things.

The sixth subject of this present letter, that is, speaking in figure, the manner in which the precious stones, representing the two Kings, must be immersed and soaked in the precious wine from the vineyards of Engadi

We said at the beginning of the imagined dream of the Old Solitary that, marvellously, the vineyards of Engadi, of which the Holy Scriptures speak in such high terms, have blossomed anew in these kingdoms of the West, in such wise that in the hopes of many good men the said vineyards will produce wine of the kind to intoxicate the two Kings and many of their brave knights; [55r] or, as we might say, that the balm and lodestone, thus figured, may be wisely and in due proportion mingled, and imbued in spirit with the wine from the vineyards of Engadi.

It is written in the Book of Properties that the flower of the vine has power to drive away serpents and other venomous creatures. If, then, serpents cannot survive in the presence of the flowers of the vines which grow in the cold West, how could they persist near the strong wine of the East from the precious vineyards of Engadi?

The Holy Spirit writes in the Book of Wisdom that the Wisdom of God has built for Himself a house, and has prepared the wine and set the table. This statement bears on our intention to examine the precious wine of the vineyards of Engadi, so let us now pass to a certain concordance between our subject and the nature of that wine, with which the two Kings and a great number of their chivalry must become intoxicated.

God's Wisdom, that is the blessed Son of God, sweet Jesus, has built in this world a special house for Himself, in which He delights [55v] to dwell, performing great wonders therein; this house is the two kingdoms of France and England, excelling all other Christian realms, and although we have here two kingdoms, they make but one house, with the two Kings descended from one parentage, that is, from the most valiant King, St. Louis. Let this truth be applied to the house and most excellent lineage which God's Wisdom has, in particular and with great love, built for Himself in this world, and also to the great evils caused by those who, through mortal war, have brought about division between the royal sons of the one holy house.

Further, it has been written that God's Wisdom has mixed and watered the wine to be given to the royal sons of the aforesaid holy house, for they could not stomach the said wine in its full strength. Although certain doctors may interpret the vines of Engadi as the shrubs which distil the fine balm, spoken of above, yet we find in the Scriptures a more precise account of the vineyards of Engadi, [56r] in the Book of Canticles, where the Holy Spirit says, *Botrus Cypri in vigneis Engady*, that is to say, The grapes of Cyprus grow in the vineyards of Engadi.

You should know that in the kingdom of Cyprus, on a certain hill lies the vineyard of Engadi, according to the account given in the said Book of Canticles and in ancient writings. This vineyard is the most famous in the kingdom and the whole Orient, and its wine is of such strength and quality that it cannot be drunk until it is three years old. In the first year it is much disturbed and thick, like black oil; in the second it begins to clear and continues to do so in the third, until, by the fourth year, it is like rock water, very potent and sweet smelling. The odour of it brings comfort both to the head and the senses. It becomes so strong and good and powerful in quality that it will keep for a hundred years without change. This wine is called *marouant*, and with it, as I hope, our two Kings will be refreshed and spiritually intoxicated.

Now let us consider a certain moral concordance concerning this precious wine from the vineyards of Engadi. It has been said above [56v] that the Wisdom of God has prepared His wine, that is to say, for three years. By the first year, in which the wine is dark and troubled, may be understood the recollection and recognition by the two Kings of the dreadful evils resulting from the wars waged by their predecessors. By the second year is to be understood the suffering of the Kings and the true repentance of their knights, both French and English, for the great wrongs which they and their fathers have perpetrated and cruelly carried out against God and their neighbours.

But by the third year is to be understood full compensation and remission for the harm and injury inflicted by one chivalry on the other. Once these three stages have been accomplished, by the goodness of God, devoutly and without pretence, and our precious wine thus prepared and diluted, the time will have come for the Wisdom of God to set the table, as was said above, and prepare the feast for our Kings and their noble chivalry, and for them to partake of this wine, thus matured and clarified, which, by its power, will maintain love for one hundred years among those who have tasted it.

This precious wine [57r] speaking in figure, is the wine made from the fine grapes that Joshua and Caleb brought from the Promised Land to a certain house to show to the children of Israel, thus encouraging the people to enter boldly into the land that abounded in these grapes and all other fruits. This is the precious wine which, according to David the prophet, makes glad the heart of man. This wine is not that which, as St. Paul the Apostle says, excites to luxury, but is that strong wine, spoken of by St. Peter, with which, in the view of the Jews, the Apostles were drunken. It is the precious wine from the vineyards of Engadi, which is, in truth, the wine of the Holy Ghost, strained and clarified, with which the Apostles were made drunk on the day of Pentecost, when they spoke in all the tongues of the world, praising God.

O blessed and thrice blessed will be our Kings and their chivalry, if they quench their thirst with this precious draught, that is, with the unction of the Holy Spirit, which reconciles discords, which brings back the wanderer to the right path, and which, by its gentle power, makes peace everywhere, so that wrongs [57v] are forgotten and enemies become friends.

Among men in general, who have been at war, to celebrate the making of peace, it is usual to offer one another wine, beer or honey. But in the case of peace made between Kings who have been fighting one another, it is fitting that the Wisdom of God should lay the table, and offer to our Kings, as the seal of true peace, the Bread of Life, kneaded and leavened in the body of the Virgin Mary, and baked upon the tree of the true Cross. After they have partaken of the holy bread and meat of angels, it is right that our Kings and chivalry should quench their thirst and drink of the cup of the New Testament, by which Testament true peace is bequeathed from Heaven, that is to say, of the precious wine from the vineyards of Engadi, the blood of the slain Lamb, by which offering peace was made between God and man.

Most mighty King of Great Britain, seated at the table prepared for you by the Wisdom of God, open your ears and hear the words of the Holy Spirit: Come, my friends, make yourselves glad [58r] with the wine I have put before you, that is, the wine of the love of God, of peace with your neighbour, and avoidance, henceforward, of the shedding of Christian blood.

It is desirable that in the quest for true peace in Christendom, for the unity of our mother, Holy Church, and for the deliverance of the Holy Land from the hand of the false prophet Mohammed, our carbuncle and our lodestone, figured as the diamond, should in spirit, be wisely and discreetly mingled and immersed, in great humility and brotherly love, without pomp, ceremony or too great caution, in the precious wine from the vineyards of Engadi, so often mentioned, that is, the love of the Holy Spirit, Author of peace, love and justice, which will give such power to the royal majesty that the serpents, that is, those who stand in the way of peace, at the scent of the flowers of the vine, and even more at the scent and strength of the figurative wine, cease to exist. May it please God to grant these things. Let this suffice concerning the significance of the wine of which our Kings and their chivalry must drink deep.

A short prayer against those who would disturb peace

[58v] Now let us pray to God, lifting up our hands to Heaven with David the holy prophet, saying, Come, O Lord, and let your enemies be scattered; that is to say, those who strive to prevent the descent of the peace of Heaven on our Kings. Let them be crushed and let them flee before the face of God. Let their backs be bowed down for ever. Lord God, scatter and destroy all those who seek war against their Christian brothers. Let the cries of the dead and wounded by heard in their houses, their wives made widows and their children orphaned; that is to say, all those who through pride, envy and avarice, and by great cruelty, kick against the goad of the Holy Spirit and are twice pierced. The Holy Spirit blows on the doors of the hearts of sinners, saying unto them, Whoso openeth unto Me, I will sup with him and grant him My peace, as is written in the Book of the Apocalypse, and whoso denieth Me, be sure he will repent thereof.

*The seventh subject of this present letter demonstrates that
if the two Kings make war on each other, they will become
the serfs of all their subjects. And if they* [59r] *make peace,
the opposite holds good*

Most excellent Prince, in making the choice between peace and war, in addition to the reasons already stated, there is another most important one for which, using your free-will, you should choose peace rather than war, namely, that if you, or your brother of France, elect to make war, you, who are now free and of free descent, by your own choice will stumble into the depths of serfdom and dangerous subjection. Indeed, there will be no-one in your kingdom to whom you do not become a slave; to the armour makers and all other tradesmen necessary for the waging of war, to your treasurers, to the communes, to clerics, and right down to the humblest of your valets, who will grumble if, because of the war, he has to get up earlier in the morning than he usually does.

What shall we say of the subjection of the royal majesty to the soldiery, whose demands are impossible to satisfy? This could easily be spoken of at length, but must remain unsaid for the sake of brevity, [59v] for you know it well enough.

Now as regards your commanders, you could suffer such abuse and subjection of the royal majesty as could not easily be put into words, and which should be noted and taken to heart by all Christian princes and true Catholics. Most wise and worthy King, if Fortune turns her wheel, as is her custom, and smiles upon your royal person and two or three of your commanders, by giving you certain victories, see how you fall into servitude. If your royal Majesty should triumph in person over your enemies, the greater the victory, the greater the number of slain, and, in the ordinary way, the souls of most of them will be borne into Hell, and all by your fault. And as to the servitude into which you will fall, we may say that usually, I don't say always, vainglory, arrogance, presumption and greed will take their seats at your royal table, on your right hand and on your left. And, as St. John Chrysostom says, it is, in practice, impossible that a great lord, [6or] placed in the seat of honour, and with many temporal victories to his credit, should not be assailed by vainglory, just as a lusty young man, often in the company of a fair young maid, sometimes looks at her with eyes of carnal desire.

Most gracious Prince, if, having gained a victory, you should be attacked by the aforesaid four vices, or even by only one of them, you would be in mortal subjection, for it is written, Whoso falls into sin, becomes the slave of his sin. And what is worse, increasing your bondage, after one victory, spurred on by ambition and greed, perhaps you will not be satified, but will seek to obtain another and greater conquest, of which you cannot be sure, for it is recorded that the outcome of battle is uncertain, as is witnessed by many a king and prince, both Christian and pagan, who, after gaining one victory, have striven for others, in which some have found defeat, and others, while being victorious, have fallen into greater servitude and have enslaved people who have done them no wrong.

[60v] Now let us turn to a great abuse in the enslavement of royal majesty by commanders who have gained victory in the King's absence. Everybody knows that a commander who has had notable conquests, believes in his heart, as do his friends, that the King owes more to him than to other commanders, who have not gained such victories. This is not surprising, for when the said successful commander returns to his lord and king, bearing a branch of olive or laurel as token of victory, and accompanied by the brave knights of his command, to receive reward from the king for his effort and valour, and to sit at the royal table, the king will be compelled to pay him great honour, lest he should incur the anger of the said valiant knights, his subjects. Now regarding this offence, in the sight of God, of royal subjection, the more of his fellow Christians the said commander and his men have slain in battle and sent to Hell, so much the more will the king feel himself constrained and bound to reward the said commander, sometimes far beyond his merits, which is a great offence in the sight of God and an enslavement of royalty.

[61r] O what evil bondage in the eys of God! The more Christian souls the chieftain has sent to Hell, the more the King becomes his slave. And if the King fails to reward the leader to the latter's satisfaction, he will be angered and may gather round him in secret a band of followers, concerning the future effect of which, to the hurt of the royal majesty, no more need be said here.

Some may say that, according to divine and civil law, to recover a heritage, to mete out justice to evil doers, or for the defence of the public good, war between Christians is justified. To these we may reply that if a man weighs in the balance of truth the main pretext for which the war is to be waged, which to human wisdom seems good, but often in the sight of God, because of man's ignorance and lack of understanding, must be seen to be unjust; and if the countless ills and cruelties which occur in war, against and outside the laws of chivalry, are also well weighed in the said scales, it will be found that, before the outbreak of war, it would have been better if one king, [61v] out of respect for God and to avoid so much harm, had freely surrendered to the other two thirds of his claim, so that they remained friends, without future grievance over the surrendered claim.

Most excellent Prince, if according to civil law the man who kills another must die, and if according to divine law the man who hates his brother is a murderer, following the words of St. John the Evangelist, and if, what is more, the man who kills but one other, and dies himself without due repentance and satisfaction made to God and those concerned, is, according to divine law, damned for ever, what shall those kings say who, in their mortal war, often lightly undertaken, have caused the death of not merely one man, but of a hundred thousand, most of these, alas, unshriven, and so in great danger of eternal punishment? He who has ears to hear, let him hear, as sweet Jesus says in His holy Gospel; for it is written that stern judgement will be passed on lords who in this world have high [62r] office, and mighty rulers will be mightily tormented. May God keep our two Kings from such a fate and strengthen them in the peace which He inspires. And this is enough in broad outline concerning the subjection of the royal majesty, if cursed war gains the supremacy.

The eighth subject of this present letter deals with two orchards, or gardens; one most pleasing and to be compared with peace, the other horrible and full of peril, to be likened to war; which are displayed before the Kings, so that they may choose the one and beware of the other

It is a natural thing for men, and especially kings, if they are wise, to shrink from and avoid all that is inimical to their royal persons, to their houses, and to their worldly authority, and to seek after the opposites, that is, personal prosperity and the increase and strengthening of their lordships. And this opposition is to be found in war and peace. Now let us relate a pleasing parable which sets forth plainly the two propositions.

The delectable orchard

The Old Solitary [62v] in his dream beheld an orchard, filled with all manner of trees and plants, bearing fruit and giving out a very pleasing scent. In this orchard, full of all sorts of flowers, there was never frost, mist, floods or thunder. The people of this orchard enjoyed good health and suffered no sickness, until they died in God's good time. All fruits were held in common by the inhabitants, to each according to his need, and the words 'my own' were never heard. These people lived so happily together, that they seemed never to grow old. All tyranny and harsh rule was banished from the garden, though there was a king, who stood for authority and the common good, and he was so loved and looked up to that he might have been the father of each and all. And no wonder, for he had such concern for the welfare of his subjects, dwellers in the garden, that neither he nor his children owned anything in person.

This pleasant orchard was surrounded on all sides [63r] by a high wall, called Tuition, furnished with many lofty towers, each named Protection. On these walls, inside and out, were depicted, in noble and enduring paintings, the golden days of times past, including the gracious rule of the Bargamains and their king, from which covetousness, pride and luxury were entirely absent. They held everything in common and were content to live in caves, and built no houses. They took no count of gold or silver or precious stones. When the women found themselves with child, they no longer co-habited with their husbands, until they had been delivered and had left their beds. The king was never troubled in the administration of justice, for the good reason that no man offended against his neighbour. King Alexander once visited these Bargamains, but because he found among them neither gold, nor silver, nor tyranny, he took little account of them.[6]

Further, on the walls was also depicted the golden age of peace of King Solomon, in whose days the benches in the streets of Jerusalem were covered with silver.

Again, there were figured the golden days of universal peace [63v] under Octavian, Emperor of Rome, who rebuilt in many coloured marble this city, which previously had consisted of old walls and baked earth. He kept the whole world at peace for full twelve years, at the end

6. Cf. *Songe* i, pp. 224–5.

of which the King of Peace elected to be born of the Virgin Mary into this world.

In these walls were four main gates, one of rare cypress wood, the second of palm, the third of cedar and the fourth of the wood of olive, of which same woods the true Cross was made. The first gate was called Peace, the second Love, the third Justice, and the forth Comeliness. Blessed shall be all they who enter into the beautiful garden through these same gates.

Further, you should know that in the midst of the garden there was a round fountain, from which flowed twelve streams, which watered the garden on all sides and caused to flourish the twelve fruits of the Holy Spirit, of which St. Paul wrote to the Galatians, that is, love, joy, peace, long-suffering, gentleness, goodness, meekness, kindness, cheerfulness, faith, temperance and chastity.

And just as bread is needful [64r] for the life of man, so, in our garden, everywhere along the banks of the watercourses there grew in plenty a certain herb, called Sanamonde, that is to say, sound and clean. The dwellers in the garden ate this herb, Sanamonde, with all their meat and fruit. And just as the heavenly manna in the wilderness was changed to such flavour as the children of Israel desired, in the same way, speaking figuratively, this herb, Sanamonde, changed the taste of the said inhabitants of the orchard, to suit their comfort and their needs.

Also from the aforesaid fountain issued four main streams, which watered every part of the garden. The first was called Safety, the second True Repose, the third Abundance of all Good Things, and the fourth Sufficiency. O blessed shall they be who labour for the construction of so noble a garden! And more blessed still all they who shall enter into possession of this garden, so longed for by all good men.

By this garden, speaking in parable, should be understood all Christian kingdoms; and by the noble fountain [64v] that true peace, hoped for by the worthy. And by the streams and their significance should be understood the blessings without compare which follow peace; not that peace spoken of by Jeremiah the prophet, when he said, Peace, peace, and there is no peace, but that true peace which Jesus gives to the world, and with which peace He gives Himself. And blessed shall be our two Kings if they accept Him. Here ends what is to be said concerning the delectable garden of peace, the garden which may be called an earthly paradise. And the King of this garden may in truth be called *Rex pacificus*.

The Garden of Horror and Perils

Now let us speak of another garden, quite different from the one described above. The Old Solitary saw in his dream another imaginary garden, enclosed in whole and in part by brambles. This garden was of such a kind that if the sun shone freely for one day, for four or five days afterwards darkness overhung it. Cold and frost, fog, rain in floods, prevailing in the garden, beat down the flowers and allowed no fruit to [65r] ripen. Winds from the north, that is, pride and vainglory, blew over the garden for the best part of the year, and for the rest of the time the wind from the south, deep-rooted avarice, prevailed. Nor was wanting the beguiling wind of the west, greed, sloth and waste. But the gentle east wind, that is, truth and consolation of the Holy Spirit, although sometimes breathing upon the garden in passing, made no long stay, by reason of the authority of the other three winds which reigned in the garden. What more can we say? In this garden the wives of the inhabitants and their beasts aborted, and all their joy was changed to grief. Some were over-fed, while others died of hunger. Therein was neither justice, love, law nor order. And no wonder, for the strong devoured the weak, and tyranny triumphed, to such a degree that the good citizens there preferred death [65v] to life.

Now there was in the midst of this garden a fountain, whose waters were dark and troubled, and from it issued fifteen streams, watering the whole garden, with no lack of vapour and foul stench. These streams may be named, according to their effect, as cruelty, tyranny, pretence, hypocrisy, rapine, vengeance and melancholy, excuse for wrong doing, lying, aggression, treason, suspicion, iniquity, bloodshed, and all inhumanity.

There flowed also from the said troubled fountain four main rivulets, from which all the inhabitants, or most of them, took their drink. The effect of the first of these was to incline the people to various heresies; the second to vile supersition and sorcery, the third to magic arts and the invocation of demons; and the fourth to replace free-will by the judgements of astrology.[7] The first rivulet bore the name of Perpetual

---

7. The last part of this sentence is obscure in construction, though the meaning would appear to be clear.

Fear, the second Labour without Rest, the third Lack of All Good Things, and the fourth Misunderstanding and Ingratitude Towards God, which names derive from the aforesaid inclinations. [66r] Further, in the middle of the garden was an old roofless palace, where in former days were depicted all the instances of the shedding of human blood since the beginning of the world. First there were the giants, who fought among themselves, shedding human blood without measure, as we are told in the Holy Scriptures.

There was figured, too, the battle of Hannibal, King of Africa, against the Romans, under the walls of Rome, in which so many Romans were slain that the victorious Hannibal gathered up three full measures of golden rings, belonging to the Roman knights who had died in the battle. There was shown, also, the battle of Octavian, Emperor of Rome, against Antony, Emperor of the kingdoms of the East, which took place at sea, between the kingdom of Cyprus and Syria; and according to the chronicles, there were present on that occasion one thousand armed galleys, without counting great ships and lesser ones without number. Antony was defeated and fled to Egypt and killed himself by poison. And Cleopatra his mistress, Queen of Egypt, for whose sake the war was waged, also killed herself by poison. In that battle so much human blood [66v] was shed, that the sea was dyed crimson therewith.

In the same palace was depicted the great battle between the three sons of Louis the Debonair, Emperor of Rome and King of France, son of the great Charlemagne. These three brothers, Louis, King of Germany, Lothair, King of Italy, and Charles, King of France, spurred on by greed, envy and ambition, fought one another near the city of Auxerre, and the slaughter was so great that there is no record since the beginning of the world of so much French blood being spilt. It is impossible for anyone to describe in full the amount of human bloodshed among pagans, Saracens and Christians caused by the mortal wars which have been since the beginning of the world. At the same time, it would be expedient for those who have in mind to start a war, and especially one against their Christian brothers, to have always before them in a mirror these examples of human slaughter, to restrain them from their dangerous path. This must suffice as an account of the instances of human bloodshed depicted in the roofless hall, all displeasing to God and contrary to the divine goodness and leading to the destruction of [67r] Christendom.

In the water of the fifteen foul-smelling streams of the garden, there grew in great abundance a certain weed, called Sanguinolence, and most of the people of the garden ate it greedily with all their food. And the nature of this weed was such that all the meat that the people ate was turned into blood, without the eaters being disgusted thereat, which to the good people dwelling in the garden was horrible to see. The said weed, Sanguinolence, did its work through the King of the garden and his commanders, who, as greedily as the starving man rushes at meat, went forth to shed the blood of their Christian brothers in the garden, by battle, murder, injustice and other ways. This unrestrained appetite turned everything into blood, and, in fulfilling their cruel office, according to the judgement of David the prophet they were justly called men of blood, and so unworthy to build God's Temple.

Further in the said streams were many leeches, large and small, which sucked the blood of those who lived [67v] in the garden, wherever they could reach them, so much so that many of these leeches burst asunder and died, and although some of the inhabitants were relieved and made healthier because of the bad blood that had been sucked away by the leeches, others lost so much that they died therefrom. In this parable, the leeches in the streams represent the commanders and their men-at-arms, who suck the blood of the poor, that is, the substance of their livelihood, by ransom, pillage, *gabelles*, taxes and oppression without measure. It sometimes happens that those who are pillaged or put to ransom have an excess of worldly goods, ill-acquired, and so, after their loss, they are healthier and live more temperately, refraining from unjust gains. All the same, some of the leeches feed so greedily that they burst asunder and die the death and risk damnation.

Again, there were in that garden a vast number of sharp-toothed locusts, [68r] which devoured and gnawed the corn, and all the fruit, and all the green things of the garden, right down to the roots. I have seen in my time, in the kingdom of Cyprus and elsewhere, a great multitude of locusts settle at one end of a field of good wheat, ready for harvesting, while at the same moment at the other end of the field the reapers, many in number, began their work. The locusts in their part of the field ate more of the wheat, down to the roots, than the reapers were able to cut down, and the reapers lost the day to the locusts, to such an extent that every single blade or ear of corn left standing was devoured by them. These are indeed foul and harmful creatures. In our parable they represent the captains, the men-at-arms, and robbers, cruel and sharp-toothed beyond words, before whom nothing survives except what is too hot or too heavy. Ill-fated are the people who, for their sins, have to dwell in that garden, under the rod or goad of these leeches and locusts.

Further, round this garden of perils, in the circle of sharp thorns, there were gates, open to all, marked by certain signs, inscriptions [68v] and banners denoting the seven mortal sins, that is, pride, envy, anger, sloth, avarice, gluttony and lust. In addition, there were four main doors, the first of which was fashioned of willow wood, which is green and bears no fruit, the second was of a wood called beech (fou), the third of aspen, and the fourth of elder, of which both leaves and fruit are foul smelling. The first of these four main gates was called Presumption, which like the willow, bears no fruit; the second was called Beyond-all-bounds like a fool; the third Lamentation, like to the aspen, which trembles with fear at every wind; and the fourth gate was called Despair, with the elder tree, whereon Judas hanged himself, according to the old wives' tales.

O what dangerous gates through which to enter a dangerous garden! Better to be a humble dweller in the gracious garden of peace, than to be a crowned king in the garden of perils, filled with so many evils. May God save us from that garden and its King and its chieftains, and house us in the blessed orchard, likened to an earthly Paradise.

[69r] Keeping to the concordance, we may understand by the garden of perils just described, any Christian kingdom which offers like conditions; and by the dark and troubled fountain in the midst of the garden, the war reigning in that kingdom. The fifteen streams, the weed, Sanguinolence, the four rivulets, the leeches and the locusts, the gates to the garden, full of danger and mystery, together signify, both in general and particular, the infinite evils and hazards which, day and night, follow in the tracks of war, and the maledictions that spring therefrom.

This garden of perils, because of its great marvels, should be called Two-faced Fortune and *Perilleuse Garde*. The true name of the King of this garden was Nimrod, the same who built the tower of Babel and was the first tyrant in the world, who subjugated all the people of his time to his tyrannous rule. Would to God that, in his office, this Nimrod had been barren and had not had so many descendants, who, today, follow to the letter [69v] and too well his example.

By comparison, in complete contrast, in the delightful garden that we have praised so highly, beautiful virgins and young girls, gently stirred thereto by melodies sounding from all parts of the orchard, sweetly sang the praises of God, and little songs of love, devoid of all impurity; but in the garden perilous, the virgins and young girls sang only songs of lamentation and woe, shedding tears and breathing sighs instead of pleasing canticles. No wonder! for often and continually were they terrified by trumpets sounding, Alarm, alarm! by bells also, summoning the people to war, and by the cries of the dead and wounded, often ill-housed. Further, there was another song which aroused much disquiet, that of the wretched inhabitants who were compelled to stand guard round the garden, and all night, without rest, in wind and rain, cried, Look out, look out. Enough has now been said concerning the garden of peril.

The concordance made between the two orchards by way of a comparison with two [70r] great hazards of the sea, Scylla and Charybdis

Most excellent and mighty Prince and worthy King of Great Britain, two gardens or orchards, set forth in great detail by the Old Solitary, are presented with great love and reverence to your royal Majesty, and to your beloved brother, Charles, King of France, to the royal Princes on both sides, and the valiant chivalry of England and France; two gardens, that is, one of light and the other of darkness, one of repose, the other of travail; one of great dangers, the other of complete safety; one of joy and the other of sadness; one fortunate, the other ill-fated; one longed for by the elect of God, the other by the ungodly cultivated diligently; one the way to Paradise, the other the road to noisesome Hell.

Most worthy and devout King, it lies in the power of the free-will of both you and your brother of France to choose the one or the other. It would be calamitous and do great harm to the whole of Christendom if you were to throw yourselves into the foul smoke of the garden perillous and leave behind the sweet perfume and gracious scents of the garden called the earthly Paradise. Most Catholic Prince, St. Augustin tells us in his book. [70v] The City of God, that in a certain region of the sea there are two rocks, two whirlpools, two great hazards, and it is prudent that ships which chance to find themselves in the midst of these perils should steer between the two rocks, for if they depart ever so slightly from a middle course, they will be lost. These two dangers are called by St. Augustin and in the writings of poets, the one Scylla and the other Charybdis.[8]

Most gracious King, you and your brother of France, by divine choice and calling are the Masters of two royal ships, the most eminent that sail the wide sea, and it is decreed by God that in your time, you shall bring these ships, voyaging to the East, to Jerusalem, but you cannot escape the risk of passing between the two hazards mentioned above, Scylla and Charybdis. And so it is expedient and of necessity that you, the two Masters, should fix your eyes ever on the northern star, the Pole Star, that is, the Virgin Mary. And to begin with you should make your assembly and preparations for the holy journey in the lovely delectable garden, that we have praised, for without [71r] its fruits you cannot begin the enterprise that you have longed to undertake, and you must shun altogether the garden perilous, with its bitter and ill-tasting harvest.

If you act thus with wisdom and courage, most gracious Princes, Chief Masters of the royal ships, in accordance with the prayer of the blessed St. Augustin, you will, I hope, pass mid-way between Scylla and Charybdis, looking neither to left nor right, that is, by the royal road, and at the last with the gentle wind of the Orient guiding your ships, laden with a rich cargo of virtues, you will complete your voyage and arrive at safe harbour. May God grant you this, your wish and my heart's desire.

Esteemed and worthy King, by these two great hazards of the sea, the oft-mentioned Scylla and Charybdis—between which from the beginning of time many royal ships and countless others have foundered, because the sea in that place boils with whirlpools and strong currents, perpetually restless and without calm—we mean the two chivalries of France and England, that is, those who have been trained in the garden [71v] of peril, and have set in motion the raging of the sea, that is to say, the cursed war. To attain once for all the desired and beautiful garden, and then to guide your ships on the way to the East, like sweet Jesus who passed through the midst of the Jews who sought to kill Him, you must travel boldly on a middle course among those habituated to the drinking of the blood of their fellow Christians, without looking to your right or left. And if they say to you, most worthy Princes, while you are trying to create the beautiful orchard, that is, peace: My Lord, to satisfy our loyalty to your Majesty, look to the

8. Scylla and Charybdis are not mentioned in the *Civitas Dei*.

honour of the crown of England (and the others, Look to the honour of the crown of France), if you accept this treaty, you are dishonoured. To these people you may well and justly reply with the common saying, The man who profits from a war has the real honour, and the real honour and victory in war is true peace, for the Emperor laid down in his civil law that the object of war is peace. If you reply in these terms, by the grace of God, when they [72r] recognise your constancy, courage and prowess, and that, in spite of what they say, you have already made the passage between Scylla and Charybdis, and when they see in you divine virtue, then they will follow you and under a new dispensation will be numbered with the fortunate dwellers in the gracious orchard and among your holy chivalry. May God grant you this. And this suffices at some length on the matter of the two gardens and their mystery, and the opportunity to choose the one and reject the other.

A short justification by the Old Solitary of the length of this letter

To conclude, then, this feeble and ill-composed writing, this long and flavourless letter, it must be admitted that the Old Solitary well recognises that the matters included in it, diverse yet inter-connected, dictated by an abler and more distinguished writer, would have been expressed in many fewer words, because the great lords of today, on account of their importance and occupation with temporal affairs, find great satisfaction in brief writings. To this charge and objection, the Poor Solitary can answer that you can only take out of the bag what is in it, that is, roughness and [72v] dull wits, feeble ideas, prolix and ill-expressed. The apostle St. Peter said to the sick man, Silver and gold have I none, but what I have, I give unto you, that is, healing. God knows that the Old Solitary longs for the good health and true peace of your royal Majesty. And so, with St. Peter and the poor widow woman, who gave her two mites, he offers what he has, that is, the strong wish that he has for peace and true friendship between the two Kings, so often expressed in this letter, and not in few words. And no wonder, for such high and great matters, concerning the two greatest Kings of Christendom, and the great good or the great ill of their persons, their kingdoms, the Church, God, and the whole Christian race, by a foolish old writer, who morn and night faces his grave, could not

have been brought together or set down in few words. And so the poor
old writer craves pardon for his excess of words and his over-long
exposition, submitting himself to the correction of the benign patience
of the royal Majesty of the three golden leopards, changed by God's
goodness from rigour into gentleness, from animosity into love, and
[73r] from cruel beast of prey into love of *Mont Joye*. May God in His
grace arouse and confirm such love, to the glory of His divine goodness
and the consolation of all Christendom.

*The ninth and last matter of this letter, namely, a brief
recapitulation of its substance and a proposed ratification of
peace and love between our two Kings through a happy
alliance and gracious marriage, which, under God, may be
the means of bringing peace to all Christendom*

Let us come, then to the ending of this uninspired letter, recapitulating
briefly the details of the wonderful dream of the Old Solitary, concerning the balm, transformed into a carbuncle, and the lodestone, transmuted into a diamond, which have been born anew at the command of
the Author of Nature in the cold regions of France and England, something which, taken after the letter, would be difficult of belief, but in its
moralised sense the dream comes true, as was shown clearly in the first
chapter of this letter.

It was said then that the pure balm, representing in the parable the
high, royal person of Charles, by the grace of [73v] God, King of
France, through its triple virtue has, on his side, up to the present,
closed the dangerous wound, so fully described in this letter, that is,
the war between the two kingdoms of France and England. It was said,
further, that according to the translation of the name Karolus, that is,
Charles, which is so to say Beloved Light, the said balm has been
changed into a rare carbuncle, giving out a shining light, of great
succour to those that sat in darkness, as was set forth more plainly in
its appropriate chapter.

Again, it was stated that the lodestone, representing in the parable
the high, royal person of Richard, by the grace of God, King of England, by his power of attraction has in great measure drawn to himself,
in love under God, his brother King Charles, that King's uncles and
brother, and the good men of the kingdom of Gaul, and, in respect of
his kingdom of England, his own uncles also, his barons, and the valiant

chivalry of Great Britain, in such wise that, through God's grace, on his side, and up to the present, the dangerous wound has been closed, and all that is lacking for the final healing of the said wound is that the last plaster should be applied for complete cure, namely, the face to face meeting in love of the two [74r] Kings in person, to ensure real health, true peace and sweet charity.

Moreover, it was stated that the true lodestone, or *aymant*, would be changed and transmuted into a rich diamond, keeping always its great power of attraction. But little has been said in this letter until now of this transformation. Now let us consider briefly the aforesaid transmutation, for a concordance in the love between our Kings, and, further, a declaration of the virtues of these precious stones, already roughly described. O Richard, worthy and noble King of England, represented in this letter by the fine, pure *aymant*, take from the word *aymant* the first 'a' and put it after the 'y' and in place of that 'a' put 'd' and you will find quite clearly '*dyamant*'. O what a happy and swift transmutation of precious stones, that is, of '*aymant*' into '*dyamant*'. But consider another change in the name, even swifter and more glorious, add one single letter to '*dyamant*', that is, a 'u' after the 'y', and you will discover plainly that our precious '*dyamant*' has been changed into '*Dieu amant*'. This final interpretation, in its [74v] great virtue, surpasses that of all other precious stones.

What a wonderful moral change is that of the person of our young King Richard into the fine *aymant*, with its power of attraction, and yet more wonderful change that of the attractive *aymant* into a rich, imperial and royal *dyamant*, but most wonderful of all is the third, that is, the conversion of the rich *dyamant* into the precious stone which can be bought neither with gold nor silver, that is *Dieu amant*, love of God, love of sweet Jesus, by means of which love the pure balm, transformed into a carbuncle, glowing with bright light, has been marvellously drawn by the *aymant* to godly love, as has been described above. Further, the diamond has preserved this love, transferred by great charity from one King to the other, in such fashion that the great wound has been staunched and, as it were, cleansed and healed. Finally, through this same love, the pure balm, changed into a fine ruby, that is, a precious carbuncle, and the lodestone, transformed into a rich diamond, have been, are, and will be, as I hope, gently steeped in and divinely intoxicated with the precious wine of the vineyards of Engadi, which is the love of the blessed Holy Spirit.

[75r] But what morals are to be drawn from the interpretation of the name of Richard, our very wise and worthy King? The meaning of the name, according to the spelling, is quite clear, it is a 'rich' and 'ard'; rich in good will towards the peace of Christendom, rich in godly power to attract his brother, King Charles, and the noble knights of France, once his enemies, rich in the virtues of justice and good government, rich in compassion for all Christian people and in the virtue of mercy, rich in the holy Catholic Faith and in hope for the restoration of the Church and all Christendom, rich in the love of God and his neighbour, rich in the cardinal virtues and the longing to attain, once for all, the eight beatitudes set forth by Jesus in His holy Gospel. So much for the interpretation of the first syllable of his name.

Now for the interpretation of the second syllable of Richard, that is 'ard'. It is hard to believe that God has been so gracious to him, that is, in turning the hearts of his enemies towards love, and in the case of the French, in restraining the action against the French of the swords of his knights, nurtured from youth up in warfare, [75v] in planting peace once again in the hearts of those well used to war, and, what is more, in bringing under his lordship, without bloodshed, a race of people as savage and uncivilised as the Irish, who live with the wild creatures in the mountains, and also the men of the islands, who, with little form of government, depend on the fortune of the sea. These events, so great, so marvellous and so unheard of in times past, brought about so gloriously by divine grace in so short a time, God would never have granted him, if, following the interpretation of the second part of his name, he had not been ardent in his love of God and, hence, of his neighbour. On the evidence of the matters mentioned above, and set forth often in this letter, it may be said, then, without using the ointment called Popilion, that, in my opinion, he is and will be ardent for the peace of his Christian brothers, for the union of the Church and, finally, for the enterprise of the holy passage, in company with his beloved brother, Charles, King of France. And may it please God to grant them this. Now this suffices concerning the interpretation of the name of Richard, most excellent King of England.

St. Augustin [76r] says that the virtue of perseverance is a work of perfection. The root of the matter here set forth is that our Kings should persevere in love, one for the other, and should let what has been well begun be continued with God's help and brought to the desired conclusion; that the carbuncle should often be changed into the attractive lodestone, the rich diamond, and the *Dieu amant*; and that the diamond, also, should often be transformed into the shining carbuncle; and that both should be anointed with the holy balm, the sweet odour of which, according to the word of St. Paul, will be spread abroad, even to Jerusalem. Because in every alliance made between great lords, and because in their holy policy, ever since Adam ate of the apple, there were never lacking those who practised sowing tares among the wheat, for this reason, it is expedient that the two Kings, both in public and in private, should sagely reveal to these dangerous people, the curses which are written in the Book of Moses against all those who sowed tares, troubled the peace and tranquility of the Israelites, and murmured against God, as has been said earlier. And if they will not restrain themselves, let such people be banished from the royal councils, and let strict watch be kept, with God's help, on these [76v] malcontents, so that they can do no harm, and the two Kings may proceed valiantly on their way, obeying the inspiration of the Holy Ghost. And the Kings should remind the well-disposed and those anxious for the peace and recovery of Christendom, of the holy benedictions of Aaron, the most holy Samuel, and the holy patriarch Jacob, called Israel, and the other holy patriarchs and prophets, and, in the New Testament, of the blessings which sweet Jesus bestowed on his gentle Mother, the Virgin Mary, on Mary Magdalen, and on His holy Apostles, when He said unto them, My peace I give unto you, not as the world gives; and the blessings also of the martyrs, confessors and glorious virgins, who follow the Lamb, whithersoever He goes. And the two Kings should, in their councils, continue to follow the wise advice of Husai, the loyal and sage counsellor of the holy King David, shunning and fleeing, with prudence and caution, the counsels of Achitofel and his followers. And may God grant all these things for the consolation of my old age.

Most worthy Kings of France and England, so that the love you have, one for the other, may be perpetuated, it is my longing that the rich diamond [77r] through the holy sacrament of marriage should become son to the shining carbuncle, and so shut the mouths of all those who ask for the five-footed sheep, that is, war, which might result from the other hazardous marriage, already discussed in its proper place. This holy aliance is the most speedy way to silence everyone. Thus the two Kings would be like father and son, dwelling in harmony in one Temple of God, in one love, and in a single will.

If anyone should argue that the daughter of the carbuncle is over young, and that it is expedient that the diamond should take to wife a woman from whom he can soon hope to have children, for the comfort of himself and his loyal subjects, to this it may be replied: Bearing in mind the will and favour of God, that is to say, that although the diamond, on the advice of his subjects, may marry a lady, good, beautiful and of the right age, yet to have issue as quickly as human beings desire does not fall within the power of man's freewill, for this gift of God to have children, and worthy ones, is reserved to the decree of Divine Providence alone, as was fully explained [77v] in the chapter on the fourth subject of this letter.

Moreover, it is well known that if a man wishes to have the greatest benefit from the use of a horse in battle, or elsewhere, it is necessary that that horse should have been well trained when young, and become obedient to the commands of the bridle and to other guidance, and, further, it is recognised that the man who has trained the horse will get more profit from it than anyone else.

The elephant is one of the largest beasts in the world, and one of the fiercest when offered the juice of the mulberry in order to excite him to mischief, as is shown in the Scriptures, in the Book of Maccabees.[9] And yet this same elephant, carrying on his back a wooden tower holding thirty soldiers, can be controlled by one unarmed man, whom he obeys at all times. How wonderful! This elephant was thus trained while young to obey one man alone, to the amazement of all; and it is beyond the power of man to train an elephant once he is full-grown.

This rough comparison may be suitably applied to both men and women, who usually retain the bent and instruction given them in their youth [78r] into their maturity, as is the case with camels.

Now let us turn to the training of women, and especially of young women of high estate. The proverb says that daughters, in good habits or bad, copy the example of their mothers. The ways they have learnt from their mother in childhood, they usually keep when grown up, and it is no easy matter to change the habits to which they are inclined by long use.

It may be said on reflection that it would be easier to entrust the guard of a great flock of poultry to Master Fox and expect him to do his duty without attacking them, than it would be to change the nature and habits of certain young women accustomed from youth up to

9. 1 Macc. 6: 34: 'Et elephantis ostenderunt sanguinem uvae et mori, ad acuendos eos in praelium.'

follow their own will and inclinations. Those who have learnt from experience, and not from books, know this well. The training of young girls, I don't say all, but some, is no less effective, if the truth be told, than the training of elephants.

Now let us deal briefly with the concordance of these examples, so that we may do with God's blessing, according to the counsel of St. Paul, all that should be done in the matter. The rich diamond [78v] of the parable, Richard, the good and gracious King of England, has already had full experience of the rules and state of the strong bond of marriage, but, as God willed, without offspring. If therefore he seeks a godly consolation for himself and, hence, for his subjects and friends, in a second marriage, would it not be better that the lady he chooses as helpmeet and wife, from her childhood, before reaching the age of discretion and before acquiring harmful habits of mind, should be well nurtured and instructed under the prudent and wise guidance of the royal majesty of the rich diamond, first in the fear and love of God, like the saintly Queen Esther, and, next, in royal behaviour, according to the station and will of her lord and husband, rather than that he should choose an older lady, who may have already acquired undesirable habits and leanings towards things forbidden? Moreover, the rich diamond could not be well and fully informed as to the upbringing of such a one, nor of the intimate morals of her mother, which is a matter [79r] of great importance.

According to the proverb it is the herb that one knows that one should bind on one's finger. He who tries to train a young sapling, has little to do, but if he waits until the wood has hardened, it will break sooner than bend. It is a great consolation to a king, and a special gift from God, to have as wife and pleasing companion a woman whom he has moulded by his teaching and brought up, by the grace of God, in accordance with his will and in agreement with his opinions, of whom he can say, This is my wife, this is my daughter. And the lady, also, who has been reared thus carefully and has not felt the goad of outside and harmful longings nor of fleeting temptations, will always feel in her heart filial obedience and reverence as to a father towards her lord and husband, as the saintly Sara felt to the holy patriarch Abraham, her lord and husband, who in her youth had reared and trained her in his way. He had no children by her before he was old and Sara was barren. In spite of this, because of his great faith, in his old age he begat the holy patriarch Isaac, which name being interpreted means laughter, which gave greater joy to his fellows [79v] than if he had begotten in his youth forty sons in the ordinary course of things.

Blessed will be our most worthy King, figured as the diamond, and sweetly comforted under God if he marries one whom he has reared in keeping with his way of life and rank, namely, the daughter of the pure balm, of the shining carbuncle, his own niece, thus obeying the commandment which God gave to the holy fathers of the Old Testament, the daughter of his elder brother, both being sons of the blessed St. Louis. By this holy alliance all unease will be banished from both countries, for in true paternal and filial love the two kingdoms will become as one, with one 'policy'; and the rich diamond, transformed into *Dieu amant*, will confirm by this act of marriage the laws of kingship of the Kingdom of Gaul, that is, that a woman cannot inherit the crown of France, thus wisely preventing, under God, any similar occasion, if it should arise in the future, which God forbid, as that for which in the last sixty years and more a hundred thousand souls, perhaps, have been borne into Hell. The two sons of the most valiant King of France, St. Louis, are bound, then, under God, to foresee and remedy any dangers which may occur in the future, by which dissention, [80r] hatred or war might arise and show themselves in the kingdoms of France and England, thus closely united by the bond of marriage between the rich diamond and the daughter of the shining carbuncle, transformed into the beautiful, white pearl. May it please God to grant this for the good of all Christendom.

And if through the machinations of the archpirate of Hell any discord grow between those of the royal line and the barons, clergy or people, our beautiful white pearl, our very rare emerald, daughter of the carbuncle, by the goodness of God, will bring peace without delay.

And through her conjugal chastity, not only will the fury of the unicorn be appeased, but the unicorn itself will be taken in the net, which has long been spread in vain, that is to say, in the net of true peace, so long desired by men of goodwill. And may God grant us this.

Now as concerns the tender years of our young marguerite, our precious stone, our beautiful white pearl, it may be said that for a virtuous and constant Prince two or three years soon pass, when the prize is the restoration and reformation of all Christendom. Do not forget, most virtuous and worthy [80v] King, the holy patriarch Jacob, who waited seven years to have the beautiful and saintly Rachel as his wife, of whom in the end he had two noble sons, Joseph and Benjamin. Remember, too, most devout King, the long wait for offspring of the holy prophet, Zacharias, who in his latter days begat the most blessed John the Baptist.

No man can describe in full the singular graces that God will bestow on your royal Majesty and on your beloved brother, and, as I hope, father, Charles, King of France, provided that you remain constant in the high task to which God has called you, that is, the government of His people, and are adorned, through God's bounty, with the virtues of patience and forebearance. May it please God to grant you this and direct your doings towards the love of God and long sought for peace.

When this proposed alliance has been, by God's goodness, achieved and put into effect, so far as the youth of our very gracious emerald, already placed on the finger of the most excellent King of Great Britain, allows, and when she has been trained in the ways described above, and sweet peace has been made and concluded [81r] under God, in the two kingdoms and between father and son, you should call to mind the words of the Holy Spirit, written by the prophet in the Psalter, saying, O how good and pleasant a thing it is to see brothers living together in harmony; that is to say, our two Kings, not only made father and son by the aforesaid holy alliance, but, as it were, blood brothers, sons of the most valiant King, St. Louis, dwelling together in one intention and one will, and having one goal, inflamed by God-sent brotherly love, which all the waters of the sea and of all the rivers of the world are powerless to quench. Thus of you two Kings, one will be worthy to be called David and the other Jonathan, who loved each other until death, as we are told in Holy Writ.

As regards companionship in arms against the enemies of the Faith, let one of you be the noble Roland and the other the very perfect Oliver; and in the matter of royal and imperial splendour, one of you may imitate the very valiant and knightly Charlemagne and the other that very bold and excellent King Arthur, when you fight against the enemies of the Faith, against [81v] schismatics and heretics. Love one another, then, with a love that is sweetly fraternal, paternal and filial, and do not rashly nourish favourites, creators of discord. As to any differences which may arise over the treaties, failing agreement among the royal councillors, arm yourselves with the shield of patience, as we have said above, in which you may possess your souls, and with the hauberk of generosity, by which you may settle between yourselves things which your councillors would never dare to attempt. What you hold in peaceful agreement is worth more than a dozen kingdoms won by war and hate. He who shows the greater generosity, manifests the greater proof of love, following the doctrine of St. Gregory, doctor of the Church, who said that the proof of love is furnished by the act.

Further, when by the grace of God you shall have conquered Turkey, Egypt and Syria, overflowing with all manner of riches and delights, through the goodness of sweet Jesus and the virtue of the Faith, you will set little store by your Western kingdoms, which are [82r] cold and frozen, and given over to pride, avarice and luxury.

Most excellent and gracious Catholic Princes, worthy Kings, chosen by God, of France and England, if as has been said above, in broad and rough terms, you stand together, continuing one with the other, and by your holy conversion illuminating all Christendom, and not for one single moment forgetting that on your finger you wear the rich diamond, or, rather, *Dieu amant*, following as far as you can the holy life of your ancestor St. Louis, and of those kings, your predecessors, martyrs and confessors, then sweet Jesus, King of kings, will, by grace, ever be with you and will lead you on from strength to strength, from kingdom to kingdom, until you reach the earthly Jerusalem, and, finally, after many a victory and a long and deserving life, will bring you to safe lodging in the heavenly city of Jerusalem triumphant. May God grant you all these things. *Amen.*

Most excellent and noble Prince, worthy King of Great Britain, my very special and much loved master under God, if in this present letter, rude and without flavour, conceived and invented in the form [82v] of an old man's dream, and composed and dictated by the benevolence and express command of the royal majesty of your beloved brother Charles, King of France, I have applied to your royal Majesty, more severely than becomes an unworthy sinner and old solitary, the ointment of the Apostles, which is acid and repressive, though in the end curative, I humbly beg that I may be forgiven, and that you should remember, most wise King, that often in the courts of great kings are to be found physicians who greatly favour the use of the unguent called Popilion, that is, a soothing plaster called a placebo.

And because this Old Solitary at times in his unworthy life has spent long periods at the courts of many kings and popes, and knows well that the said ointment, Popilion, leaves the wound unhealed, for this reason, he, trusting in the sovereign Physician, sweet Jesus, His gentle Mother, and the holy teaching of His Apostles, is here and now emboldened to make full use of the ointment of the Apostles, although it may be, to some extent, over mordant, in order to assure complete healing [83r] of the wound, so fully described in this letter.

Therefore I pray good Jesus, quietly and devotedly, and with my whole heart, as my final prayer, that, although He was willing to use on Himself this very strong and mordant unguent to cure the universal wound, to redeem souls from Hell, and to open the gates of Paradise to His elect, when He shed His precious blood on the tree of the true cross, yet, in order to efface completely and close for ever the mortal wound dividing the two kingdoms, so often spoken of, to seal true peace and heartfelt love between our two Kings and their valiant chivalry, He may be pleased, of His pity and special favour, to send down from Heaven on our Kings that sovereign plaster called *Gracia Dei*, and, in His holy mercy, inspire them to make good use thereof.

Most excellent, gracious and rightful King of England, my special and much loved master in sweet Jesus, may the God of peace and love, through the supplication of the blessed Virgin Mary, remain with you always, and bring you into Paradise after long life. *Amen.*

Here ends the letter touching the matter of peace and true love [83v] between the Kings of France and England, addressed to the King of England.

Epistre au Roi Richart

1395

PHILIPPE DE MEZIERES

Epistre au Roi Richart

[2r] Une povre et simple epistre[1] d'un vieil solitaire des Celestins de Paris, adressant a tresexcellent et trespuissant, tresdebonnaire, catholique, et tres devost prince, Richart, par la grace de Dieu roy d'Angleterre, *etc.*, pour aucune confirmacion, tele quele, / de la vraye paix et amour fraternelle du dit roy d'Angleterre et de Charles, par la grace de Dieu roy de France.

O bone Jhesu, scribe in corde meo vulnera tua preciosissimo sanguine tuo; ut semper cognoscam quid [2v] desit michi, legam, scenciam, et intelligam dolorem et amorem tuum, bone Jhesu. *Amen.*

Ci apres commence le prologue de l'espitre

Pour empetrer de la bonte divine, la benivolence et pacience de vostre audience royale, tresdebonnaire prince, je vous suppli treshumblement et devotement qu'il vous plaise avoir en ramembrance comment le Roy des roys, le doulz Jhesu, fort traveille d'aler a pie et apres longue jeune, reposant soy sur le puys de Sicar, non tant seulement benignement ouy la pecherresse Samaritaine, / mais oultre plus il li fist un grant et lonc sermon, au sauvement de son ame et, par consequent, au salut des habitans de la cite de Samarie, sicomme plus clerement il est escript en la sainte evvangile.

Et combien que je ne soie pas digne d'ouvrir ma bouche, tresdevot roy, de parler ou escripre a vostre grande sapience royale, pour mes pechiez et que je suy beesgue avec Moyses, toutefois, en confiant de Celuy qui fist parler l'anesse de Balaan le prophete, je ouverray ma bouche avec David le tres saint roy prophete, et adresseray ma penne

---

1. The transcription here presented is a faithful copy of the *Letter* as it reached Richard II. In the 35,000 or so words of the text there are roughly 75 errors, due, we may suppose, to the carelessness of the copyist, and these may be classified briefly as including: (*a*) repetition of syllables or words; (*b*) omission of syllables or words; (*c*) lack of agreement between past participles and their nouns; (*d*) indiscriminate use of 'se' and 'ce'; and (*e*) a few miscellaneous errors.

For detailed description of this handsomely decorated manuscript, its dimensions, illustrations, etc., see Sir George Warner and Julius P. Gilson (eds.), *Catalogue of the Western MSS. in the Old Royal and King's Collections in the British Museum*, vol. ii (1921), MS. Royal 20 B VI. The analysis of the contents given by the above-named is cursory and not without error.

envers le Saint [3r] Esperit, en luy suppliant devotement qu'il le veulle adressier a ce que je puisse escrire aucunechose grossement, qui soit a sa loenge, au bien de pais de la crestiente, et consolacion de vostre royale majeste; en appelant a ce faire l'aide de la tres doulce Vierge Marie, qui enfanta et nous presenta le Dieu de paix, qui est appeles la droite voie, verite infalible, et pardurable vie; en sousmettant auxi ceste foible escripture, rudement composee, a la correction de vostre sapience royale et debonnairete, partout bien renommee.

Tresexcellent prince, / il est escript en la sainte escripture par Joel le prophete que les josnes enfans verront les visions et les vieilles gens songeront les songes. Joseph, l'espous de la Vierge Marie, vit en songe que Herode queroit la mort du doulz enfant Jhesu, et pour luy sauver de mort, il le mena en Egypte. Daniel le prophete, josne homme, vit l'avision du songe de l'estatue du roy Nabigodenosor et, apres l'interpretacion de la dicte estatue, le roy pour son orgueil fu prive de son sens, et condampnes vii. ans de mangier fain avec les buefs ou [3v] bois, et apres, par la priere de Daniel, il fu rapeles a son sens et a sa royale majeste. Que refist Dieu de Joseph, filz de Jacob le saint patriarche, qui par les songes du roy Pharaon et l'interpretacion d'yceulz fu fait prince d'Egypte et garda tout le peuple de famine vii. ans entiers? Combien que tous les songes ne soient pas veritables, ne les vrays crestiens catholiques generalment n'y doivent pas ajouster foy, toutefoiz aucunefois on en a veu l'effait d'aucuns songes en tout ou en partie veritable, comme il est apparu par le songe des iii. roys de Couloingne, qui, pour / eschaper le malice du roy Herode, par une autre voie sagement s'en retournerent en leur pais d'orient. Ce se puet asses demonstrer par les anciennes ystoires, comme il appert ou livre des songes du tresvaillant prince, Cypion Aufrican, et en plusieurs autres croniques autentiques.

Il est assavoir que en ceste foible epistre sont traitiez ix. materes, a la sainte memoire des ix. ordres des angels. La premiere si est une concordance de pierres precieuses, et certaines medicines, as tres haultes personnes du roy de France et du roy d'Engleterre, par maniere d'un songe [4r] figuratif, pour doulce confirmacion de la paix et vraye amour l'un a l'autre, en recitant les maulz qui sont advenus de la guerre de leurs predecesseurs, et qui pourroient advenir se la guerre se recommencoit, que ja n'aviengne, faisant conclusion partout de la paix des dis roys et de toute la crestiente. La seconde matere si est du fait et sisme de l'eglise, des maulz qui en sont advenus et adviennent tous les jours, et du remede et union de l'eglise par le moien de la vraie paix des ii.

roys. La tierce matere si est touchant au saint passage d'oultre / mer, pour la preparacion duquel saint passage le vieil solitaire offre au roy d'Angleterre une nouvelle chevalerie, tresnecessaire pour le dit saint passage et pour la reformacion de toute la crestiente. La quarte matere si est un petit traitie touchant au mariage de la royal majeste du roy d'Angleterre, par lequel la sainte paix des deux roys pourroit estre empeschiee, et le remede du dit empeschement. La quinte matere si est une exemple intelligible qui condampne les roys crestiens d'espendre le sanc humain de leurs fre-[4v]res crestiens. La vi⁶ si est que, pour confirmacion de la vraye paix des ii. roys, la fine escharboucle figuree et le fin dyamant figure doivent estre trempe, arouse, et enyvre du precieux vin des vingnes d'Engadi. Et les autres iii. sont plusieurs exemples tendans a la conclusion et paix tant desiree des proudomes de la crestiente.

Tres debonnaire prince, cestui solitaire escripvain en sa vieillesse a veu un songe en sa contemplacion, parlant moralment, dont l'effait par maintes gens ne seroit bien creable, voire qui vouldroit / interpreter le dit songe a la lettre. Mais a l'esperit, selonc la doctrine de l'apostre saint Pol, le dit songe est veritable, c'est assavoir que le fin baulme, qui en un seul lieu de ce monde croist par la grant vertu et chalour du soleil desu ou midi, c'est assavoir au Caire en Babiloine, de nouvel a pris sa naissance, par la grace de l'aucteur de nature, en ceste region froide et souvent engelee, c'est assavoir ou royaume de France. Encores une autre grant merveille est apparue ou dit songe, c'est assavoir que la precieuse pierre d'aymant, non pas samblable as pierres d'aymant qui se [5r] treuvent es parties du north, c'est assavoir de la terremontaine, qui attraient le fer a elles, mais une autre singuliere pierre d'aymant, qui se treuve tant seulement es haultes parties d'Inde la majour, laquele auxi de nouvel a pris sa naissance encore en plus froide region es parties d'occident, c'est assavoir ou royaume d'Angleterre. Et qui plus est grant merveille, les vignes d'Engadi, dont la sainte escripture fait une grant mencion, de nouvel sont flouries es dessus dis royaumes, par telle maniere que, selonc ce que plusieurs proudommes ont esperance, / les dittes vingnes porteront tel vin que les ii. roys et grant partie de leur tres vaillant chevalerie saintement seront enyvres du dit vin, comme il apparra si dessouz plus a plain, par la misericorde de Dieu, qui par sa grace veuille garder le dessus dit precieux baulme et la pierre d'aymant en leur plaine vertu, et les dittes vignes proposees d'estre en nostre temps engelees. Et ce souffice du dit prologue.

Cy commence l'espitre

Or entrons ou nom de Dieu en la matere gracieuse de la grant vertu du fin baulme, [5v] moralisant grossement pour venir a la concordance du songe proposee, par laquele concordance il se trouvera par la bonte de Dieu que ce ne sera pas le songe d'une nuit, engendre par habondance de vin, qui est oublie au matin.

Entre les grans vertus du fin balme qui est une liquour precieuse, descendans goute a goute d'un petit abrisel, et nourry de la rousee du ciel, iii. vertus du dit balme a nostre propos soient recitees, laissant les autres pour cause de briefte.

La premiere vertu du dit balme / si est, c'est assavoir que tantost qu'il est mis sur la plaie, par sa vertu il oste la douleur de la plaie et le mondifie en tele maniere que pourreture ou morte char dessoubz luy ne puent longuement arester, en confortant les nerfs, s'il estoient bleciez, en les ramenant a leur premiere vertu.

La seconde vertu du balme sollempnelle si est qu'il fait en brief temps rejoindre ensemble les ii. parties de la plaie merveilleusement et plus tost que nulle autre medicine.

La tierce vertu si est que le fin balme cure et deffait entierement les cicatrices des [6r] plaies par tele maniere qu'il semble que onques n'y ait eu plaie et, que plus est, se en la cicatrice aura defaulte de char, le balme la fera croistre jusques a sa premiere fourme, en ostant toute defformite de la plaie. Et ce soit dit et moralise de la vertu du fin balme par maniere de medicine, pour aucune ramambrance des grans plaies qui ont este mal curees en nostre temps depuis xl. ou lx. ans.

Pour venir donques a l'exposicion du dit songe et de la figure du dit balme, en l'ymaginacion du vieil solitaire proposee, pour parvenir a la concordance de la paix des preudommes / desiree, il est assavoir, parlant moralment, et a correction de vostre royale majeste, tres devost roy catholique, que depuis lx. ans en enca en la crestiente a puissaument regne une plaie ouverte et mortele, et si plaine de venin que elle a envenime toutes les parties de la crestiente, et par especial les regions parties occidentales, ne par la doctrine de Galien, d'Ypocras, ou d'Avicenne, ne par tous les fisiciens de Salerne, la dicte plaie n'a peu estre curee, voire par defaulte de fin baulme. Par la dicte plaie proposee, moralisant puet estre assez clerement entendue la mortelle guerre, qui a este commen-[6v]ciee et maintenue par vos grans peres, le tres vaillant roy Edouart, et par vostre pere, le tres vaillant prince de Gales, auquelz Dieu soit debonnaires, encontre leurs freres crestiens, et freres en lignage, les roys de France iii., Philippe, Jehan, et Charles, auquelz Dieu face pardon.

Lamentacion

O, quele male plaie mortele et perilleuse, par le venim de laquele tant de roys, duchs, contes, et barons, et la vaillant chevalerie ancienne de France et d'Engleterre et d'ailleurs si douloureusement ont este et mort et envenime, et les plussieurs en corps et en ame. Helas, / helas, quantes eglises par le venim de la dicte plaie ont este destruites, quantes cites, chastiaux, et viles arses et abatues, quantes vierges ont este deflourees, quantes dames de religion hors de leurs monastiers ravies et a pechie livrees, quantes vesves et orphelins y ont este crees, mors de fain et mal menees. Et, qui pis est, la sainte foy catholique en grant partie a este oubliee et perie; et tout par orgueil, avarice et envie, et pour possessions transitoires et temporelles, qui par un roy ne puet onques estre possedee lx. ans en un trait, qui n'est pas un moment au regart [7r] de l'ame qui est eternelle, et qui, a tousjours mais, possedera tele possession, bonne ou male, que laboure en ce monde elle aura.

Ha, plaie de Dieu maudite et pour les pechiez mandee, de laquele le venim mortel, qui tant de pueple crestien a mis a mort, ne se pourroit descripre. La journee que la dicte plaie fu ouverte soit deffacie du nombre des jours de l'an. La dicte plaie par langue d'omme en son malice ne pourroit estre a plain recitee, combien que par les preu-dommes devant Dieu, pour sa garison empetrer, elle doit estre fort plouree. Quel merveille, / car elle a este plus perilleuse et fait pis assez que les plaies d'Egypte, qui firent mourir le roy Pharaon et son pueple ydolatre. Mais ceste a fait mourir les roys catholiques et le pueple crestien, membres de l'eglise de Dieu et de nostre vray chief Jhesucrist.

Il est escript es loys divines, civiles et morales, que le filz qui tient la possession du pere est tenus de paier ses debtes et adressier les torfais de son pere. Qui pourra satisfaire par les hoirs a tant de maulz qui ont este faiz par les peres? Certainement il y fauldroit bien du fin balme pour [7v] la cure de la dicte plaie, qui n'est pas encores reclose ne bien sanee. Et ce soufice briefment d'aucune lamentacion de la dicte plaie proposee.

Naturelment chascun malade, qui longuement a languy, desire de trouver un bon fusicien par lequel il puist empetrer du dit fusicien aucune medicine singuliere pour la garison de sa maladie. Et pour ce que cestui vieil solitaire pour ses pechiez a este aucunesfoys ferus et envenimes du venim souvestesfoiz repete de la dicte plaie, et a present, par la bonte de Dieu, il a aucune compassion des trespassez pour / la dicte plaie, et encores plus grant doubte et compassion de ses freres crestiens qui sont en vie et que en temps advenir ilz ne soient entechez du dit venim mortel de la plaie, qui n'est pas encore du tout estanchiee. Et en querant plussieurs fusiciens, il c'est retrait au grant fusicien, a Celui qui donne la vertu et la force aux paroles, aux pierres, et aux herbes, en luy priant souvent, et non pas si devotement comme il deust, qu'i li plaise a mander du ciel aucune medicine singuliere, en apaisant son yre, par laquele la dicte plaie, souventesfoiz et non pas sans larmes repetee, soit du tout par sa [8r] misericorde sanee et reparee.

Apres plussieurs larmes espandues devant Dieu, souverain fusicien, par les preudommes des ii. royaumes de France et d'Engleterre, pour la garison pleniere de la dicte plaie, au povre solitaire, abortif et inutile et non digne d'estre nomme, en son esperit, par grant et ardant desir, en son songe ymaginatif a este revele que Dieu, par sa grace et par la priere de la tres doulce Vierge Marie, a mande singulierement en France le fin balme cy dessus desclarie, qui a mon vouloir par son effait sera transmue en une escharboucle relui-/sant. Et en Angleterre il a mande des parties d'orient, c'est du ciel, la dicte pierre precieuse, aymant appelee, laquele a mon vouloir, se elle sera en sa vertu essauciee et eslevee, et par le balme confortee, elle attraira a luy par grant compassion la moitie de la grant maladie qui est issue de la dessus dicte plaie, voire mais que le dit balme et pierre d'aymant discretement soyent bien proporcione et adjouste ensemble et bien trempe en esperit ou vin, cy dessus propose, des vignes d'Angadi.

Or venons a aucune concordance morale des figures propo-[8v]sees, pour parvenir unefoiz a la sante de la plaie, souventefoiz repetee et des preudommes redoubtee, c'est assavoir a la vraye paix des ii. roys occidentalz de France et d'Engleterre. Et combien que a present la ditte plaie ne respant pas publiquement son venin, pour les trieves qui ont este accordees, toutefoiz la dicte plaie en sa substance au jour duy, quant a l'opinion d'aucuns, puet estre ditte comme une apostume, qui n'apert pas dehors et se nourrist dedens, cavant et pourrissant la char entour luy, ou comme le feu qui est couvert des cendres / et n'atent autre chose que estre descouvert et ardoir entour luy, en faisant boulir le venin, si dessus repete, qui fait fort a doubter, voire se le Dieu de paix et de charite par sa tresgrant pitie n'y met remede par le moyen du fin balme et de la pierre precieuse aymant.

Se les sages et preudommes de France et d'Engleterre, par grant desir devant Dieu, voudront bien peser en la balance de leur consideracion les vertus si dessus proposees du fin balme et, moralisant, apliquer les a aucune personne, il se puet dire clerement que ou royaume de France ne se trouvera [9r] pas personne royale a laquele les dictes vertus au propos puissent estre mieulx appropriees ou ymaginees, ne si proprement, comme a la haulte, tresnoble, et tres gracieuse personne du roy Charles, vi^e de son nom, sicomme il apparra par les similitudes du fin balme au dit roy Charles assez convenientes.

Quant a la premiere vertu du fin balme, c'est assavoir qu'il oste la douleur de la plaie et la mondefie et fait retraire, et enchasse son venin, chascun scet, et Anglois et Francois, que depuis le gouvernement du josne roy Charles, en son royaume de France, / par la grace de Dieu, la douleur de la dicte plaie, c'est de la male guerre, a este plus apaisie et mains gette de venin par batailles et effusion de sanc que la plaie n'avoit fait en xxx. ou en xl. ans devant; qui est un tres bon signe de crisis en medicine, c'est a dire terminement ou convalescence de la maladie. Et, en rendant graces a Dieu, ce soit atribue a l'aucteur de nature, qui a nostre fin balme a singulierement atribue ceste grace especiale, de laquele ses predecesseurs en l. ans ne porent onques finer. Et ce souffise de la briefve concordance du fin balme a la personne du [9v] roy Charles, c'est assavoir d'oster la douleur de la plaie.

Quant a la seconde vertu du balme, c'est assavoir qu'il rajoint les ii. parties de la plaie ensemble, par tele maniere qu'il semble qu'il n'y ait eu point de plaie, or veons qui sont les ii. parties de la mortele plaie, tant de fois repetee. Certainement ce sont en chief les personnes des ii. roys, de France et d'Engleterre. Et tout auxi quant une grant plaie est ouverte, les ii. parties sont eslongiees l'une de l'autre, de tant a il plus de venim, de morte char, et de pourretu-/re entre les dittes parties ou bordures de la plaie. Mais par la bonte de Dieu, nostre fin balme, Charle, par sa vertu et grant bonte, et par sa royale et singuliere debonnairete, de sa part fera rajoindre les ii. bordures de la dicte plaie, c'est assavoir sa noble personne royale a la personne de son tresame frere Richart, le roy d'Engleterre, en vrai conjonction d'amour et de charite, par telle maniere, a mon vouloir, que le venim d'orgueil, d'envie, ou de indignacion, de murmuracion, ne recordacion de vieille hayne ou inimiste entre les ii. roys, dessoubz eulz, ne entre eulz, n'y pourront [10r] arrester, voire par la vertu et doulce amour du fin balme et de la precieuse pierre aymant. Et par ainsi la rousee du ciel, descendant sur les ii. parties principales de la plaie, par la grace de la divine bonte, elle se trouverra sanee. Et les ii. parties de la plaie, qui longuement ont este eslongiez et divisees, en grant amour seront rajoustees, par tele maniere que en brief temps le mortel venin, en nostre temps a grans ruisseaux courans, sera restraint, et la plaie sanee. Laquele chose Dieu par sa grace nous vueille ottroier. Et ce souffise de la concordance du fin balme a la personne du roy Charles, / c'est assavoir de rajoindre ensamble les ii. parties de la plaie.

Or venons ou nom de Dieu a la tierce vertu du fin balme. Il fut dit que le fin balme deffait et anientist les cicatrices des plaies, et sont les signes par dehors d'une plaie mal seans apres la garison, et que le balme, par sa vertu, de la cicatrice oste toute la defformite du signe de la plaie. Encore fait plus, car, se deffaulte de char aura este en la plaie, le balme le fait croistre, par tele maniere que la cicatrice sera remplie naturelment a la qualite du membre qui aura este navre.

Toutes ces condici-[10v]ons et vertus du fin baulme, moralisant doulcement, puent estre assez clerement appropriees a la personne de Charles, roy de France, voire aidie et conforte par la puissante sapience et debonnairete de son frere Richart, roy d'Engleterre. Il est vray que les grans cicatrices et signes apparans de la dicte plaie, c'est assavoir de la guerre, apres la paix et la jointure des parties comme dit est, materielment ne a la lettre ne se pourroient deffaire ne reparer, sicomme des eglises, citez, chastiaux, et villes, qui sont destruites pour la guerre, ne les corps ne les ames sans nombre, / qui par le venin ont este mortes et dampnees, ne pourroient estre resuscitees, mais les signes et cicatrices de la plaie, tant de fois repetee, quant a l'esperit, qui tousjours dure, du tout en tout, par la bonte de Dieu et grace infuse des ii. roys, seront deffais, planees, et anullees, c'est assavoir les haynes, les rancunes, les malivolences des subgiez des ii. royaumes, qui par le venin de la plaie aucunefoiz auront este offendu l'un de l'autre.

Nous devons doulcement esperer que si grant vertu sera du baulme a l'aymant, et si grant amour l'un a [11r] l'autre, parlant obtativement, que, par la grace de Dieu, il devendront un cler mirouer, ouquel tous leurs subgies, et par especial ceulz qui souloient esmouvoir et acroistre le venin, et auxi les estranges, vueillent ou ne vueillent, se regarderont ou dit mirouer, et seront contrains de Dieu de conformer soy a l'exemple de leurs chiefs et seigneurs et roys natureulz. Et que plus est, la deffaulte de char et les fosses de la plaie, qui pourroient engendrer aucune defformite a la plaie curee, comme dit est, se mestier fera, il feront racroistre et remplir, chascun de sa partie, par tele maniere / que, par la misericorde du doulz Jhesu, les parties seront contentees et lors les cicatrices du tout en tout seront deffaciees et anullees, Et lors sera acompli ce qui est dit en la sainte escripture, c'est assavoir, Les vielz et malz temps sont passez, et le monde en bien et en joye de nouvel est renouvelez; laquele chose Dieu par sa sainte grace nous vueille ottroier. Et ce souffise assez prolixement de la concordance de la tierce vertu du fin balme, moralisie telement quelement a la tresgracieuse et amoureuse personne royale de Charles, roy de France, et a sa royale majeste, c'est as-[11v]savoir de deffacier la deformite de la plaie.

La vertu du fin aymant moralisie a la personne du roy d'Engleterre

Il seroit temps par la bonte de Dieu de descrire aucunement et brief-ment les condicions et vertus singulieres de la precieuse pierre aymant, pour la concordance a nostre propos de la treshaulte, tresnoble et tres-gracieuse personne royale, Richart, par la grace de Dieu roy d'Engle-terre. Et pour aucune introduction de la matere, sans aleguier ystoires apocriffes, il est assavoir que le noble philosophe et docteur, un des plus sages phi-/losophes qui ait depuis le temps Aristote, c'est assavoir le grant Albert de Couloingne, en son livre des pierres precieuses, recite solempnelment que es darraines parties d'Inde la majour, a grant diffi-culte se treuve la fine pierre d'aymant, qui est de tele vertu que non tant seulement elle attrait le fer a luy, comme font les pierres d'aymant des parties d'occident, mais oultre ce elle atrait merveilleusement et amour-eusement a luy la char de l'omme. Et pour la recommandacion de la dicte pierre precieuse orientelle aymant, le dit docteur ou dit livre recite une de ses merveilleuses vertus, [12r] c'est assavoir:

Se la ditte pierre d'aymant sera mise dessoulz le cheves, c'est assavoir dessoulz la teste, d'une dame dormant avec son mary, sans ce qu'elle en sache riens, tantost qu'elle sera endormie, se elle se sera mal portee de son corps envers son mary, et fause le sacrement de son mariage, par la vertu de la dicte pierre elle sera si troublee en son dormant, et verra songes et visions si horribles, que elle ne se pourra plus tenir en son lit, mais convendra que elle se laisse cheoir du lit a terre, et tout en dormant. Mais au contraire, se elle aura bien garde envers son ma-/ry le sacrement de son mariage, sans mesprendre de son corps, tantost elle sera contrainte en dormant de acoler et baisier son mary par vraie amour de mariage, qui est bien contraire chose a la premiere, qui s'est laissie cheoir en la ruelle de son lit.

Grant vertu a la dicte pierre d'aymant, selonc le dit du philosophe susdit, le grant Albert. Quel merveille, car qui veult user et jouir de la vertu des pierres precieuses, il les fault porter nettement et sanz pechie mortel, comme il appert par la belle esmeraude, conforterresse de chastete, qui par l'euvre de luxure se treuve tost fendue et [12v] brisie. Par l'exemple donques de la vertu du fin aymant cy dessus recite, nous est demoustre qu'il attrait la char de l'omme a luy mais que l'aymant soit dignement porte sanz pechie, comme il est apparu par la dame chaste et preudefemme envers son mary, qui par la vertu de l'aymant fu attraite a l'amour et a la char de son seigneur et mary.

Encores, la dicte pierre d'aymant a une autre vertu bien solempnelle, combien qu'elle soit assez commune, et par especial aux maronniers de la mer Adriane ou Mediterraneane, c'est assavoir que l'aiguille / de fer, frotee et atouchee a la pierre d'aymant, a tousjours son regart a l'estoille du north, c'est assavoir a l'estoille tresmontaigne, par la vertu de laquele aguille de fer, frotee a l'aymant, les maronniers de la dicte mer ont tousjours leur regart a la dicte estoille, recongnoissant leur chemin en la mer, et s'il s'en sevent bien aidier, communelment il parviennent a port de salut.

Encores, selonc ce que aucuns dient, la pierre d'aymant est propre pour restraindre le sanc. Et ce souffice en brief des iii. vertus du fin aymant, pierre tresprecieuse.

Qui vouldra donques [13r] moralisier des dictes iii. vertus du fin aymant, il n'a personne royale, a mon avis et a mon vouloir, ou royaume d'Engleterre a laquele les similtudes du fin aymant puissent estre mieulx appropriees que a la digne et royale personne de Richart, par la grace de Dieu roy d'Engleterre. Or entrons ou nom de Dieu en la matere gracieuse et joyeuse de la concordance des dictes similitudes de l'aymant et de la tresgracieuse personne du roy, souventesfois a grant joye repetee, en commencant ou nom de Dieu a la premiere vertu, c'est assavoir d'atraire la char de / l'omme, c'est l'omme tout entier, a son amour en Dieu.

Chascun scet, et Francois et Englois, comme il fut dit du fin baulme que, depuis le sacre et gouvernement du dit josne roy Richart, la male plaie, cy dessus tant de foys repetee, a mains gitte de venin qu'elle n'avoit fait en tout le temps de lx. ans devant. Quel merveille, car Dieu, aiant en abhominacion l'effusion du sanc des crestiens baptisiez, qui a este crueusement espandu par les princes et generacions d'Engleterre, en rafreschissant sa mi misericorde, de grace es-[13v]peciale a fait naistre des espines poingnans la rose bien fleurant en Engleterre, par l'oudour de laquele, c'est par la vertu de l'aymant figure, elle a attrait, et chascun jour merveilleusement atrait, non tant seulement le cuer de ses subgiez, mais des estrangiers, a son amour en Dieu. Quel merveille, la ditte gracieuse rose vermeille, le noble roy Richart, rafreschissant la memoire du precieux sanc de Jhesucrist, et enflambee de l'amour de Dieu et du proesme, par la vertu de l'aymant en son cuer a abhomine l'effusion du sanc humain, c'est le tresvertueux aymant / qui aime paix et unite, et par grace est denus filz de Dieu par adoptacion et par charite, selonc le dit de saint Jehan l'evangelistre en son evvangile, *In principio erat verbum.*

Sa grant vertu de l'aymant propose, c'est la vertu de la pierre precieuse de saint Pol l'apostre, descendue en nostre aymant figure d'Engleterre, c'est en la personne du tresdebonnaire josne roy Richart, non tant seulement a attrait a luy et a son amour ses subgiez et autres gens d'estat, conversans et parlans avec sa royale majeste, mais, que plus est, il a attrait a luy ses anemis, reputez par [14r] longue possession comme anemis natureulx, c'est assavoir les preudommes de France, et, que plus est, la personne de nostre tres ame roy Charles, par la grace de Dieu roy de France, et ses oncles auxi, lesquelz il ne vit onques. Or plaise a Dieu que la fin aymant oriental unefois soit mis dessoulz les chiefs des ii. roys et des princes, et d'un coste et d'autre, affin qu'il soient en Dieu contrains d'embracier l'un l'autre, pour doulce conclusion de vraie amour et de paix des preudommes desiree.

Aucuns anemis de la paix pourroient dire que cestui vieil solitaire a la loenge du gracieux aymant figure / eslargist trop sa penne, et que l'avugle ne puet jugier des coulours. Et a ce y puet respondre que des iiii. evvangelistres les ii., c'est assavoir saint Jehan et saint Mahieu, furent tesmoings des oeuvres du doulz Jhesucrist de veue, et les autres ii., c'est assavoir saint Marc et saint Luc, furent tesmoings d'ouye, avec lesquelz, au propos, cestui vieil solitaire, en parlant et trop briefment loant l'aymant figure, a empris a escripre, enfourmes diligaument de la vertu attrative du dit josne roy Richart par tous les messages, secres et publiques, qui ont este mande au dit roy d'Engleterre par [14v] son tresame frere le roy Charles. Et par especial de la dicte vertu actrative cestui escripvain a este a plain et longuement en Dieu enfourme par le preudomme de Dieu, Robert l'ermite, message de Dieu singulier as ii. roys cy dessus proposes.

O glorieux roy d'Engleterre, a l'aymant figure, avec mon maistre le glorieux saint Jeromie, docteur de l'eglise, escripvant a monseigneur saint Augustin, en disant, Laisse moy loer ton engin et les vertus de fin aymant cy dessus proposees, que Dieu a en ton ame plantees. Il est escript que la vertu loee croist tousjours / es cuers de grant magnificence vertueuse, mais es cuers des presumptuex et vaine glorieux la vertu loee est convertie en orgueil et en vaine gloire. De laquele chose, noble roy, amys de paix, Dieu vous vueille garder.

Encores, pour demonstrer la vertu actrative du glorieux aymant figure, sa vertu en Dieu est si grande, voire confortee et arousee du fin baulme figure, qu'elle a merveilleusement atrait, auraie conjonction d'amour les ii. vertus, l'une de par pere et l'autre de par mere, de la septisme generacion du tresvaillant saint Loys, roy de [15r] France, c'est assavoir les ii. freres, filz du dit saint Loys, Charles roy de France et Richart roy d'Engleterre. Et ne fault autre chose pour la confirmacion en Dieu de la dicte conjunction que l'asamblee et presence mutuele des ii. freres ainsi doulcement attrais l'un a l'autre. Et bien seront maudit en Dieu, comme Cayin et Lamech, qui la dicte assemblee destourberont. Et ce souffise assez briefment de la vertu actrative de nostre vertueux et gracieux aymant figure.

Quant a le seconde vertu du fin aymant, c'est assavoir qu'il atrait le fer a luy et que l'aiguile de fer, frotee a l'aymant, a tousjours son regart / a l'estoille du north, c'est a l'estoille tresmontaine, qui maine les naves a bon port de salut: Or venons a aucune concordance, parlant moralment, de ceste seconde vertu et similtude du fin aymant au roy Richart, aymant figure. Il a este dit dessus comment nostre aymant atrait le cuer et la char des gens a luy et a son amour en Dieu.

Or veons donques comment il attrait le fer a luy et comment il transporte sa vertu a l'aiguile de fer. Il se puet dire, et non pas sanz larmes en nostre crestiente, que la vaillant chevalerie d'Engleterre environ [15v] lx. ans, pour chastoier les pechiez par la sentence divine, a este transmuee et convertie en une aguille ou aguillon de fer, voire si tres poingnant que ames infinies en sont dampnees et boulent en enfer; et que les noirs sengliers, crueux a leurs freres crestiens, sur fourme de prouesse et de vaillance mondainne, ou d'aucun droit apparant, ont aguisie leurs dens aus maistres citez des royaumes d'Espaigne, de Gaules et d'ailleurs, selonc ce que Merlin l'avoit escript en son livre. Et toutefoiz il se puet dire que apres la cruaute redoubtee du dit aguillon, et / apres victoires moult merveilleuses, et honnour mondaine et transitoire, aux diz noirs sengliers peu de proufit temporel leur en est demoure. Quel merveille, car Dieu les avoit mandez permisisvement es dis royaumes pour corrigier les roys, princes et communes des dis royaumes de leurs pechiez et non pas pour avoir la plaine seignourie des dis royaumes; car, comme il est dit en proverbe, Lombardie demourra as Lombars, Espaigne aus Espaigneux, France aus Francois, et Engleterre aux Anglois. Et ce soit dit affin que par le petit avis de cestui vieil escrip-[16r]vain solitaire, la vaillant chevalerie d'Engleterre et de France de cy en avant doye laissier le dit office du dit aguillon de fer, ainsi poingnant comme dit est dessus, encontre leurs freres crestiens, et radrecier le dit aguillon, par le commandement de Dieu et des roys, encontre les anemis de la foy, pour satisfaire a Dieu des grans maulz qui ont este fais par le dit aguillon.

Retournant donques a la concordance des vertus proposees de nostre aymant figure: Il se puet dire a grant joye que au jour duy par la grace de Dieu l'aymant propose a merveilleusement attrait a luy le fer, c'est / assavoir la chevalerie et d'Engleterre et de France, figure par l'aguillon et son cruel effait cy dessus proposee; et, que plus est, la dicte aguille de fer, ou aguillon, bien frotee et atouchie au roy Richart, aymant figure, en laissant ses pointures par l'adressement de l'aymant, a son regart, comme les maronniers en mer, a l'estoille du north, c'est a l'estoille tresmontaine, par laquele estoille tresmontaine, parlant doulcement, je n'entens autrement, ne autre chose, que la tresdoulce Vierge Marie, appelee estoille de mer, ravoians les maronniers desvoians, selonc le dit de monseigneur [16v] saint Benait; par le moien et adressement de laquele en tous perilz, s'elle sera bien regardee et contemplee devotement sans intermission, a l'exemple de celuy qui garde la boiste de navier en la nef quant on a perdu veue de la terre, l'aguillon de fer, c'est a la dicte chevalerie et principaument l'aymant figure, qui tousjours a son regart envers la dicte estoille, elle enseignera la droite voie de retraire soy de l'office a Dieu desplaisant du dit aguillon; et sussitera la vraie pais et amour des ii. roys et de leur vaillant chevalerie; et finablement la doulce estoille amou-/reuse, apres victoires infinies encontre les anemis de la foy, les fera ariver a vray port de salut. Laquele chose

Dieu leur vueille ottroier et ma vieillesse esleessier. Et ce souffise assez briefment et rudement de la concordance de la seconde vertu du fin aymant, et comment il atrait le fer a luy.

Quant a la tierce vertu du fin aymant, c'est assavoir qu'il restraint le sanc, il se puet dire, parlant moralment qu'il n'ot pierre precieuse figuree a aucun roy ou prince du royaume d'Engleterre, lx. ans cy arriere, qui ainsi restrainsist le sanc humain [17r] d'estre espandu comme a fait le roy Richart, au fin aymant figure. Les lapidaires dient que la pierre onicle, le corail, la belle pelle, et la fine esmeraude pour sa froideur, et plussieurs autres pierres, ont grant vertu de restraindre le sanc, mais non pas si grant comme nostre aymant figure. Ses subgiez les Anglois souloient espandre le sanc de leurs freres crestiens en Espaigne et en Bretaigne, en Escosse, en Normandie, en France, en Guianne, en Champaigne et en Picardie, par tele maniere que la plus grant partie de nostre crestiente, de la dicte espee des Anglois, a este toute ensanglantee en / en grant malediction de la crestiente catholique. Mais par la bonte de Dieu a present, par sa grace, et par la vertu de nostre aymant, le dit sanc est restraint; et Dieu vueille qu'il soit bien et a tousjours mais restraint par tele maniere que la prophecie d'Isaye en nostre temps soit acomplie, et que les espees et les lances en fers de charues soient converties, et que par la doulce paix et amour du fin baulme et du fin aymant soit acompli le dit de David le prophete, c'est assavoir, Misericorde et verite se sont entrencontrees et justice et paix se sont entrebaisiees; laquele chose Dieu nous vueille [17v] ottroier.

Nous devons devotement croire, et Anglois et Francois, que la vertu de restraindre le sanc humain a nostre gracieux aymant est descendue la doulce estoille proposee, a laquele il a eu continuelment son regart, c'est a l'estoille tremontaine, qui porta virginalment en son precieux ventre le fin ruby, qui respandi son sanc en l'abre de la vraie croix pour racheter le monde, en satisfacion du sanc humain qui avoit este espandu des le temps que le sanc d'Abel le juste avoit este espandu de son frere Cayin jusques a sa sainte passion; et pour / restraindre auxi le sanc humain du temps de sa resurrection jusques a la fin du monde. Et devoit bien souffire le dit sanc precieux espandu pour l'umaine generacion, et par especial a la generacion crestienne, voire pour l'amour et reverance de nostre tres doulz Redempteur, sans espandre ainsi le sanc l'un de l'autre, comme il est dit dessus. Et pour ce que le roy Richart et le roy Charles ont eu eu leur regart et leur devocion a la precieuse estoille, c'est assavoir a la Vierge Marie, elle leur a doulcement empetre la vertu de restraindre l'effusion du sanc humain et de leurs freres et parens crestiens. [18r] Si se doivent bien garder et l'un et l'autre roy et leur vaillant chevalerie de rencheoir en la dicte maladie par conseil desordene. Car il se dit en proverbe que la renchiete d'une grant maladie aucunefois vault pis que la premiere maladie.

Noble roy, aymant figure, il vous plaise a souvenir de la noble et sainte parole que disoit le tresvaillant et preudomme Theodocien, l'empereur de Romme. Aucuns de ses barons et collateraux li raporterent que un de ses chevaliers par maniere de blapheme avoit dit mal de luy, et disoient a l'empereur / qu'il estoit digne de mort, et qu'il le fist mourir. Lors le vaillant empereeur catholique leva les yeux et les mains au ciel a Dieu et dist ainsi: Or pleust a Dieu, dist il, que je peusse faire les mors revivre et non pas faire mourir ceulz qui sont en vie. Bien avoit son regart cestui saint empereur a l'estoille de mer cy dessus proposee, et bien avoit en grant abhominacion l'effusion du sanc humain en terre et de faire mourir les gens.

Encores, tresnoble prince et tresgracieux roy, il vous souviengne de Titus, filz de Vaspasien, empereur de [18v] Romme, et apres empereur, et comment, luy estant au siege de la cite de Jherusalem, en laquele furent mors de fain et de glaive xi. fois c. mile hommes, exceptes iiii^{xx} et vii. mile qui furent vendus, xxx. pour i. denier en vengence et ramambrance des xxx. deniers qu'il vendirent le benoit Filz de Dieu; et quant le tresvaillant et debonnaire Titus vit si grant mortalite de ses propres anemis et anemis de sa loy, car il estoit ydolastre comme estoient les Rommains et ceulz dedens estoient Juyfs, et vit que les Juyfs de Jherusalem jetoient les mors sans nombre / par dessus les murs, en emplissant les fosses, le tresdebonnaire Titus, ce veant, ot si grant compassion qu'il leva les yeux et les mains au ciel et ploura tendrement, disant a Dieu, Sire Dieux, tu vois bien ma douleur que je de ceste gent, car c'il se vousissent estre rendus a l'empire de Romme et le recognoistre comme il faisoient devant, un tout seul n'en fust mors.

Ce fu celuy Titus, empereur de Romme, qui un jour au vespre en lamentant dist a ses chevaliers, Helas, nous avons perdu ceste journee, pour ce qu'il souvient que celle journee [19r] il n'avoit fait aucun don ou grace aucune a ses chevaliers et subgiez. Bien fu large et piteux cestuy empereur payen et ydolastre, aiant compassion des mors. Et comme le roy et pueple de Ninivee condampneront les Juyfs au jour du jugement, comme il appert en l'evangile, il fait fort a doubter au propos que ce vaillant paien, Titus, ne doie condampner les roys des crestiens, qui n'ont pas faite la penitence de leurs pechiez comme fist le roy et pueple de Ninivee, mais se sont efforciez, et a petite occasion, de faire mourir leurs freres crestiens.

Or y / prenez example, tres devot roy, aymant figure, et auxi vostre frere, le roy Charles, au fin baulme figure. Et vous gardez bien que par le conseil de la chevalerie, en effusion de sanc nourrie, le sanc de vos dois ne soit trouvez courant devant le souverain Juge, en la presence duquel vous rendres conte de tous vos pechiez, jusques a une petite pensee et jusques a un quadrant. Et ce souffice de la concordance tele quele de la tierce vertu du fin aymant a la personne du tres debonnaire roy Richart, aymant figure, et de aucune induction et amonicion de restrain-[19v]dre le sanc des crestiens de si en avant et d'avoir compassion des mors.

Tout ce qui est dit dessus, grossement, prolixement et rudement, n'entent a autre chose finable que a la vraie paix et amour sans faintise des ii. josnes roys, au fin baulme et au fin aymant figurez. Pour la confirmacion de laquele amour, il vous doit souvenir comment il fut dit vers le commencement de ceste foible escripture que le fin baulme figure sera converti en une reluisant escharboucle et le fin aymant en un precieux dyament.

Or veons / premier du fin baulme. Il est assavoir que Charles, en latin c'est assavoir *Karolus*, par son interpretacion vault autant a dire comme *kara lus*, c'est a dire chiere lumiere. O, O, que longuement et a grans larmes et prieres a Dieu ceste chiere lumiere en France a este desiree, par laquele les tenebres d'ignorance et de la male guerre, qui tant a dure, par la grace de Dieu peussent estre enluminees, en recognoissant les Francois et Anglois, freres et cousins crestiens, l'un l'autre, en vraye amour et pardon des offenses passees.

Parlant moralment, entre les pi-[20r]erres precieuses l'escharboucle est la plus reluisant, car quant elle est grosse et fine, de nuit elle rent grant clarte entour luy. Ceste precieuse escharboucle, enointe du fin baulme, c'est de l'oyle du ciel, dont elle a este sacree, par la bonte de Dieu et par l'aide et vertu du fin aymant, sa clarte, a luy participant, rendera et rendront telle lumiere a mon vouloir que le temple de Dieu, qui est en Jherusalem, en sera renlumine, le saint sepulcre du doulz Jhesu et le mont de Calvaire a la gloire de la foy catholique glorieusement en seront restaure.

Ceste lumiere par aven-/ture en figure est le feu que Neemias et Esdras trouverent ou temple, qui longuement avoit este couvert; par lequel feu reluisant de nouvel le temple fu renlumine a sa gloire, dedie et restaure, et la sainte cite en sa force reedifiee.

O quele precieuse lumiere de la fine escharboucle et de l'aymant, converti en fin dyamant, conjoins ensemble par vraie amour, paix et charite en Dieu; desqueles benoites pierres les ii. cuers et les ii. ames seront converties en un vouloir en Dieu; par laquele lumiere toutes les generacions des crestiens catholiques qui [20v] jusques a ores par les guerres et divisions se sont trouvez en tenebres, recognoistront la droite voie qui va en Jherusalem. Et qui plus pres pourra approchier a la clarte de la dicte lumiere, c'est a la presence des ii. roys, a confirmacion de paix generale et au service de Dieu soubz l'ombre de la dicte clarte, il se reputera bien eureux. Et bien seront mauldis de Dieu, comme il fut dit autrefois, tous ceulz qui sur fourme apparant ou bien temporel ou honnour reluisant s'esforceront d'estaindre les rays de la dicte lumiere. Il vauldroit trop mieulx pour leurs ames que en ce mon-/de n'eussent onques este nez. Et ce souffice de la conversion et concordance du fin baulme a l'escharboucle precieuse.

Or entrons ou nom de Dieu en la matere gracieuse de la conversion du fin aymant en un fin dyament. Le fin dyamant apres l'escharboucle, c'est le fin ruby, est la pierre precieuse qui est plus precieuse et plus prisiee et solempnelment portee des grans princes de ce monde; et qui vouldroit moralisier au propos de toutes ses vertus, il y fauldroit un grant volume. Mais pour cause de bri-[21r]efte ii. des ses vertus a nostre propos soient a present recitees. La premiere si est, selonc les lapidaires, que le fin dyamant a grant vertu contre le venin. La seconde vertu si est qu'il conserve l'amour de celuy qui le donne a l'amour de celuy a qui il est donne. Or venons a la doulce concordance de nostre fin aymant, devenu et converty a la nature du fin dyamant. Quant a la premiere vertu, c'est assavoir qu'il vault contre venin: Le plus grant venin et le plus perilleux et aus corps et aus ames, qui pourroit plus nuyre a la royale majeste de Richart, tresnoble et puissant roy / d'Angleterre, si est la guerre et occision des crestiens et de France et d'Angleterre; par laquele les creatures humaines et batisiees sans nombre en seroient mortes et detranchieez, et les ames de plussieurs a tousjours mais seront dampnees et peries. Cestuy mortel venin vault pis assez que le venin qui est appele le boucon en Ytalie et en Surie, car cestuy venin du boucon ne fait mourir que celui qui le prent, mais le venin propose en fait aucunefois mourir en un jour a milliers et a cens. Il se puet dire par la bonte de Dieu jusques a ores nostre aymant, converti [21v] en fin dyamant, en luy a eu telle vertu que le dit venin, c'est la guerre proposee, n'a eu nulle puissance, et ce se puet dire auxi de la vertu de la fine escharboucle. Et non obstant que le dit venin ait este presente par plusieurs fois sur fourme de laituaire au fin dyamant figure, toutefoiz par sa vertu, acquise de l'aucteur de nature, il s'en est bien garde. O quel merveille, car tout auxi que la flour de la vigne enchasse les serpens devant luy, tout auxi devant nostre dyamant figure le dit venin n'a peu arrester ne son office exercer.

Et ce souffice de la / briefve concordance de l'aymant au fin dyamant et de sa vertu contre venin; duquel venin Dieu nous vueille garder.

Quant a la vertu du fin dyamant et qu'il engendre et conserve l'amour du donnant a l'amour de celuy a qui il est donne, voire mais qu'il soit donne et receu en bonne entencion, sans malice, convoitise, ou corrupcion: Les personnes secrettes de la premiere amiste et doulce aliance d'amour et de paix cordiale du fin baulme et de l'escharboucle au fin aymant et, a present, dyamant, sevent que la [22r] ditte amour fu par le moien du fin dyamant, en signe d'amour, mande l'un a l'autre. Quel merveille, car le tresgracieux et amoureux roy Richart, ensuivant sa vocacion, a laquele le doulz Jhesu, Aucteur de paix, l'avoit appele et predestine, de la nature des noirs sengliers dont il estoit issu fu transmue, parlant moralment, en la pierre precieuse d'aymant, merveilleusement atraiant comme il est dit dessus; et puis apres se transforma en la pierre du riche dyamant, et se transporta, parlant figuralment, par amour fra-/ternelle a son frere, le roy Charles; dont par la bonte de Dieu le transport fu tel et de si grant vertu que l'escharboucle reluisant en un moment auxi fu transmuee en la vertu et amour du fin dyamant, par le moien duquel en figure et doulce volente elle fu tantost transportee en l'ame et ou cuer de nostre dyamant figure, par telle maniere et vertu singuliere que l'amour des ii. pierres figurees, par la grace de Dieu est encore toute entiere; sicomme cestui vieil solitaire et les preudommes le desirent.

Or preignent bien garde donques le fin dya-[22v]mant et l'escharboucle reluisant que par conseil du contraire, ne par les menistres du dieu de Mars, ne du dieu de Mercure, leur grant vertu cy dessus desclarie ne soit aucunement ameurriee, divisee, ou souillie. Car se tel cas advenoit, que ja n'aviengne, ce seroit signe que les dictes pierres n'auroient pas pris leur fondement et naissance en la riche miniere dont la pierre fu prise de la grant montaigne et taillie sans mains; sicomme Daniel le prophete le recite en ses prophecies. Nostre gracieux dyamant figure en perseverant face bien son / office et deca et dela, afin que par sa vertu l'amour soit perpetuelle et le dit venin, tant de foiz repete et redoubte, soit bany des cuers des roys, des maistres cites, et de toutes les frontieres; afin que les ii. roys par grace soient dignes d'oir la gracieuse cantique des angels que les pastours oirent, c'est assavoir que en nostre temps gloire soit a Dieu lassus ou ciel, et en terre la paix as hommes de bonne volente. Et ce souffice de la concordance du fin dyamant et comment il conserve l'amour en figure de nos ii. roys.

Dieux scet que se cestuy vieillart solitaire [23r] eust peu trouver choses ou joyaux plus riches et de plus grant pris en ce monde que le fin baulme et les pierres precieuses, en ceste povre epistre telement quelement moralisiee, pour la confirmacion de la doulce paix tant desiree des proudommes, et de l'amour des ii. filz par droite lignie du tresvaillant roy saint Loys, volentiers l'eust fait. Et est a croire doulcement que Dieu estendra sa grace es dictes personnes royales, par luy esleues des principales en la crestiente, et qui noteront les vertus des dictes pierres precieuses a eulz apartenans, en / metant la main a la paste pour reparer et soustenir la chose publique des royaumes catholiques. Laquele chose Dieu leur vueille ottroier.

La seconde matere de ceste presente espistre, c'est assavoir du mortel sisme de l'esglise et du remede d'iceluy par le moien de la paix des ii. roys

Selonc l'art de medicine, qui sur une grande plaie ouverte et toute pourrie metroit tousjours l'oingnement qui est apele popilion, jamais la plaie ne se reclorroit, mais tousjours crestroit. Il est expedient [23v] d'user souvent es plaies perilleuses, et a present, de l'oingnement qui est apeles *unguentum apostolorum*, c'est l'oingnement des apostres, qui est ou premier degre corrosif et ou secont degre mondificatif. Et, tresexcellent roy de la Grant Bretaingne, il a une plaie ouverte en la crestiente, de laquele le venim qui ensault a envenime toutes les parties de la crestiente; laquele jusques a ores a este bien garnie de l'oingnement popilion, c'est assavoir des flateurs, qui par sa doulceur apparant tient tousjours la plaie ouverte. Ceste plaie malditte, sans / parabole ou figure aleguier, est le mortel sisme de nostre mere sainte eglise, c'est la propre mere principale des ii. filz saint Loys, qui gist en son lit malade, plaie, et detranchie, et en ii. moities partie. Et que pis est, chascun des ii. filz de roy cy dessus proposes de sa ditte mere en a pris la moitie, pour maniere de creance et cure de sa grant maladie; voire en habandonant l'autre partie as chiens et as oysiaux, afin qu'elle soit devouree, et que de sa plaie, se autrement ne se fera, jamais ne soit sanee.

Il est escript en la sainte escripture, [24r] Honnoure ton pere et ta mere, afin que tu puisses vivre longuement sur la terre. Encores est il escript, Qui maudira son pere ou sa mere, de male mort il mourra. O parole divine, comminative et perilleuse a tous ceulz qui ne font pas l'onneur qu'il doivent faire a leur pere ou a leur mere. Or venons a la concordance et declaracion de la plaie proposee, usant toutefois de l'oingnement des apostres corrosif, a grant amour et reverance des ii. filz royaux proposez, qui si longuement ont laissiee languissant leur mere, qui les a engendrez et regenerez par le sacrement de baptesme / et par les autres sacremens, pour estre ii. roys en Paradis.

Dittes moy, tresgracieux enfans royaux, je vous pri, que respondres vous a l'Aignelet occis, quant en fourme de Dieu et de homme il vendra au jugement et vous arguera de vostre grant negligence et de vostre grant cruaute, que vous avez laissiee s'espouse, pour le mariage de laquele il espandi son sanc en l'abre de la crois, si longuement ainsi languir et en ii. moitiez estre divisee? Par laquele plaie et horrible maladie tant de sanc a este respandu, et l'unite de l'eglise et la charite de [24v] Dieu entre les crestiens a este si longuement, et est encore, par grant hayne troublee et divisee; et, qui pis est, les settes en la foy et les heresies, helas, sont ja partout multipliees, les crestiens catholiques, faisans un monstre de leur mere a ii. tetses, respondans l'une l'autre, non pas par charite mais par indignacion, et disans, Je suy de Paul, je suy de Apollo, c'est a dire, Je suy de Boniface, je suy de Benedic.

Certainement l'un roy et l'autre devroient avoir grant paour de la sentence cy dessus de Dieu fulminee. Que vous vault vostre grant / puissance de multitude de vaillans chevaliers et vostre gloire royale, qui trespassera comme l'ombre du soleil, quant vostre mere, ainsi divisee et malade, gist en chartre en languissant et attendant l'ayde de ses enfans, les roys catholiques qu'elle a sacrez et enoint de son saint oille de misericorde, et allaitie de ses mamelles; et par especial suspirant l'ayde des roys qui sont les premiers nez en l'eglise quant a puissance et a dignite reputee par toute la crestiente?

Et combien que la negligence des grans prelas de l'eglise, qui par ambicion et convoi-[25r]tise ont faite la dicte plaie et ont estez negligens de la cure d'ycelle, pour ce que chascun disoit de sa part, *Qui tenet teneat*, c'est a dire, Qui tient, si tiengne, et se doubtoient fort et par aventure doubtent encore d'estre refourmez de leur grant symonie et de leur petite vie, s'il avoient sur eulz un saint pape de Romme, seul vicaire souverain de Jhesucrist, nostre tres doulz Createur, toutefois en tel cas survenant, en defaulte manifeste des prelas, il aperent as roys de reparer l'eglise, comme le tres saint roy David fist vaillaument et devotement en la synagogue, laquele / il repara et amplia quant es serimonies et du service divin. Et tout ce n'estoit que l'ombre et figure dont vous autres roys estes venus a la clarte de la vraie lumiere.

Tres gracieux et tres debonnaires princes, et l'un et l'autre, se vous seres bien enformez par les proudommes et grans clers de vostre royal conseil de la dicte plaie, souventefois et non pas sans larmes repetee, et des maulx qui en sont advenus et qui croissent tous les jours, vous trouverres que la dicte plaie et sisme mortel n'est autre chose que une parfonde fosse d'ignorance et de maledicion.

[25v] O quel merveille, car il a ouailles, brebis, chievres et moutons sans nombre en la crestiente qui cuident estre menees en pasture par vray pastour, et toutesfoiz devant Dieu il ne sont pas drois pasteurs, mais sont mercennaires. Probacion: Il voient clerement venir les leux pour devourer leurs brebis et s'enfuient, car ilz sont mercenaires comme il est dit en l'evangile. Ceste fosse et abysme d'ignorance, helas, est au jour duy si parfonde que on n'en puet trouver le fons.

Tres debonnaires princes, par maniere d'example, il vous / souviengne la parfonde et horrible fosse qui soudainement apparu en la cite de Romme, laquele fosse rendoit une puour si mortele que tous ceulz qui en estoient abuvre, il mouroient soudainement; et fu la plaie et mortalite si grande que nulz n'y savoit mettre remede. Toutefois, a la parfin les Romains demanderent conseil a leurs dieux, pour empetrer aucun remede; et leur fut respondu par leurs dieux qu'il convenoit, pour remedier a la dicte plaie et a la chose publique des Romains, que le plus bel et le plus noble de [26r] la cite de Romme, arme de toutes armes et a cheval, sausist en la dicte fosse, et tantost la plaie seroit sanee. Et pour abregier l'istoire, apres plussieurs consultacions de trouver personne telle que dit est entre les Romains. qui vousist sa personne offrir a mort pour la delivrance de la cite, entre les princes et nobles des Romains se trouva un appele Curcius, qui franchement et a grant triumphe et victoire, tout arme et a cheval, en la presence de tout le pueple de Romme, sailly dedens la fosse, et tantost elle fu reclose et l'epidimie cessee, a memoire glorieuse et paradura-/ble quant aus Romains du tres noble Curcius, comme il appert plus clerement es ystoires des Romains.

A nostre propos il se puet bien dire que encore est plus perilleuse la fosse du sisme propose que ne fu la fosse des Romains. Quel merveille, car la dicte fosse ne nuisoit forsque la cite de Romme, mais la fosse proposee en l'eglise, non tant seulement absorbist et devoure les citoiens de Romme, mais gens sans nombre par toute la crestiente.

Aucuns voudroient dire, en lamentant, que la dicte fosse figuree, de laquele jusques [26v] a ores on n'a peu congnoistre le fons, comme il seroit expedient, les cardinaulz, apres la mort du pape Gregoire xi^e, y midrent la main et foirent et creerent par la beesche et chappe d'ambi- cion et de bien propre et singulier, ou prejudice de l'union de leur mere, sainte eglise. Si est expedient a present de trouver aucun remede par les roys, afin que la dicte fosse soit reclose et ne face plus mourir les gens.

Or veons doulcement en la cite de Romme, c'est a present en la crestiente, la ou nous pourrons trouver le plus bel et le plus noble des princes crestiens pour remedier a / ceste perilleuse epydimie et des corps et des ames, ceste fosse maldicte et plaie mortelle a ii. parties divisees. Et pour ce, parlant moralment, il est expedient de trouver ii. personnes, teles comme dit est, qui soient tres nobles et tres belles. Il puet estre que par election des preudommes de la crestiente, s'il se trouveront ensemble, devant tous autres il esliront l'escharboucle reluisant et en sa compaignie le vertueux dyamant souventefois recite. O nobles roys, a bien faire des preudommes desirez, n'attendez pas de cy en avant que du monde a ce vous soies appelez, car [27r] Dieu ja pieca vous a esleus a ce faire, et le vous a expressement mande. Prenez le frain aus dens et noblement armez de toutes armes de vertus et de grant humilite, tout a cheval, par lequel est entendue vostre puissance royale, pour racheter le pueple crestien de la mort, et premiere et seconde vaillaument et a grant triumphe vueillies saillir en la fosse, c'est a dire a remedier et de fait, sans aucun regart ne acceptacion de personne, au grant mal qui tous- jours sourt de la dicte fosse, sans prester les oreilles a ceulz de l'eglise qui veullent regner, et non pas de par Di-/eu, comme il est dit par le prophete. Et soies certains que se devotement et diligaument vous entreprendres ceste divine prouesse pour le salut de vostre mere, sainte eglise, Dieu vous fera grace et reclorra la fosse, a plaine garison de toute la crestiente et a plus grant gloire pardurable qu'il n'est dit cy dessus du tres noble Curcius.

Tres noble roy de Cornuaille et tres puissant prince de Gales, aourne de la digne majeste royale d'Angleterre, ceste tres sainte emprise et vaillance divine de ravivier l'eglise par vous ne par vostre tres ame frere, le roy de Gau-[27v]le bonnement ne se puet acomplir selonc l'opinion d'aucuns, et de cestui vieil escripvain, se par la bonte de Dieu le feu, qui ja assez longuement a este aucunement couvert, ne sera plainement ardent et descouvert, c'est assavoir la paix et vraye amour monstree en publique de vous et du roy Charles, vostre tresame frere. Et pour ce, a grant reverance, pour le zel du bien de la crestiente, je, vieillart, ose dire que suppose, que ja n'aviengue, que la guerre de France et d'Angleterre fust au jour duy auxi male et auxi forte comme elle fu ou temps de la correction divine, regnant le roy Edouart / et le roy Jehan, auxquelz Dieu soit debonnaires, si devries vous, sans barguegnier, ou faire paix ou prendre une trievez de c. ans et un jour, pour remedier ensamble a la male plaie, tant de foys repetee et si perilleuse aux ames.

A ce que se dira a present, que respondres vous a Dieu quant au jour duy vous amez l'un l'autre par la vertu du fin dyamant commun et si n'avez nulle guerre? En verite je doubte fort que ce vous serez negligens, Dieu le vous monstrera de fait et sentires sa verge, et que fort ly desplaira; de laquele negligence Dieu par sa grace vous vueille [28r] garder et vous doint grace que aux consaulz du contraire vous puissies vaillaument resister. Et ce souffice grossement et rudement d'aucune lamentacion de la maladie de nostre mere sainte eglise et de la cure d'icelle, longuement des preudommes catholiques desiree.

La tierce matere de ceste presente espiltre, c'est assavoir du saint passage d'oultre mer qui doit estre fait par nos ii. josnes roys de France et d'Angleterre

Il se lit ou Livre des Moralitez une parabole, c'est assavoir qu'il fut un roy moult pu-/issant, qui avoit nom Malavise, et avoit guerre a un autre roy son voisin, qui estoit apele Vigilant. Le dit roy Malavise se fioit plus en sa puissance humaine qu'il ne faisoit en son bon droit, ne en sa diligence, ne en la vertu de son Dieu. Et petit a petit devint negligent en la vertu de justice et en la discipline de chevalerie, par tele maniere que en la fin de la guerre il perdi sa maistre cite et, apres, son royaume. Et convint qu'il se retraisist en une estrange et lointaine contree qui li estoit demouree, laquele estoit souvent et froide [28v] et angele.

Le roy Vigilant, estant en la maistre cite de son anemi qu'il avoit acquise, fist iii. choses solempnelles, en aprobacion de sa victoire. Premierement toutes les banieres, armes, et enseingnes du roy Malavise il fist ardoir et destruire publiquement. Secondement au son de ses trompes royales il fist banir du dit roiaume son anemi, le roy Malavise. Et tiercement il retint tous les hommes du dit royaume en servage.

Apres un temps, le roy Malavise en son cuer recognut son pe-/tit gouvernement, et vit clerement que par sa deffaulte il avoit pardu son royaume sans aucune esperance de pooir le recouvrer en grant temps, pour la grant puissance de son anemi. Toutesfois, afin qu'il eust souvent fraiche memoire de l'injure que le roy Vigilant li avoit faite es iii. choses cy dessus recitees, il fist une loy en sa court roiale, c'est assavoir que un povre et vieil chevalier, qui avoit este desert de tout son heritage ou dit royaume, a toutes les festes solempnelles et assemblees royales du dit roy Malavise, quant il estoit a table ou [29r] milieu de sa chevalerie, le dit vieil chevalier en povre habit venoit parmi la sale, cornant fort d'un grant cor de chasse, jusques a la table du roy Malavise, et a haulte voix li disoit, O, O, sire roy, es temps passez malavise, souviengne toy des grans injures et damages et vilenies que le roy Vigilant t'a faites et a toute ta lignie; et souviengne toy que par petit gouvernement et par especial par defaulte de justice tu as perdu ton royaume et tes loyaux subgies sont desers. Et ce dit, le dit vieil chevalier sanz plus parler a homme, ne sanz faire autre reverance / se partoit de la court et s'en aloit a sa povre habitacion. Ceste parabole, assez clere ce elle est bien entendue en bon entendement, monstrera clerement la fin auquel elle entent.

Tres excellent et tres devost prince et digne roy d'Angleterre, par vostre grace et licence de vostre benignite royale, cestui povre et vieil solitaire parlera en personne du povre et vieil chevalier cy dessus recite, tousjours a grant reverance de la royale majeste de vous et de vostre frere, le roy Charles, et des autres roys crestiens, en desclarant et exposant, et a son propos allegant, la dicte parabole proposee, dont [29v] il est assavoir, parlant moralment et grossement, quant a l'exposicion de la dicte parabole, que par le roy Malavise puet estre entendue la personne d'un roy crestien et catholique, representent en sa personne l'empereur de Romme et tous les roys crestiens catholiques. Et par la personne du roy Vigilant puet estre entendu proprement le souldain de Babiloine, comme il aparra cy dessus par les similitudes et concordances de l'efect des ii. rois.

Or venons, ou nom de Dieu, a la concordance de l'exposicion du roy

Malavise, c'est assavoir des roys crestiens qui / longuement ont estez malavisez, et encore sont. Et par deffaulte de bon gouvernement, c'est assavoir principalment par defaulte de justice, en laquele est comprise la foy de Jhesucrist et ses saintes oeuvres, et par defaulte auxi de discipline chevalereuse, la maistre cite du royaume general des crestiens, c'est assavoir la sainte cite de Jherusalem, le premier fondement de la foy catholique, et, apres, tout le royaume, et toute la terre de promission, a este pardue, et acquise a grant victoire par le roy Vigilant, c'est assavoir par le souldain de Babiloine, qui en a eu la pos-[30r]session et c. ou iiᶜ ans, a grant honte et vitupere des roys crestiens, helas, malavises.

Et se paraventure aucun roy crestien de cestui malavis et de ceste grant perte de la terre sainte se vouldra excuser, et dire que par luy ne par ces predecesseurs la terre sainte n'a pas este pardue, mais par le roy de Jherusalem qui lors regnoit quant elle fu perdue, a ce se puet respondre assez clerement que se Guy de Lizignen, lors roy de Jherusalem par sa femme, eust eu le secours de ses freres et cousins, les roys de la crestiente, il est a croire doul-/cement que la sainte cite de Jherusalem n'eust pas este pardue, qui fu perdue en son temps. Et a la fin, auxi, se Henri de Lizignem roy de Jherusalem, eust eu l'aide comme dit est dessus, il n'eust pas perdue la cite d'Acre et tout le remenant du royaume de Jherusalem et de la terre sainte. Quel merveille! La dicte cite de Jherusalem et le royaume, commencement et fondement de la foy, et royaume singulier, tout autour avironne des anemis de la foy, c'est assavoir pais et terre pubique de la crestiente, quant a la foy et quant a l'onnour, non tant seulement des pueples [30v] crestiens mais de tous les roys et princes de la crestiente, ne devoit pas estre separe de la garde et tuicion de tous les roys crestiens pour l'onnour de la foy. Ne ou dit royaume, gardant bone policie, ne pouoient pas demourer iiii., v., ou vi. roys ensemble pour la garde d'iceluy. Et pooit assez souffire que un des roys crestiens, pour luy et pour tous les autres roys, en eust le gouvernement, par tele condicion que tousjours en ses necessitez il fust aydiez de ces freres, les autres roys de la crestiente. Et pour ce que les dessusdis roys de Jherusalem et les au-/tres roys entredeux qui regnerent es parties du dit royaume, es citez de la marine, n'orent pas le secours sicomme il est dit dessus, tout fu pardu, a grant honte et vergoingne de tous les roys crestiens, et a confirmacion du nom Malavise. Encores il fut dit dessus du roy Malavise qu'il perdit son royaume par defaulte de justice et de petit gouvernement de la discipline chevalereuse, qui se puet dire a la lettre des dessus diz roys de Jherusalem depuis la perte de la sainte cite; lequel petit gouvernement estoit nottoire a l'empereur et au pape de Romme [31r] et a tous les roys de la crestiente, qui pour l'onneur de la foy de Jhesucrist ilz devoient mettre remede, et de fait, ou dit gouvernement, comme a la chose publique de tous les crestiens. Et par ceste rayson, qui pourroit estre legierement prouvee par les loys divines, civiles et morales, il se puet dire que tous les diz empereurs, papes et roys, par leurs negligences furent en cause de la perdicion de la terre sainte, non excusant pour ce les dessus diz roys de Jherusalem. Et pour ce auxi qu'il ont tant attendu de recouvrer la terre sainte, en espandent le sanc l'un de l'autre, / par le moien de la parabole dignement il puent estre apelez les roys malavisez, qui est une grant honte a la gloire de leur cedre royal, car selonc les drois les filz sont tenus de reparer les defaultes de leurs peres, voire celles qui sont possibles d'estre reparees.

Encores a concordance de la parabole, le roy Vigilant a confusion des crestiens dormans, c'est assavoir le souldain de Babiloine, en Jherusalem fist ardoir et destruire les banieres, les enseignes et armeures du roy Malavise, c'est assavoir le signe de la vraye croys et toutes [31v] les precieuses enseignes et autres de la foy crestienne. Encores il fist banir a trompes, c'est a dire publiquement, le roy Malavise, c'est assavoir tous les roys crestiens du royaume de Jherusalem. Et pour conclusion, de grant despit et mesprisement de la gloire de la crestiente, il retint, et encores retient, tous les subgiez du roiaume crestiens en servage, si-comme il appert au jour duy, qui n'est pas petite vergoingne a la grant puissance et orgueil des roys crestiens.

Encores fu dit en la parabole que le roy Malavise, qui avoit / perdu son royaume sans esperance de le recouvrer, se retray en une lointaine region qui li estoit demouree, laquele estoit souvent engelee. Ce sont les grans roys crestiens, representans a la lettre le roy Malavise, qui se sont retrais, et leurs predecesseurs, en la region d'occident, souvent froide et engelee de vertu et de l'amour de Dieu, qui deussent habiter en Jherusalem et es parties d'orient pour la multiplicacion de la foy; entre lesquelz roys d'occident, selonc l'ymaginacion et ardant desire du vieil solitaire en poursui-[32r]vant son songe contemplatif, ii. roys y a qui, par la bonte de Dieu, ont recogneu devant Dieu que leurs pre-decesseurs et eulzmeismes en ceste presente epistre n'ont pas este nommes et appelez sans cause les roys malavisez.

Et pour ce que par la grace de Dieu le nom de Malavise soit mue en Bien Avise en esperit, il ont faite la loy du povre et vieil chevalier cy dessus propose, pour avoir souvent remambrance de l'injure que le roy Vigilant, c'est le souldan et ses predecesseurs, ont fait et font encores au benoit Filz de Dieu et a leurs royales majestes. Ce / sont les ii. roys en ceste presente epistre par l'escharboucle et par le fin dyamant moralisant figurez, qui de ii. diverses et lointaines regions, anemies et morteles l'une a l'autre, par la doulce amour et inspiracion du Saint Esperit, en esperit sont conjoins en leurs cuers a vraye paix et amour l'un a l'autre; voire en entencion de vengier en leurs personnes royales l'injure du Crucefix et la grant vergoingne envieillie de tous les roys crestiens, au propos malavisez apelez.

Cestui vieil solitaire donques est reconforte en esperit de la haulte prouesse et magnani-[32v]mite royale des ii. roys et princes proposes, c'est assavoir Charles et Richart, roys de France et d'Angleterre, et de leur haulte et sainte volente; et reconforte auxi en Dieu de la parole du prophete David, qui nous demonstre clerement que le temps est venu de pardon et de redifier de nouvel Jherusalem la sainte cite, le dit solitaire a grant humilite prendra la personne du dit povre et vieil chevalier, qui a perdu son heritage quant a la foy ou royaume de Jherusalem, en entrant en la sale en esperit devant les dessusdiz roys, et a present devant la royale majeste du / tresgracieux et tresdevot roy d'Angleterre, cornant d'un grant cornet de chasse, duquel il ne fina xl. ans de corner as empereurs et roys et princes de la crestiente, voire pour assembler a la chasse de Dieu les grans levriers et chiens courans pour envair la riche proie, par laquele le nom de Malavise soit mue; et a haulte voiz et de cuer fervant dira a present comme il a dit ailleurs et darrainement au tresvaillant et tresdebonnaire roy Charles et a sa tresnoble lignie, c'est assavoir:

O gentil et tres noble roy de la Grant Bretaingne, prince de [33r] Gales et Norgales, seigneur de la grant Hybernie, et roy de Cornuaille, il vous souviengne, et non pas sanz larmes, de la grant injure envieillie que le roy Vigilant, c'est le souldain, a fait a nostre Dieu, le doulz Jhesu crucefie; il vous souviengne du Mont de Calvaire, du saint sepulchre, et des sains lieux arousez du precieux sanc de l'Aignelet occis, qui sont souilliez chascun jour par la faulce generacion de Mahommet, devant Dieu reprouvee. Il vous souviengne, non pas en songent, que vos armes et enseignes et banieres par lesqueles vous avez puissance / en esperit de desconfire et enchassier les grans anemis de humaine nature, les anemis d'enfer, et comment elles ont este tenues longuement en vilte, et sont encore, en Jherusalem, vostre esperituel royaume quant a l'ame en ce monde; et comment il ont arses, destruites, et vilenez ou quart degre les saintuaires de vostre foy, c'est assavoir la vraye croix et les tres nobles et tres saintes enseignes de la passion de vostre redempteur et sauveur, Jhesucrist. Tres excellent et tres puissant roy, il vous souviengne que voz predecesseurs et vous estes honteusement banis de vostre [33v] royaume et propre heritage quant a la foy, c'est la terre sainte que le doulz Jhesu vous avoit acquise par la monnoie de l'effusion de son precieux sanc et de sa mort precieuse. Tres devost roy, il vous souviengne que vos subgiez, alans et demourans ou dit royaume, par le roy Vigilant sont retenus en servage, batus et malmenez, et comment il paient les grans treuages et subvencions, a grant honte et vergoingne de tous voz freres, les roys crestiens, et par especial de la majeste royale de vostre tresame frere, Charles, roy de France, et de vous, tres / devot et tres debonnaire roy d'Angleterre. Il vous souviengne auxi, et non pas sanz souppirer, de la tres sainte foy catholique, pour laquele tant de vos grans peres, les tressains roys d'Angleterre, se sont laissiez martirer, au jour duy en Jherusalem et en Surie, en Egypte, et en Turquie, et par tout orient, est foulee et deshonnouree, destruite, laissie et abandonnee, et les temples de Dieu partout en orient prophanez, destruis et abandonnez, et le divin sacrefice et office oubliez et en abhominacion reputez. Qui est celuy, ou nom du doulz Jhesu baptisie, qui ait le cuer [34r] d'acier, oyans les grans injures de la foy reciter et ne soit meu a compassion, en presentant devotement a Dieu son corps, son avoir et tout ce qu'il pourra faire, pour aidier a reparer les tres grans maulz et la deshonneur de la crestiente, cy dessus en briefve sustance recitees? Il est grant peril que les crestiens qui n'en auront compassion ne soient privez de la consolacion en Jherusalem triumphant, par l'apostre saint Pol recitee, aus preudommes desiree. Et ce souffice assez briefment de l'office du vieil solitaire et de son effect en esperit et en escript, pris a concor-/dance du vieil et povre chevalier en la parabole recite quant a la reparacion des injures faites a tous les roys crestiens par le souldain de Babiloine, et par especial a vostre tres devote et puissante royale majeste.

Tres excellent prince et tres debonnaire seigneur, il est doulcement a croire que par vostre inviolable foy catholique, ensuivant les voies et vertus des sains roys vos predecesseurs, et par especial de vostre grant pere, saint Emont, et le vaillant roy de France, saint Loys, que vous cognoissies assez que les injures cy dessus recitees, par le roy Vigilant faites a vous et a tous voz [34v] freres roys crestiens, puent estre dites et reputees une grant plaie, et trop plus grande assez que la male plaie de ceste povre epistre cy dessus rudement proposee. Quel merveille, car de tant comme une plaie est plus universelle, de tant fait elle plus a redoubter et est plus forte a saner. Ceste plaie principalment est destruction de la foy et touche a l'ame sanz moien, voire de tous les crestiens, et catholiques et sismatiques, et par consequant as roys. Et trop plus grant honte est des damages et injures de l'ame immortele et d'en-/ fraindre les loys de sa possession, que ce n'est de la honte du corps, ne d'enfraindre ou corrompre les loys de sa temporelle possession, pour laquele la plaie des roys d'Angleterre et de France a male journee fu creee et a tresgrant joye et a journee bieneuree par vous et par vostre frere de France restrainte de son venin; et se puet dire a grant desir qu'elle est au jour duy presque sanee. Et Dieu veulle en vous ii. roys parfaire a consolacion des bons, tout ce qui est a parfaire.

Comment le vieil solitaire presente au roy d'Angleterre une nouvelle chevalerie [35r] du Crucefix qui doit estre mandee oultremer devant les ii. roys, qui par la grace de Dieu feront le saint passage

Tres puissant roy de la Grant Bretaingne, saint Jehan Bouche d'Or dit par maniere de sentence que a un grant seigneur souffrir ses propres injures par la vertu de pacience est chose meritoire, mais souffrir les injures de son Dieu, quant / il les puet bien amender, c'est chose tres mauvaise et plaine de iniquite. Cestuy vieil escripvain est assez enfourme de la haulte et ardant volente de vostre tresame frere Charles, roy de France, qu'il a de reparer et de fait les injures sustoucies faites a son Dieu, le benoit Filz de Dieu, le doulz Jhesucrist, par le roy Vigilant, c'est le souldain. Encores, le dit vieil solitaire a este enforme par le message de Dieu, Robert l'ermite, ja par plussieurs annees, de vostre treshaulte volente et prouesse samblable, comme vrais champions de la foy, qui a leur Dieu se doivent presenter [35v] pour vengier son injure.

Et pour ce que a la plaine cure de la plaie darrainement proposee, si universelle et si damagable a la chose publique de la crestiente comme a la foy catholique, il y fault grandes et sollempnelles medicines et puissans et sages phisiens, lesquelz pour leur grant humilite ne refusent pas aucunefois pour la cure de leurs paciens aucune petite medicine composee par les petis varles de l'apoticairie; ceste humilite des grans fusiciens supposee, avecques la bonne volente qu'il ont de la cure de la plaie univer-/selle, tres debonnaire prince, cestui vieil solitaire, a present poursuivant medicin, s'est enhardy de presenter a vostre tres-ame frere le roy de France, et a present a grant reverance a vostre royale et devote majeste d'Angleterre, une petite medicine pour la dicte plaie, par maniere de preparacion precedent a la grande medicine qui est necessaire pour la cure de la dicte plaie universelle.

Dont il est assavoir, parlant moralment, que par la grande medicine sustoucie puet estre entendu le saint passage d'oultremer, qui par la bonte de Dieu a mon voloir se fera par la haul-[36r]te prouesse de vostre frere et de vous, a la gloire de Dieu et exaltacion de la foy catholique. Pour lequel saint passage de ii. si puissans roys, il y fault grandes, longues et meures preparacions, entre lesqueles cestui vieil abortif, vostre tres indigne orateur en esperit et en escript, tres debonnaire et tres devot roy, vous offre une petite medicine preparative, non tant seulement pour aidier a la cure de la dicte plaie, mais a refourmacion et cure en Dieu des grandes maladies et passions au jour duy courans par toute la crestiente. /

Ceste petite medicine preparative au grant passage qui se doit faire par vous, vray aymant au fin dyamant figure, et par vostre tres ame frere, l'escharboucle clere lumiere apele, n'est autre chose que la gracieuse et nouvelle chevalerie de la passion Jhesucrist, ja xl. ans inspiree de Dieu, sicomme doulcement se puet croire, pour la presenter a present a la devocion de vos ii. royales majestez. Ceste petite medicine, doncques, preparative, par la bonte de Dieu et par vos ii. royales majestez, doit estre composee, confite, et cree de nouvel des vaillans chevaliers et hommes [36v] d'armes de vii. langages de toute la crestiente catholique, tousjours a vostre bonne ordenance, voire pour iiii. choses principales; c'est assavoir pour rapeler les hommes d'armes, souilliez et mal nourris en l'effusion du sanc de leurs freres crestiens, a une gracieuse penitance chevalereuse et a la bataille de Dieu. Secondement doit estre cree pour estre fourriere de voz ii. royales majestez, et aler devant en la terre des anemis de la foy, prendre les pors et les places pour vous requeillir quant vous vendres au saint passage, en descendent a ter-/re sans aucun peril ou dangier des anemis de la foy. La tierce cause et principale si est pour la conqueste de la terre sainte, par la grace de Dieu, avec le favour, aide, et benedicion de vos ii. royales majestez. Et la quarte si est pour multiplier la sainte foy catholique partout es parties d'orient.

Sicomme de l'entencion de la puissance et de l'efect de la dicte sainte chevalerie et des clers motifs expediens pour lesquelz la dicte chevalerie a present est tresnecessaire a la crestiente, et par especial au service de la royale majeste de vous et de [37r] vostre frere le roy de France, et des grans biens qui raisonablement doivent advenir d'icelle chevalerie a l'onneur et reparacion de toute la crestiente, vostre tres debonnaire et royale devocion puet avoir este enfourmee plus plainement par vostre tres loyal serviteur et orateur le dit Robert l'ermite, plainement enforme de la dicte chevalerie, et darrainement par le livre de la sustance abregie de la dicte chevalerie, que le vieil solitaire humblement et a grant devocion bailla nagaires a vostre tres ame frere, le conte de Hontintone, tres puissant roy, pour le vous presenter et / vous enformer du bien a advenir de la dicte chevalerie; et pour ce auxi que par vostre tresame oncle, le duc de Wyork, et par messire Jehan de Harlestone, et autres tres vaillans chevaliers, vos loyaux subgies, vostre debonnairete en pourra estre enformee, pour ce est il que le dit vieil solitaire de la declaracion de la dicte chevalerie en ceste presente epistre s'en passe plus briefment; en recommandant la dicte chevalerie, sa creacion et tous ces affaires a vostre tres excellente royale devocion, tres catholique prince, et principaument au doulz Jhesu, patron et maistre princi-[37v] pal de sa chevalerie singuliere; auquel doulz Jhesu il ly plaise par sa doulce pitie de inspirer en vostre cuer la creacion et exaltacion de la dicte chevalerie a vostre gloire et a son saint service; laquele chose Dieu vous vueille ottroier.

Tres noble et tres catholique roy, parlant tousjours a grant reverance de vostre roiale majeste et a grant confiance de vostre devocion et grande humilite, iii. choses sont assez cleres qui vous devroient mouvoir en Dieu de doulcement embracier par les bras de vraye amour et de charite ceste gacieuse / et nouvelle chevalerie, nommee et apelee du nom de la passion du benoit Filz de Dieu. La premiere si est le grant desir que vous avez au salut des ames de vos freres les crestiens, qui, par l'example de la sainte vie de la chevalerie, seront contrains en Dieu de laissier les pechiez, de servir a Dieu, et d'amander leurs vies; lequel desir du salut des ames vous avez bien monstre en la grant et sainte volente que vous avez monstre, c'est assavoir d'avoir paix a vos freres les Francois, et par consequent a tous les crestiens. La seconde cause qui vous devroit mou-[38r]voir, tres devot prince, si est pour satisfaire aucunement as grans debtes de vos tres amez peres, auxquelz Dieu soit debonnaires, qui en mon temps ii. fois ont empeschie le saint passage d'oultre mer par la malediction de leur guerre, voire en mandant devant par vous oultremer, comme il est dit dessus, ceste sainte chevalerie, pour le salut des ames de vos devant diz peres, et pour la vostre auxi; afin que par ceste premiere offrance a Dieu, il vous face grace d'acomplir vos sains desirs, c'est assavoir d'avoir vraie paix a voz freres crestiens et de non estre des-/tourbe par pechie de faire le saint passage personnelment, en la compaignie de vostre tresame frere, le roy de France. La tierce cause qui vous devroit mouvoir, tres sage roy, si est que par l'example et effect de ceste sainte chevalerie, vostre roiale majeste, faisant le saint passage comme dit est dessus, quant a finances, qui ne seront pas petites, vous despenderes mains un million de florins que vous ne feries se de la dicte chevalerie n'estoit riens, et ce se puet dire auxi de vostre frere le roy Charles, qui seroit et sera, se a Dieu plaist, un grant avantage au bien publique de [38v] l'ost de la crestiente. Quel merveille, car mains despenderes, plus vous demourera de finance pour parfournir le saint passage et vostre tres sainte emprinse, sicomme de la verite de ceste tierce cause vostre debonnairete pourra estre enfourmee clerement par le dit Robert l'ermite et par les vaillans chevaliers qui sont en Dieu disposez de commencier la sainte chevalerie. Et se souffice briefment et en gros de la nouvelle chevallerie du benoit Crucefix et des grans biens qu'elle produira en la crestiente, a la loenge de Dieu et de tous ceulz qui li seront en Dieu favourables. /

La quarte matere de ceste presente epistre, c'est assavoir
aucuns mariages touchans au roy d'Angleterre, par lesquelz
la paix desiree pourroit estre empeschee: et le remede au propos.

Tres excellent prince et digne roy de la devote crestiente d'Angleterre, parlant tousjours a grant reverance de vostre dignite royale, le vieil solitaire, nourris longuement indigne es cours des papes et des roys, et jusques a sa vieillesse, en conversant souvent avecques les sages fusiciens des dessusdiz papes et roys, se delittoit fort de faire questions, aucunesfois diver-[39r]ses, touchans a medicine et a astrologie, pour apprendre tousjours et retenir aucune conclusion de medicine, desqueles il peust et sceust user en temps de maladie. Et pour ce, en poursuivant son songe figuratif, le dit solitaire, en la fiance du doulz Jhesu, souverain fusicien, s'est enhardis en ceste povre epistre de parler a vostre royale majeste par maniere de medicine, de plaies, et de la cure d'icelles, combien qu'il ne soit pas licenciez en la dicte science, sous-metant soy tousjours a la correction de vostre debonnairete.

Or est ainsi, tres / aimable roy, que nouvelles sont ja esparses ou royaume de Gaule que aucuns fusiciens, grans et moiens, de vostre royaume et d'ailleurs, meus de *prime face* pour bonne consolacion, nouvelle generacion, et consolidacion des maladies advenir, et a fortification auxi d'une des bordures de la grant plaie occidentale, en ceste epistre largement desclariee, pensant bien faire, vous ont offert et offrent un laictuaire assez alectif aux choses cy dessus proposees. Dont il est assavoir, tres debonnaire prince, que selonc le dit des aucteurs de me-[39v]dicine aucuns laictuaires sont qui au prendre samblent si doulz pour le succre qui cuevre l'amertume de la medicine, laquele est amere, sicomme scamonnee, dyagridi, ou aloue, qui sont fort et amer et corrosif; et est un grant peril de prendre teles medicines, qui sont moult perilleuses, voire se la medicine preparative n'aura este bien ordenee devant, et se la garde des contraires, apres la medicine prise, ne sera bien observee et regulee. Encores avient aucunefoiz que, non obstant bonne garde apres la medicine prise, les dictes medicines, scamonnee et les autres, de leur nature / sont si fortes que nature ne les puet pas bien souffrir ne digerer, et font aucunefoiz rencheoir le pacient en plus forte maladie que la premiere ne fut. Ce soit dit a bonne fin a ce que l'omme ce doye bien garder, tant qu'il pourra, de prendre si fortes medicines, pour les grans perilz qui en puent advenir; et puet estre qu'il vauldroit mieulz, pour conservacion de la sante, de user des medicines gracieuses et non perilleuses, sicomme de cassiafistre, manne et du gracieux laictuaire catholicon, en aidant et laissant faire nature, petit a petit, ses operacions, qui ne dort pas, de faire [40r] sa purgacion et de acquerir sante. Et ce souffice par maniere d'un petit prologue du laictuaire propose.

Tres sage et tres humble roy, par le laictuaire propose, avecques ses ordinacions descriptes, qui vous est presente comme il se dit par les fusiciens, vos loyaux subgies, et par autres, parlant moralment et par maniere du songe propose, puet estre entendu certain mariage pour la haulte personne de vostre royale majeste, qui est un laictuaire assez alectif, maiz qu'il soit bien confis; duquel lectuaire alectif et mal confit le tres sage roy Salemon en fist / mal son proufit, voire la scamonnee tresamere, couverte de succre, de la fille du roy d'Egypte, poingnant et corrosant et son office faisant. Dont il est assavoir, tres noble prince, que selonc les drois divins, civilz et moralz, les roys se doivent marier pour iiii. causes principales, c'est assavoir pour avoir lignie, pour acquerre aliance honnourable, pour acquerre ou pour conserver bonne paix ou royaume, et, la quarte, pour eschiver fornicacion et vivre honnestement et chastement ou saint sacrement de mariage. Et se puet dire par les sages preudommes que tous les [40v] roys sages et amis de Dieu, en leur mariage devroient bien peser les iiii. condicions sustouciez appartenans a mariage, plaisans a Dieu et a tous les subgiez preudommes du royaume. Et se l'une ou les ii. condicions y failloient, tel roy, avant que tel mariage fust consomme et parfaiz selonc Dieu, devroit fort tirer son frain, recommander soy a Dieu, muer conseil comme sage selonc la doctrine de la loy, et non soy precipiter legierement en la fosse perilleuse, dont on vient trop tart au repentir quant la perilleuse roe est bien / empainte et ara pris son cours.

Tres debonnaire prince, cestui vieil solitaire et radote escripvain, par ce que dit est dessus n'entent pas a reprouver le saint sacrement de mariage, lequel Dieu le Pere ordena de sa bouche et commanda, et son doulz benoit Filz, Jhesucrist, es noces d'Archedeclin aprova; maiz il li sovient, par maniere de contemplacion au propos, des iii. estas que le doulz Jhesu en sa sainte evvangile principalment aprouva, c'est assavoir l'estat de mariage, l'estat de chastete ou de vesvete, et le souverain [41r] estat de virginite. Au premier estat, selon la sainte escripture, pour guerredon de son labour en la gloire de Paradis est deue la couronne trentisme; aux chastes ou aux vesves est deue la couronne sesantisme; mais as vierges est ottroiee la couronne centisme, et suivent l'Aignelet occis tout partout ou il va.

Tres renomme roy en vertu et en grant sapience, qui bien aime un seigneur d'amour vertueuse et sans en attendre guerredon en ce monde, il desire de tout son cuer que le dit seigneur par la grace de Dieu soit vertueux de fait, et parez des / vertus souveraines qui en ce monde puent estre acquises. Le doulz Jhesu scet que cestui vieil solitaire, amant en Dieu les vertus que Dieu a semees en vous, selonc la renommee publique, et auxi largement enfourme des dictes vertus par la relacion du povre hermite Robert; amant pareillement en vostre personne royale le doulz Jhesu, Roy de vraye paix, qui a inspire en vostre cuer le doulx fruit de vraye paix de la crestiente; considerans donques le vieil solitaire que des iii. estas de perfection, cy dessus recitez, par aventure vous estez privez du souverain, sans vostre pe-[41v]chie, c'est assavoir de virginite; et pour ce il c'est enhardis a present de recommander telement quelement en vous l'estat de chastete, pour ce que devant Dieu c'est le plus grant apres virginite, non entendant par ce a blasmer l'estate de mariage.

Qui vouldra bien avoir remembrance des vertueux hommes de ce monde du vieil testament et du nouvel, et des ystoires anciennes des le commencement du monde, il trouverra que ceulz qui ont vescu en chastete et continence vertueusement quant a l'onneur du monde et sauvement de leurs a / ames, il ont eu entre les hommes vertueux une grant prerogative et glorieuse renommee. Que se dira du premier filz de nostre pere Adam, Abel le juste, qui morut vierge et, par consequant, chastes, et sanz laissier lignie? Et Helye le prophete, qui est en paradis terrestre a grant joye, se passa bien de laissier enfans en ce monde par procreacion, combien qu'il fust pere de pueple sans nombre par vraye doctrine et par ymitacion. Daniel le prophete, esleu de Dieu, chaste selonc la sainte escripture, pour sa sainte continence deservi d'estre gouverner du roy Nabugodenosor et du roy-[42r]aume des Assiriens. Et le saint patriarche Joseph, pour sa chastete flourie, deservi estre prince d'Egypte et d'avoir la sapience et l'interpretacion des songes du roy Pharaon. Que se dira encore de la tres sainte vesve Judich, qui par la vertu de sainte chastete trencha la teste de Holofernes et delivra de mort le pueple d'Israel?

Qui pourroit nombrer les vaillans roys et princes de la crestiente qui ont vescu chastement en ce monde, desquieulz il est plus glorieuse memoire ou ciel et en la terre que de mile autres qui ont este mariez? Sicomme le tres preux Godefroy de Buillon, qui par / la vertu de chastete trencha parmi le Sarrasin a la bataille d'Anthioche; et le premier empereur Henry, qui demourra vierge et sa compaigne l'empereis Radegondis auxi. Se fu celuy qui par grant vertu enchassa de sa court tous les hyraux et les menestereux, et l'argent que on leur souloit donner il fist donner aux povres. Quans roys ont este en Angleterre, en France, et es autres roiaumes, qui ont vescu chastement, dont les aucuns ont este vray martyr, desquelz la memoire est trop plus doulce que de c. autres qui ont este mariez. Et ce soit dit a la loenge de Dieu quant a l'estat de [42v] chastete, de laquele il est escript, Qui la puet prendre, si la preingne. Et a confirmacion de vivre chastement, l'apostre saint Pol dist a ceulz qu'il avoit convertis, Je vouldroie que vous fussies tous comme moy, c'est assavoir vierges ou chastes, car la figure de ce monde si trespasse et va a nient.

Or entrons briefment en la matere de la premiere cause pourquoy les rois et tout bon crestien se doivent marier, c'est assavoir pour avoir lignie, et trouverons qu'il n'est pas en puissance d'omme marie d'avoir lignie, ou tele lignie comme il vouldroit, / car Dieu l'a reserve a luy tout seul, et donne lignie ou la retrait comme il li plaist, selon sa grace ou sentence divine, pour le merite ou desmerite des roys ou des pueples. Quar il est escript que pour le pechie du pueple Dieu consent regner l'ipocrite, c'est assavoir, selonc la glose, le tirant.

Quans vaillans hommes ont estez en ce monde qui n'orent oncques lignie de leurs corps qui succedast apres eulz. Melchisedeth, le grant roy de Salem, c'est de Jherusalem, par les docteurs de l'eglise et par la sainte escripture est descrips, Sans pere et sans mere, [43r] —figure de Jhesucrist, ne sans pere en ce monde, car du Saint Esperit, et sans mere a la fourme des autres meres, car de la Vierge Marie—et toutesfoiz de la lignie du dit Melchisedeth l'escripture n'en fait aucune mencion. Qui ot plus grande renommee en ce monde que le roy Alixandre, duquel les enfans en sa grant seignourie ne regnerent pas apres luy? Qui fu plus preux en son temps, ne plus puissant en ce monde, que Julius Sezar et son nepveu Ottovian, empereur de Romme, qui tint la monarchie du monde et trespasserent sanz laissier nulz hoirs de leurs corps qui reg-/ nassent apres eulz? Quans vaillans hommes ont este du nouvel testament, empereurs, roys et princes, confes et martirs, qui sans hoirs de leurs corps sont trespassez de ce monde, desquelz la memoire est trop plus doulce et trop plus renommee que de mile autres qui ont laissie lignie.

Il est chose naturelle et plaisant a Dieu que l'omme marie doie desirer lignie. S'il aura lignie et elle sera vertueuse, le pere aura grant joye, et tous les jours de sa vie demourra en grant doubte et amere suspicion de perdre sa lignie; et s'il [43v] la pert, il n'aura jamais joye, sicomme il est a croire du vaillant roy Edouart, vostre aieul, qui n'ot onques si grant joie des haultes victoires que Dieu envoia et ottroia a vostre tres ame pere, le tres vaillant et tres victorieux aisne filz du roy, le tres noble prince de Gales, comme il ot amere doulour de son trespassement. Et se le roy ou prince aura par aventure, qui avient souvent, lignie reprovee, qui ne soit pas de bonnes meurs, s'il est sages jamais n'aura joye, et mile foiz souhaidera que onques n'eust marie.

Il est assez cogneu en ce / monde que combien que les grans princes mariez et autres soient preudommes, toutefois, pour les causes cy dessus recitees, il engendrent les enfans aucunesfoiz tous contraires a la bonte de leurs peres; comme il appert en la sainte escripture et ailleurs par Cayin, qui occist Abel son frere. Ezechias, tres saint roy de Jherusalem, engendra Manasses, qui fist soier parmi Ysaie le prophete, d'une soye de bois, et, qui plus est, il arousa toutes les rues de Jherusalem du sanc des prophetes de Dieu, et finablement perdi tout son royaume et fu mene [44r] prisonnier en Babiloine. Qui fut plus saint et meilleur roy ou pueple d'Israel que David? Et toutefoiz il engendra Absalon, qui enchassa son pere du royaume. Et Salemon engendra Roboam, qui par mauveste de xii. royaumes enperdi les x. en une seule journee. Jolias, le tres saint roy duquel le prophete Jeremie fait si grande lamentacion, engendra Jechonias, tres mauvais roy, qui perdi son royaume et fu mene prisonnier en la transmigracion de Babiloine. Que se dira entre les crestiens de Constancieux, frere de l'empereur Constantin, / qui engendra Julius Apostata? Et le roy Henry, vostre grant pere, engendra Henry, qui se revela contre luy. Et Loys, le tres debonnaire filz du grant Charlemaine, empereur de Romme et roy de France, engendra Lothaire, qui tint en prison son pere le dit Loys, empereur et roy de France, en la cite de Soissons. Qui vouldroit descripre les mauvais filz que les grans roys, princes et autres vaillans et preudonnes ont engendrez, il seroit comme impossible. Ceste consideracion et dubitacion d'avoir mauvaiz enfans pour les pechiez du monde, des sages roys ne doit [44v] estre ignore.

Et se aucun vouldra dire auxi bien puet un vaillant roy et preudomme par loyal mariage engendrer un preudomme et vaillant, comme il fait un mauvais, a ce se puet respondre qu'il est bien verite. Mais au jour duy, parlant moralment, quant les bons et sages laboureurs veullent semer le fourment en une champ, il examinent fort tout avant la nature du champ, car aucune terre est si bonne que qui y seme segle, elle aporte fourment. Helas, ce n'est pas en occident, car / la region est trop froide. Tres debonnaire prince, les terres de par dessa sont en possession, combien que aucunefoiz que elles soient bien labourees, de porter les espignes poingnans, comme elles ont fait longuement en France et en Angleterre. Et pour ce, qui par grace puet estre garni du forment que Joseph assembla en Egypte pour passer la famine, c'est assavoir du pain de vie qui est descendu du ciel, il sera mieulx soustenus et sans peril que de semer de nouvel ou champ d'Alchedemach, qui est appele champ de sanc, lequel est acou-[45r]stume de aporter les espines poingnans, dont maint Francois et Anglois sont descendus en enfer. Et pour ce est il expedient, tres debonnaire prince, que par la grace de Dieu vous doies bien examiner le champ ouquel vous semerez le fourment, pour avoir une sainte et gracieuse lignie, qui ne saute pas la nature des espignes de

la terre de sa mere. Quel merveille, car il n'a au jour duy, helas, si biau
champ, ne si bien floury, ne si bien laboure, ne de si bonne renommee,
que aucunefois, pour les pechiez des peres ou des meres, le dit chan ꝑ
n'aporte des espi-/nes, qui sont aucunesfoiz si poingnans que les ver-
meilles roses et les blanches flours de lis par les dittes espingnes ne
soient suffoquiez, qui est une grande pitie et cruaute en nature que si
nobles flours par la pointure des espingnes doient perdre leur gracieuse
oudour.

Quant a ii. autres causes pour lesqueles les roys se doivent marier,
c'est assavoir pour acquerre aliance honnourable et, par consequant,
possessions temporelles, par lesqueles paix soit nourrie ou roiaume, qui
est une chose qui fort plaist a Dieu, que se dira donques a ceste propo-
[45v]sicion qui, selonc l'opinion d'aucuns sages et doubtans Dieu, n'est
pas si clere en la matere comme elle est cy proposee? Et Dieu vueille
que en la balance de vostre haulte sapience royale, et en la doubtance de
Dieu, elle soit bien pesee, et que precipitacion, sur fourme apparant de
dilater et accroistre possessions transitoires a vostre seignourie, n'y
preigne seignourie, voire ou prejudice de vos freres crestiens; pour
lesqueles possessions et aliances, par plussieurs suspicioneuse, les espines ameres, en ceste epistre selonc Dieu assez reprouvez, de nouvel
ne soient resuscitees, et la grant plaie, en / cestui traitie par maniere de
lamentacion recitee et a vostre gloire auxi comme sanee, par la dicte
aliance ne soit ouverte de nouvel et de mortel venim envenimee. Et ne
devez pas oublier, tres devot roy, que les fusiciens qui vous offrent le
dit laictuaire alectif pour l'acroisement et multiplicacion de vostre
puissance et roiale seignourie mondainne, ne rendront pas conte a Dieu
pour vostre ame precieuse quant elle sera devant le juge souverain, a la
presence duquel il vous convendra rendre conte des ames qui seront
dampnees pour vostre occasion, par le dit mariage et par la pointure des
[46r] espines, souventefois repetees; de laquele chose Dieu, par sa sainte
misericorde, vous en vueille garder, et vous vueille reserver d'espandre
le sanc humain de vos freres crestiens.

Encores, tres debonnaires prince et amy de Dieu, en la memoire de
vostre devote contemplacion il vous devroit souvenir devant Dieu, et
non pas sans larmes, du mariage, lors bieneure repute, de la mere du
vaillant roy Edouart, vostre aieul tres ame, dont vous estes issus, et des
morteles espines qui sont issus du dit mariage trop poingnans, qui ont
point lx. ans par tele malediction que les / belles flours de lis, dont vous
estes issus, horriblement ont este foulees et en grant partie sechieez et

degasteez, et grant partie de la crestiente troublee et malmenee, et sans aucun grant proufit final qui vous en soit demoure du dit mal. Et combien que, par la sentence et permission divine, vos predecesseurs en la pointure des espines aient eu et recepu solempnelles victoires sur leurs freres crestiens, il se puet dire, a grant doulour, que les dictes espines ont administre victoires trop plus solempnelles a l'anemi de humaine nature, pour les ames infinies, et d'un coste et d'autre, qui ont este perpetuelment dampnees.

[46v] Saint Gregoire dit que par les fais precedens aucunement on puet juger des faiz advenir, et es faiz perilleux avoir une bonne garde. Cestui vieil solitaire, tres gracieux roy, qui de tout son cuer desire la confirmacion de la vraie paix que Dieu a inspire es ii. cuers de vous et de vostre tres ame frere, le roy Charles, comme en un cuer et en une ame, a en Dieu esperance debonnaire qu'il vous preservera de recepvoir laituaire quelconque, dont l'amertume couverte doie engendrer ou temps advenir nouvelles espines, samblables aux autres perilleuses repetees et des preudommes redoubtees. /

Tres puissant prince, quant a la quarte cause pour laquele les roys se doivent marier, c'est assavoir pour passer la jonesse et vivre honestement et chastement ou saint sacrement de mariage, il est assavoir que, combien que la vie de chastete viduale et continente vertueuse aucunement et grossement cy dessus par examples ait este devant Dieu aprouvee comme la plus parfaite apres virginite, se la ditte vertu donques de chastete il vous plaisoit a eslire pour acquerre l'aureole, c'est la couronne, trentisme, pour estre reconforte, tres devot roy, vous pourries dire avec [47r] l'apostre saint Pol, Toutes choses me sont loisibles, mais toutes choses ne me sont pas expedientes pour le salut de mon ame; c'est assavoir en sustance, Il m'est loisible de marier, mais pour acquerre plus grant vertu il ne m'est pas expedient, car la vertu de l'ame passe celle du corps et des choses temporelles. Et combien auxi que les grans perilz et inconveniens qui souvent avienent aux grans princes mariez, et aux autres auxi, cy dessus par plussieurs examples assez clers, a la confirmacion de la vertu de chastete, aient este recites, toutesfois il est escript par le dit saint / Pol que qui ne puet estre continent si se marie ou nom de Jhesucrist; et a nostre propos, pour satisfaire a subgiez, et par especial a ceulz qui ont presente le laictuaire souventefoiz repete; voire, offrant de nouvel par les dis fusiciens a vostre majeste royale, ou vous meismes eslisant de vostre propre et sainte volente, un autre laictuaire, qui ne soit pas si alectif ne preparatif a effusion de sanc, ne remplis dedens d'une amere amertume couverte de succre, comme il est dit dessus. Mais par la bonte de Dieu soit quis et trouve par grant amour, et de Dieu et des freres crestiens, un gracieux laic-[47v]tuaire pour nostre josne roy de la Grant Bretaingne, ouquel laittuaire n'ait scamonnee, dyagridy, ne aloue, mais soit rempli, et dedans et dehors en sustance, et procree, du precieux balme, en ceste presente escripture assez moralisie. Et soit confit le dit laictuaire de la manne du ciel, qui jamais ne puet nuire, afin que le dit laictuaire par la divine bonte soit si generatif que de luy naisse bon fruit a la loenge de Dieu, conservacion de paix, consolacion de vostre royale paternite, de tous vos loyaux subgiez, et par especial de vostre tres ame frere, Charles, roy de France, et de tous vos bons / amis; laquele chose Dieu vous vueille ottroier.

Aucuns fusiciens, qui fort se travaillent comme il fut dit de confire le premier laittuaire propose, pourroient dire au vieil solitaire par maniere de interrogacion, Ou sera trouva le second laictuaire propose, qui soit si fin et si plaisant qu'en luy n'ait amertume ne tant ne quant? A ce puet respondre par le moien du proverbe commun qui dit, Avoir bonne femme avec laquele tous biens viennent, c'est singulier don de Dieu. Se les fusiciens eussent auxi grant cure des ames de leurs paciens [48r] comme il ont de leurs corps, il seroient tost garis. Mais pour ce que souvent, et trop souvent au jour duy, nous, sages de ce monde, laissons l'esperit a part et mettons la charue devant les buefs, pour ce est il que le champ aporte les espines.

Saint Anthoine, en la Vie des Peres, dist a un autre abbe, Tout ce que tu feras, fay le par le conseil de sainte escripture. Il n'a si sage homme en la crestiente qui sceust donner meilleur conseil a un roy de luy marier que la sainte escripture. Quel merveille, car en la sainte escripture le Sainte Esperit parle, / qui est le vray docteur, et enseigne aux loyaux crestiens tout ce qu'il ont a faire. Tres debonnaire roy et ami de Dieu, vous trouveres que en la sainte escripture les grans roys et hommes vertueux pour leur mariage ne regardoient pas tant a puissance, ne a richesse, ou a haulte lignie des femmes, comme il faisoient a la vertu d'icelles. Les puissant roy Assuerus, roys des Assuriens, prist a royne et espouse une povre, gentil femme, niece de Mardocheus, de la lignie des Juifs, c'est assavoir la belle et bonne Hester, qui par sa vertu fist delivrer de mort le peuple d'Israel. David, le tres saint roy, prist a femme [48v] Abigail la tres sage, apres la mort de son mary, laquele avoit apaisie la pointure des espines apareillies de fort poindre entre David et Nabal Carmelli. Et Ruth, pour sa prudence et tres grande humilite, deservi d'estre espouse de Booz, grant pere de Jesse, duquel et de laquele le doulz Jhesu par droite lignie descendi.

Or venons ou nouveau testament. Constantin, empereur de Romme, pere du grant Constantin, prist a femme Helaine, lors une hosteliere, tres sage et aournee de grans vertus, laquele, selonc l'opinion de plussieurs, estoit fille du roy d'Angleterre, et toutesfois pour sa vertu Constantin la prist, / non pas comme fille de roy, mais comme une povre femme; laquele sainte Helaine deservi par grace de trouver en Jherusalem la sainte vraie crois, a confirmacion de l'empire de Romme qui devint crestien. Et, tres gracieux roy, le tresvaillant prince de Gales, vostre tres ame pere, prist a femme la princesse qui n'estoit pas fille de roy, dont tant de bien en est advenu, que par vous, qui de luy estes issus, la paix de la crestiente, l'union de l'eglise, et le saint passage d'oultremer, a l'aide de vostre frere de France, par la bonte de Dieu, a mon vouloir seront mises sus, en vraie lumiere de la foy et de toute [49r] la crestiente. Et lors les Anglois et Francois d'un commun acort diront a vous, tres noble roy Richart, Benoit soit le ventre qui te porta et les mamelles qui t'aleterent. Laquele chose Dieu nous vueille ottroier.

Or pleust a Dieu, tres debonnaire prince, que, pour nourrissement de paix de la crestiente et consolacion de vostre royale personne, il vous vousist ottroier et mander une tele espouse et compaingne comme il fist au marquis de Saluce, apelee Griseldis, qui fu fille d'un povre laboureur, et toutesfoiz, selonc la cronique autentique du dessus dit marquis / de Saluce et de Griseldis sa compaingne, escripte par le solempnel docteur et souverain poete, maistre Francois Petrac, depuis le commencement du monde jusques au jour duy, apres les saintes, ne se treuve pas femme si vertueuse en escript, ne si merveilleuse en l'amour de son seigneur, et merveilleuse vertu de pacience, comme fu la dicte noble marquise Griseldis, sicomme vous poez avoir veu, ou verres ou temps advenir, par la cronique d'icelle.

Or vous plaise, tres noble et tres debonnaire prince, aucunement noter et estudier la foible escriptu-[49v]re d'un povre et vieil homme ydiot sur les condicions touchans au mariage de vostre royale majeste, et priez a Dieu qu'il vous vueille adrecier par son saint ange, comme il fist Thobie par l'ange Raphael, qui delivra Thobie des vii. anges mauvais, et en la fin luy enseigna de loer Dieu et comment il devroit vivre. Et priez a Dieu que par foible conseil vous ne soies pas de ceulz qui s'escuserent de venir au convit du grant roy pour ce qu'il avoient prins nouvellement femmes, voire charnelment ou par avarice, et non pas selonc Dieu, qui apreuve les mariages. Et ce souffice assez prolixement / du petit et foible traitie de mariage touchant a vostre royale majeste, parlant tousjours a grant reverance, et des condicions qui pourroient empeschier la sainte paix desiree et le bien general de la crestiente.

La quinte matere de ceste presente epistre, c'est assavoir un exemple par lequel les roys devroient fort doubter d'espandre le sanc de leurs freres crestiens; et par i. autre example de Moyses et Aaron

Tres excellent prince et tres gracieux seigneur, la principale sustance de ceste povre epistre si est, c'est assavoir la confederacion et aliance en Dieu perpetuele, la vraie paix et [50r] doulce amour fraternelle des ii. filz saint Loys, roy de France, c'est assavoir de Charles et de Richart, par la grace de Dieu de France et d'Angleterre dignes roys, et de tous leurs subgies, et par consequant la paix et unite de l'eglise et de toute la crestiente. Laquele amour et paix desiree puent estre empetreez du ciel par la misericorde du doulz Jhesu, se vostre royale majeste, tres debonnaire roy, et vostre frere auxi, par grant vertu meteres vaillaument a son effet la sustance de ceste foible escripture; et que par mariage suspicioneux ou par sugestion et enhorteurs des anemis de la paix, sur four-/me apparant encontre la vocion a laquele Dieu vous a esleus et apeles, vous ne soies decepuz et desconfis, dont Dieu vueille garder et l'un et l'autre roy. Laquele chose il fera par sa sainte grace et vous gardera, se en vostre ame precieuse vous aueres vraie compassion et amere doulour du sanc humain des crestiens, qui a este espandu par vos predecesseurs; et se vous aures auxi doubtance et horreur devant Dieu du sanc de vos freres crestiens qui sera espandu se la guerre se recommencera; dont Dieu par sa grace vueille garder la crestiente et d'Angleterre et de France.

[50v] Les docteurs de l'eglise plussieurs dient que les examples esmeuvent plus fort les cuers des gens que ne font les paroles, et pour ce il semble expedient au vieil solitaire qu'il doie presenter a vostre devocion royale et a vostre chevalerie, ja grant temps a en sanc nourrie, un example assez au propos pour avoir de cy en avant abhominacion de espandre le sanc humain des crestiens, en monstrant clerement la grant

inhumanite des crestiens qui se delitent en l'effusion du sanc de leurs freres crestiens.

Il est escript en un livre moult solempnel, apele / Dicionaire, que ou desert d'Inde, en un lieu qui est appelez Stragopales, pres de la mer, a un oysiau appele arpia, grant et cruel oultre mesure, qui a la face d'omme et vit de proie. Cestui oyseau cruel le premier homme qu'il vit, il l'occist. Et apres aucun temps, il se treuve d'aventure la ou il y a yaue, en laquele il se mire et contemple sa face, qui est samblable a face d'omme. Et lors il li vient au devant et li souvient qu'il a occis l'omme et, sans arrest, il fait si grant duel que aucunefois il en muert. Et c'il ne se muert, tous les jours de sa vie il demourra [51r] en tristesse et doulour, plorant l'omme qu'il a mort. Cestui oysiau, arpia cruel, parlant moralment au propos de ceste presente epistre, condampne les crestiens, qui sont encores plus crueulz, et par especial les Anglois et Francois, combien qu'il se pourroit dire que les Francois l'ont fait en deffendant leur royaume. Quel merveille de la ditte cruaute, car par l'effusion du sanc de noz freres, et les uns et les autres, nous avons occis, quant de nostre part, Jhesucrist, par nos pechiez, pour lesquelz il souffri mort amere. Et toutefoiz nous, et Anglois et / Francois, tous les jours veons le doulz Jhesu que nous avons mort, selonc le dit des sains, ou mirouer des yaues ameres de sa sainte passion, et le contemplons auxi ou mirouer de la sainte escripture. Et veons Celui qui a la face d'omme, samblable a nous quant au corps, vray Dieu et vray homme, qui est venus a nous ou desert de ce monde pour nous et pour nostre salut, et ne le recognoissons pas comme nous deveresmes, maiz sommes plus cruel assez que l'oisiau dessus dit, appele arpia. Si seroit expedient pour empetrer la paix et vraie amour l'un de l'autre que nous prinsiesmes [51v] example au dit oysiau arpia, voire pour avoir fresche compassion de la mort de nostre tres doulz Redempteur Jhesucrist et horreur cordiale de l'effusion du sanc de nos freres crestiens, afin que l'oysiau arpia, parlant devotement, ne doie condampner au jugement les roys et les chevaliers qui auront este plus crueulz de lui. De laquele cruaute Dieu vueille garder les ii. roys innocens et toute leur vaillant chevallerie, par la bonte de Dieu et priere de la tres doulce Vierge Marie.

Tres catholique roy et tres debonnaire prince, en la Grant Bretaingne dominant, pour l'acqui-/sicion et conservacion de l'amour et vraie paix de l'escharboucle au fin dyamant, et pour la paour d'estre prive du benoit fruit de la dicte pais, il vous souviengne doulcement des ii. freres en la sainte escripture, qui furent chevetaines de vi^c mile chevaliers combatans, auquelz ii. freres Dieu de sa bouche dist, Vous manres les enfans d'Israel en la terre de promission que je juray donner a vos peres. Ce fu a Moyses et Aaron, chevetaines du pueple d'Israel.

Toutesfois, non obstant que Dieu eust promis, et par serement, as ii. freres, Moyses et Aaron, qu'il menroient et condui-[52r]roient le pueple de Dieu en Jherusalem et en la terre de promission, pour ce qu'il ne saintefierent pas Dieu comme il devoient as yaues de contradiction, pour ce furent il prive de cestui grant honneur. Et leur dist Dieu, c'est assavoir a Moyses et Aaron, Pour ce que vous ne m'avez pas saintefie devant mon pueple as yaues de rebellion et de contradiction, vous ne manres pas mon pueple en la terre que je leur doy donner, et mourres en cestui desert. Sicomme il appert plus clerement en la Bible.

Or venons ou nom de Dieu a aucune concordance / des ii. freres, chevetaines du pueple d'Israel, as nos ii. roys proposez. L'escripture dit que Moyses et Aaron, freres, furent de la lignie de Levi, qui estoit toute atribuee a Dieu. Moyses, amy de Dieu, fu le plus debonnaire homme qui fust sur la terre, et Aaron fu des plus vigillans au gouvernement du pueple. Qui vouldroit et sauroit bien moralisier ces ii. freres, Moyses et Aaron, aux ii. freres roys, c'est assavoir a Charles et a Richart, chevetaines du peuple de Dieu de France et d'Angleterre, certainement il auroit large matere de gracieuses concordances en la matere proposee. Mais pour [52v] la prolixite de ceste presente epistre, et pour non ennuyer a vostre royale majeste de longue escripture, le vieil solitaire abregera la figure. Il se puet dire pour concordance que le roy Charles et le roy Richart, freres, sont issus de la lignie de Levi, c'est assavoir du benoit saint Loys, et des autres sains roys de France et d'Angleterre, dedies principalement au service de Dieu, conservacion et multiplicacion de sa sainte foy catholique. Et se puet dire que le roy Charles est le plus debonnaire homme qui soit sur la terre, et le roy Richart, son frere, est des plus vigilans sur le gouver-/nement de son pueple qui se pourroit trouver.

Tres excellent prince, O vous Richart et Charles, freres, et filz des benois sains, il vous devroit souvenir sovent comment le doulz Jhesu vous a fais chevetaines ensamble de son pueple d'Israel, c'est assavoir de la crestiente d'occident, pour la mener en la terre de promission, et, par propre message, le vous a mande par son message, le povre hermite Robert, le benoit apostre saint Jaque commandant; et a confirmacion de la dicte messagerie, vous savez comment depuis que vous ouystes la dicte messagerie, la doulce [53r] amour et la paix en vos ii. cuers a este doulcement affirmee et nourrie.

Il a este revele a vous ii. roys que par vous sera faitte la paix, et de vous et de la crestiente, l'eglise raunie, et conquise Surie. Or vous gardez bien que as yaues de contradicion vous n'ensuives pas en ce cas Moyses et Aaron, mais que aus dictes yaues de rebellion Dieu soit par vous saintefiez solempnelment en la presence du pueple d'Israel, a vous commis pour le mener en la terre de promission. Par les dictes yaues de contradicion, ou de rebellion encontre Dieu, a nostre propos, parlant / moralment, puent estre entendus tous ceulz qui empescheront la paix desiree, et d'un coste et de l'autre, demandant importunement a Moyses et Aaron, c'est a Charles et a Richart, habondance d'yaues mondaines pour eulz, pour leurs familiers, et pour leurs brebis, c'est assavoir or et argent, terres et possessions, par lesqueles Dieu soit de nouvel offendu et guerre contre luy recommenciee.

Telz murmurans encontre Dieu et la paix devroient fort doubter la sentence horrible que Dieu monstra ou desert aus murmurans contre Moyses et [53v] Aaron, sicomme il appart par Dathan et Abiron, qui a toutes leurs femmes, enfans, familes, bestes et tabernacles, furent engloutis ou parfont de la terre et dampnez pardurablement. Et Marie, la suer de Moyses et Aaron, pour sa murmuracion fut ferue soudainement d'une horrible mesellerie, toute blanche, et mise hors de l'ost de Dieu a sa grant confusion. Qui pourroit escripre les examples et vengences de Dieu encontre ceulz qui ont murmure et destourbe la paix des crestiens?

Or venons a la pratique, briefve et devote, comment, en tant de contradicions que l'anemi de nature pre-/sente chascun jour, vostre royale et vertueuse magnificence, tres devot roy, et vostre frere auxi, le roy Charles, pourres et saueres saintefier et magnifier Dieu, avant que la pierre soit ferue ii. fois de la verge.

Vostre saintificacion, tres debonnaire roy, n'est autre chose que confermer vous a la volente divine, qui vous a esleus chevetaines de paix et non de guerre. Dont l'apostre saint Pol vous dit que la volente de Dieu est vostre saintificacion, c'est la vraye paix, laquele par le moien de son precieux sanc il offri au monde. A laquele paix [54r] la guerre des crestiens et les discencions ou quart degre sont contraires. Dont le dit apostre dit que Dieu n'est pas Dieu de discencion, maiz il est Dieu de vraye paix, sicomme saint Jehan l'evvangeliste le tesmoingne et largement desclaire. Comment poez vous mieux saintifier Dieu en cest monde que apres l'office des anges et des sains, qui chantent sans intermission, *Sanctus, Sanctus, Sanctus, etc.*? Vous aies paix en terre comme princes catholiques et de bonne volente a vos freres crestiens. Le doulz Saint Esperit, aucteur de paix, selonc le dit du prophete, ne puet reposer se n'est sur ce-/lui qui sera humble et en repos, c'est assavoir en vraye paix de son proisme.

Or gardez bien, tres eureux princes, que la dicte paix, a vous offerte par le souverain Dieu du ciel, ne vous eschappe de vos mains, et que par defaulte de la saintificacion, souvent repetee, Moyses et Aaron ne soient privez du tres noble office de leur chevetainerie, et qu'il ne meurent en ce desert, sans acomplir en Dieu ce qui leur a este offert, et que par leur deffaulte, qui ja n'aviengne, Dieu doie eslire un autre vaillant prince, Josue, et Caleph en sa compaignie, pour mener une-[54v]foys son pueple en la terre de promission. Et se souffice assez brief-ment d'avoir abhominacion de l'effusion du sanc crestien par l'example de l'oisel arpia, et du peril d'estre prive de tant de biens par defaulte de saintifier Dieu, duquel la vraie paix et tous les biens offers a vos royales majestes viennent comme d'une fontaine pardurable, en laquele fon-taine vous verres par grace unefoiz la vraye paix et lumiere qui jamais ne fauldront; laquele chose il vous vueille ottroier.

La vi matere de ceste presente epistre, c'est assavoir, parlant moral-/ment, comment les pierres precieuses, aus ii. roys figurees, doivent estre trempeez et enyvrees du precieux vin des vignes d'Engady*

Il fut dit au commencement ou songe figuratif du vieil solitaire, par grant merveille que les vignes d'Engandy, dont la sainte escripture fait une grant mencion, de nouvel sont flories es diz royaumes d'occident, par tele maniere que, selonc ce que plussieurs preudommes ont esper-ance, que les dictes vignes porteront tel vin que les ii. roys et grant partie de leur tres vaillant chevalerie seront en-[55r]yvres du dit vin, voire que le baulme et pierre d'aymant prefigures discretement soient bien proporcione et ajouste ensemble et bien trempe en esperit ou dit vin des vignes d'Angadi.

Il se lit ou Livre de la Propriete des Choses que la flour des vignes enchasse les serpens et les bestes venimeuses. Se donques les serpens ne puent arrester devant les flours des froides vignes d'occident, comment pourront il arrester devant le fort vin d'orient des precieuses vignes d'Engady?

Le Saint Esperit dit ou Livre de Sapience que / la sapience de Dieu a edifie pour luy une maison et a melle son vin et mise la table. Ceste proposicion fait assez a nostre propos pour avoir cognoissance du precieux vin des vignes d'Angady. Or venons, ou nom de Dieu, a aucune concordance de la matere emprise et de la vertu du dit vin, duquel nos ii. roys et grant plante de leur chevalerie a mon voloir doivent estre enyvres.

La sapience de Dieu, c'est le benoit Filz de Dieu, c'est le doulz Jhesu, en ce monde a edifie singulierement une maison pour luy, en laquele il c'est fort deli-[55v]tes de habiter en la dicte maison, faisans de grans merveilles, c'est assavoir la maison de France et d'Angleterre, maison tres exellente entre tous les royaumes des crestiens. Et combien que ce soient ii. royaumes, toutesfois ce n'est que une maison, dont les ii. rois sont issus et d'un pere et d'une mere, c'est assavoir du tres vaillant roy saint Loys. Et ce soit dit quant a la maison et tres exellente lignie que la sapience de Dieu, en especial et par grant amour, pour luy a edifie en ce monde, et quant auxi au grant mal qui a este fait par ceulz qui ont fait la division par / mortele guerre des enfans royaux d'une si sainte maison.

Encores fu dit que la sapience de Dieu a melle son vin et trempe pour abuvrer les enfans royaux de la dicte sainte maison, car le dit vin en sa plaine forte ilz ne pourroient digerer. Combien que par aucuns docteurs, parlant moralment, les dictes vignes d'Engadi soient entendues par les arbreciaux qui distillent le fin balme, comme il fu desclarrie dessus, toutefois nous trouvons en la sainte escripture plus expresse memoire des dictes vignes d'Engady, [56r] c'est assavoir ou Livre des Cantiques, la ou le Saint Esperit dit, *Botrus Cypri in vigneis Engady*, c'est a dire, le roison de Cypre es vignes d'Engady.

Il est assavoir que ou royaume de Cypre en une montaigne est proprement la dicte vigne d'Engady, selonc la relacion du dit Livre des Cantiques et des anciennes escriptures. La dicte vigne est la plus renommee que soit ou royaume ne es parties d'orient, et est de tele condicion que, pour la force de son vin, on n'en puet boire qu'il ne soit passe iii. annees. La premiere annee il est si troubles et si espes / comme oyle noire, la secunde il se commence a purifier, et la tierce auxi, mais a la quarte il devient blanc comme yaue de roche, tres fort et rendant bonne oudour, lequel oudour conforte la teste et tous les sens natureux. Et devient si fort et si vertueux et si puissant que il se conserve c. ans en sa plaine vertu. Cestui vin est appele marouant, duquel a mon voloir nos ii. roys en esperit seront doulcement abuvrez et saintement enyvres.

Or venons a aucune concordance morale de cestui precieux vin des vignes d'Engady. Il est dit cy dessus [56v] que la sapience de Dieu a melle son vin, voire par iii. annees. Par la premiere annee, que le vin est noir et trouble, puet estre entendue par les ii. roys la fresche memoire et vraie cognoissance des horribles maulz qui sont advenus par la guerre des predecesseurs de nos ii. josnes roys. Par la seconde annee puet estre entendu la doulour des roys et la vraye repentance de la chevalerie, et de France et d'Angleterre, qu'il doivent avoir des grans maulz que eulz et leurs peres ont perpetrez et crueusement exercez encontre Dieu et leur proesme.

Mais par la tierce annee / puet estre entendue vraie satisfacion et plaine remission des injures et offenses de l'une chevalerie a l'autre. Ces iii. choses cy dessus par la bonte de Dieu devotement et sanz faintisse acomplies, et nostre precieux vin ainsi trempe et melle, il sera temps que la doulce sapience de Dieu mette la table, comme il fut propose, pour faire collacion ensemble par les ii. roys et par leur tres vaillant chevalerie, du dit vin ainsi trempe et finablement clarifie, qui par sa vertu conservera l'amour, a mon voloir, c. ans et plus de ceulz qui en auront gouste.

Cestui vin precieux [57r] parlant en figure, est le vin qui issi du gros roisin que Josue et Caleph aporterent a un tinel de la terre de promission au pueple d'Israel, en confortant le dit pueple de hardiement entrer en la terre de promission, qui ainsi estoit garnie et remplie de gros roisins et de toute habundance. Cestuy precieux vin est le vin qui eslesse le cuer de l'omme, selonc le dit David le prophete. Cestui vin n'est pas le vin ouquel est la luxure, selonc le dit de l'apostre saint Pol, maiz est le vin non pas moust appele, selonc le dit de saint Pierre, duquel les apostres furent enyvrez se-/lonc le dit du commun des Juifs. C'est le precieux vin des vignes d'Engady, qui est proprement le vin du Saint Esperit, clarifie et purifie, dont les apostres furent enyvrez le jour de la Penthecouste, en parlant clerement a la loenge de Dieu tous les langages du monde.

O benois seront et tres benois nos ii. roys et leur chevalerie, se par grace il pourront estre abuvrez et doulcement enyvrez de ceste precieuse liquour, c'est assavoir de l'onction du benoit Saint Esperit, qui rapaise les decordez, qui ravoie les devoiez, et qui par sa doulce vertu fait paix par tout, oublier les in-[57v]jures et amer ses anemis.

Entre les communes gens qui ont eu guerre l'un a l'autre, a la perfection de la paix par paix faisant, l'un presente a l'autre le vin, la servoise, ou le miex. Maiz a la paix faire et parfaire des grans roys qui ont eu guerre l'un a l'autre, il est expedient que la sapience de Dieu, a nostre propos, mette la table, en propinant a nos ii. rois, pour confirmacion de vraye paix, le pain de vie, qui fu petris et nourris ou ventre de la Vierge Marie, et cuis et roustis en l'abre de la vraie croix. Et apres la prinse du pain sacre et de la viande des anges, il est / expedient que nos roys et leur chevalerie soient abuvrez et par grace doulcement enyvrez du calice du nouveau testament; par lequel testament la vraie paix nous est offerte du ciel, c'est assavoir le precieux vin des vignes d'Engady du precieux sanc de l'Aignelet occis, par l'oblacion duquel sanc la paix fu faite entre Dieu et l'omme.

Tres glorieux roy de la Grant Bretaingne, assis a la table que la sapience de Dieu vous a appareillie, ouvres un pau vos oreilles et entendez ce que le Saint Esperit vous dit, Venez mes amis et enyvrez [58r] vous du vin que je vous ay appareillie, c'est assavoir de vraie amour a Dieu, de vraie paix a vostre proesme, et de bonne garde de cy en avant d'espendre le sanc de vos freres crestiens.

Il est expedient que pour empetrer la vraie paix de la crestiente, pour l'union de nostre mere sainte eglise, et pour delivrer la terre sainte de la main du faulz prophete Mahommet, que nostre escharboucle figuree, la pierre d'aymant et nostre figure dyamant soyent melle et trempe sagement et discretement ensemble en esperit, sans pompe, sans serimonies, et sanz gait, en grant humi-/lite et amoureuse fraternite, ou precieux vin des vignes d'Engady, tant de foyz reciteez; c'est assavoir en l'amour du Saint Esperit, aucteur de paix, d'amour et d'equite, qui donnera telle vertu a la royale majeste que les serpens, ce sont ceulz qui empeschent la paix, a l'oudour des flours de la dicte vigne, et par plus fort a l'oudour et a la force du precieux vin figure, ne pourront arester; laquele chose Dieu nous vueille ottroier. Et se sofice assez grossement du vin moralisie, dont nos ii. roys et leur chevalerie doivent estre abuvrez.

Une orison briefve contre ceulz qui destourberont la paix

[58v] Or offrons donques nostre oroison a Dieu, avec le tres saintisme David le prophete, en levant les mains au ciel, disant, Viengne,

Dieu, viengne, Dieu, et soient dissipez et dispers ses anemis; c'est assavoir ceulz qui c'efforceront d'empeschier la paix du ciel, aus ii. roys inspiree. Ilz soient acravante, et soient fuians devant la face de Dieu, et leur dos soit tousjours encourbe. Sire Dieux, dissipe et destruis tous ceulz qui vuellent les batailles encontre leurs freres crestiens. La clamour des mors et des navrez soit oye de leurs maisons, et leurs femmes soient faites vesves et leurs enfans / orphelins; c'est assavoir ceulz qui par orgueil, par envie, et par avarice, et par tres grant cruaute, recalcitrent contre l'aiguillon du benoit Saint Esperit, et se sont ferus d'une double pointure. Le doulz Saint Esperit heurte son vent a l'uys des cuers des grans pecheurs et leur dit, Qui m'ouverra, je soupperay avec luy et li doinray ma paix, comme il est escript ou Livre de l'Apocalipse; et qui me refusera, soit certains qu'il s'en repentira.

La vii[e] matere de ceste presente epistre demonstre comment les ii. rois, s'il auront guerre, devendront sers a tous leurs subgiez. Et s'il a-[59r]uront paix, tout le contraire

Tres excellent prince, en election de la paix et de la guerre, cultre les raisons en ceste escripture souventefois recitees, une chose y a solempnelle, par laquele en vostre franc arbitre vous deveries eslire la paix plus tost que la guerre; c'est assavoir que se vous, ou vostre frere de France, eslires la guerre, vous, qui a present estes franc et de lignie franche, de vostre propre volente vous vous trebucheres publiquement en la fosse de servage et de dangereuse servitude. Quel merveille, car il n'aura nul en vostre roy-/aume a qui vous ne deveines serf, a ceulz qui font les armeurs, et a toutes autres gens de mestier pour la guerre, a tresoriers, a communes, a gens de l'eglise, et jusques a vostre petit vallet de chambre, qui murmurera aucunefoiz si le convendra lever plus matin pour la guerre qu'il n'aura acoustume autrefois.

Mais que se dira de la servitude de la royale majeste quant aus gens d'armes, ausquelz il est auxi comme impossible de satisfaire a leur volente, comme il se pourroient desclarier largement? Laquele desclaracion soit laissie pour cause de brief-[59v]te car vous l'entendez assez.

Or venons a vos chevaliers de la guerre, et orres une tele abusion et orrible servage, quant a la royale majeste, qui par aventure en sa fourme ne fu onques ecripte; laquele fait fort a noter et a doubter a tous princes crestiens et vrais catholiques. Tres sage et tres debonnaire roy, se fortune tourne sa roe comme elle a acoustume, et fera aucune risee a vostre personne royale, a ii. ou iii. de vos chevetaines, par aucunes victoires, or oies comment vous en vostre personne charres en servitude. Car se vostre royale ma-/jeste aura eu victoire de ses anemis en personne, de tant comme elle aura este plus grande, de tant y aura il de vos freres crestiens plus de mors, et de commun cours une grant partie des ames seront portees en enfer, et tout par vostre occasion. Or venons au servage ouquel vous seres en grant peril d'encheoir. Il est comme impossible de commun cours, je ne dy pas tousjours ne simplement, que dame Vaine Gloire, Oultrecuidance, Presumpcion, et Avarice, ne soient souvent assises a vostre table royale, a destre et a senestre; car sicomme dit saint Jehan Bouche d'Or il est auxi comme impossible que un grant seigneur, [6or] assis en la chair d'onneur et de plussieurs victoires mondaines, puist demorer sans avoir vaine gloire, comme il seroit a i. josne et fort homme, assis souvent empres une tres belle vierge et non giter les yeux au viaire de la vierge aucunefois par charnelle concupiscence.

Tres gracieux prince, se apres la victoire vous seres ferus des iiii. dames sustouciez, ou de l'une toute seule, vous demoures en servage mortel; car il est escript, Qui fait le pechie, il demeure serf de pechie. Et que pis est, en multipliant servage apres la dicte victoire, par aventure vous ne seres pas con-/tent tant seulement d'icelle, voire ambicion et avarice ce pourchassant, mais enquarres et pourchasseres d'avoir une autre plus grant victoire, de laquele vous ne seres pas certains. Car il est escript que les advenemens des batailles sont doubteux, comme il appert par maint roy et par maint prince, et crestien et paien, qui apres aucunes victoires se sont efforciez d'avoir aucunes autres victoires, ausqueles les uns y ont failly et les autres, qui les ont obtenues, sont cheus en plus grant servage et ont aservi les pueples qui riens ne leur avoient mesfait.

[6ov] Or venons a la grant abusion du servage de la roiale majeste envers les chevetaines qui auront eu les victoires en l'absence de leur roy. Chascun scet que celuy chevetaine qui aura eu la plus grant victoire tendra en son cuer, et tous ces privez amis, que la royale majeste sera plus obligiee a luy que aus autres chevetaines, qui n'auront pas eue si grant victoire. Quel merveille, car quant le dit chevetaine, le plus victorieux, retournera a son seigneur et roy, une branche d'olivier ou de lorier en sa main en signe de victoire, acompaignie des vaillans chevaliers de sa charge, pour estre guerdonne du roy de / son travail et vaillance, et seoir a la table royale, le roy sera contraint de faire tresgrant honnour au dit chevetaine victorieux, se le roy ne veult encourre

l'indignacion des vaillans chevaliers ses subgiez. Et quant a l'abusion devant Dieu et servage royale, de tant que le dit chevetaine, par luy et par les siens, aura mort en la bataille plus de ses freres crestiens et mande en enfer, de tant le roy sera plus obligie et aservi au dit chevetaine, et de luy faire plus grant guerredon, et souventesfoys oultre la merite et vaillance de la personne du dit chevetaine, ci a grant abusion devant Dieu et servage royal.

[61r] O quele male servitude royale devant Dieu! De tant que le dit chevetaine aura mande en enfer plus d'ames crestiennes, de tant li demourra le roy plus son serf. Et se le roy ne guerredonnera au dit chevetaine a sa volente, il demourra indignes et forgera secretement par aventure une bande, a l'efect de laquele ou temps advenir, ou prejudice de la royale majeste, le frain soit mis a ceste pane.

Aucuns pourroient dire que selonc les loys civiles et divines, pour recouvrer son heritage, pour faire justice des mauvais, ou pour la deffension de la chose pu-/blique, les guerres des crestiens sont licites. A ce se puet respondre que qui vouldroit bien peser en la balance de verite le principal de la cause pour laquele la guerre sera commenciee, laquele cause sera jugiee par la sapience humaine estre juste, qui aucunefoiz devant Dieu, pour les circonstances et ignorances d'icelles, sera reputee injuste; et de l'autre part, se les maulz sans nombre et cruaultez qui seront faites en la guerre, contre et oultre la loy et discipline de vraie chevalerie, seront bien pesez en la dicte balance, il se trouvera que, avant le commencement de la guerre, il eust este expedient que l'un roy a l'autre [61v] eust quittie franchement et liberalment, pour la reverance de Dieu et pour eschever tant de maulz, les ii. pars du principal de la cause, en demourant vrais amis, sans aucune reprouche ou temps advenir de la dicte cession des ii. parties sustoucies de la cause.

Tres excellent prince, se par la loy civile qui occist un homme, il doit mourir selonc la loy; et selonc la loy divine, qui het son frere, il est omicides, selonc le dit de saint Jehan l'evvangeliste; et, que plus est, qui aura occis un tout seul homme et mourra sanz avoir faite digne penitance et satisfacion a / Dieu et a partie, selonc les loys divines tel homme est dampnes perpetuelment; que respondront donques les roys qui, pour leurs morteles guerres, aucunesfois legierement emprinses, auront este occasion de la mort, non pas de la mort d'un seul homme, mais de c. mile qui seront mors en la guerre, une tresgrant partie, helas, sans confession, en grant peril evident d'estre dampne pardurablement? Qui a les oreilles pour oyr, si escouste, comme le doulz Jhesu en sa sainte evvangile dit, car, selonc ce qui est escript, riguereux jugement se fera aus grans seigneurs qui en ce monde ont les grans [62r] presidences, et les puissans seigneurs puissaument seront tourmentez. De laquele chose Dieu vueille garder nos ii. roys et les vueille confourmer en sa vraie paix, par li doulcement inspiree. Et ce souffice assez briefment et en gros de la servitude de la royle majeste se la guerre maldicte prendera la seigneurie.

La viii[e] matere de ceste presente epistre demonstre ii.
vergiers, ou jardins, l'un tres delicieux et compare a la paix,
et l'autre horrible et perilleux et compare a la guerre, presentes
aus ii. roys, afin qu'il preignent l'un et se gardent de l'autre |

Il est chose naturelle que tous hommes, et par especial les roys, s'il seront sages, doivent ressoingner et fuir toutes les choses qui puent estre contraires a leurs personnes royales, a leur lignie, et a leur grant seigneurie, en desirant le contraire, c'est assavoir prosperite de leurs personnes, augmentacion et confirmacion de leur seigneurie; lesquelz ii. parties doivent estre trovez en la paix et en la guerre. Or soit recitee une gracieuse parabole, en laquele les ii. proposicions sustouciez seront assez plainement desclariees.

Le vergier delitable

Le vieil solitaire [62v] en son songe figure vit un vergier, rempli de toutes manieres d'arbres et d'erbes, portans fruis et rendans un tres gracieux oudour. Ou dit vergier, rempli de toutes manieres de flours, ne se trouvoit gelee, brume, elevasses d'yaue, ne tonnoire. Les habitans du dit vergier usoient de planiere sante et n'y avoit nul malade, jusques a tant qu'il deust mourir en Dieu. Tous les fruis du vergier estoient communs aus habitans, a chascun selonc sa necessite, et ceste parole, c'est assavoir 'propre' et 'mien', estoient banis du vergier. Les habitans du dit vergier en si grant / joye vivoient l'un avec l'autre, qu'il leur sembloit qu'il n'en veillissoient point. Toute tyrannie et crueuse seignourie estoient banies du vergier, et toutesfoiz il y avoit un seigneur et roy ou dit vergier qui representoit la seignourie et la chose publique des dessusdiz habitans, et estoit tant amez et reveraument doubtez, comme s'il fust pere a chascun habitant. Quel merveille, car il avoit plus grant cure du bien de ces subgiez, habitans ou vergier, qu'il n'avoit du propre bien de luy ou de ses enfans.

Cestui vergier gracieux estoit avironne tout entour [63r] d'un hault mur, qui estoit appele tuicion, a grant plante de haultes tours, qui estoient appelees chascune protection. Es dis murs, dedens et dehors, estoient figures, en painture solempnelle et permanable, les temps dores de ce monde, c'est assavoir la gracieuse policie des Bargamains et de leur roy, esquelz convoitise, orgueil et luxure, du tout en tout estoient banies. Il vivoient en commun et estoient content de cavernes, sans edifier maisons. Il ne faisoient aucune mension ne d'or ne d'argent ne de pierres precieuses. Et quant les femmes se sentoient grosses de leurs maris, il n'abitoient plus / l'un avec l'autre charnelment, jusques a tant qu'elles avoient enfante et estoient relevees. Leur roy n'estoit point empesche de faire justice. Quel merveille, car il ne mesfaisoient riens l'un a l'autre. Le roy Alixandre visita les dessus dis Bargamains, et pour ce qu'il n'y trova n'or ne argent ne seignorie tirannique, il ne fist contes des dis Bargamains.

Encores, es dis murs estoient figures les temps dores et de paix du roy Salemon, en temps duquel les sieges enmy les rues de la cite de Jherusalem estoient couvers d'argent.

Encores, y estoient figures les temps dores et de la paix universelle [63v] de ce monde ou temps de Othovien, empereur de Romme, qui la cite de Romme, qui estoit edifiee de vieilles parois et de terre cuite, redifia de fin marbre de diverses coulours, et tint la monarchie du monde en vraye paix xii. ans entiers, ouquel temps le Dieu de paix vost naistre en ce monde de la Vierge Marie.

Encores, es dis murs avoit iiii. grans portes, l'une si estoit du precieux bois de cypres, la secunde de palme, la tierce de cedre, et la quarte d'olive, desquelz bois la vraie crois fu composee. La premiere porte estoit appelee alegresse, la secunde amoureuse, la tierce / bonne aventure, et la quarte biau semblant, et benois seront tous ceulz qui par les dictes portes enterront ou biau vergier figure.

Encores est assavoir que ou milieu du vergier avoit une fontaine toute ronde, de laquele xii. ruissiaux partoient, qui arousoient de toutes pars le gracieux vergier, et faisoient produire doulcement les xii. fruis du Saint Esperit que l'apostre saint Pol recite a Galathas, c'est assavoir, charite, joye, paix, pacience, longanimite, bonte, pitie, benignite, debonnairete, foy, atrempance, et chastete.

Et tout auxi comme le pain est neces-[64r]saire a la vie de l'omme continuelment, tout ainsi ou dit vergier, par tout sur les rives des ruissiaux, croissoit une herbe precieuse a tres grant habondance, qui estoit appelee sanamonde, c'est a dire saine et nette. Les habitans du dit vergier avec toute leur viande et tous leurs fruis mangoient de la dicte herbe sanamonde. Et tout auxi comme la manne du ciel ou desert estoit convertie en tel goust comme les enfans d'Israel le desiroient, et tout ainsi, parlant moralment, la dicte herbe sanamonde faisoit convertir le goust des dessusdis habitans du vergier a leur volente et doulce consolacion. /

Encores, de la dicte fontaine partoient iiii. ruissiaux principaux, qui arousoient toutes les parties du jardin. Le premier ruissiau estoit appele seurte, le second vray repos, le tiers habundance de tous biens, et le quart estoit appele souffisance. O benois seront tous ceulz qui travailleront a l'edificacion d'un si noble vergier! Et encores plus bieneureux qui en leur temps auront plaine possession du gracieux vergier, desire des preudommes.

Par cestui vergier, en parabole figure moralisant, puet estre entendu chascun royaume des crestiens. Et par la gracieuse fontaine puet [64v] estre entendue la vraye paix de tout preudomme desiree. Et par les ruissiaux et les misteres d'iceulz puent estre entendu les grans biens imcomparables qui viennent et procedent de la paix; non pas de la paix recitee par Jeremie le prophete, qui dit, Paix, paix et non est paix, mais de la vraye paix que le doulz Jhesu donne en terre, avec laquele paix il se donne il meisme. Et benois seront les ii. roys qui doulcement le recevront. Et ce souffice du biau vergier a vraie paix en ce monde figure, lequel vergier puet estre appele en ce monde, par figure, un paradis terrestre. Et le roy du dit vergier par son droit nom / est appeles *rex pacificus*.

Le jardin horrible et perilleux

Or venons a la descripcion briefve d'un autre vergier, tout contraire au vergier propose. Le quel vieil solitaire, en son songe figure, vit en la dicte parabole un autre jardin, clos et demi clos d'espignes trespoingnans. Le dit jardin estoit de telle condicion que se le soleil donnoit sa clarte une journee, iiii. ou v. jours apres tenebres estoient par tout le jardin. Froides gelees, brumes, habondances de pleuves, regnans ou dit jardin, abatoient les flours et ne laissoient venir les fruis a [65r] maturite. Le vent de north, de septentrion et d'acquillon, c'est assavoir orgueil et vaine glorie, les ii. pars de l'an regnoit ou dit jardin et avoit plaine seignourie; le vent de sudaustre, c'est assavoir le vent de mydi, c'est avarice enracinee, le remenant du temps, et tousjours excersoit son office. Le doulz vent d'oist, d'occident et de ponent, c'est assavoir gloutonnie, paresse et gastement de tous biens, n'y estoient pas oubliez. Mais le doulz vent d'est, d'orient et de levant, c'est assavoir la verite et la consolacion du Saint Esperit, combien que aucunefoiz il arousoit / le jardin en passent, toutesfoiz il y faissoit petite demeure, voire pour la seignourie des autres iii. vens, qui ou jardin avoient la plaine seignourie. Que se dira? Ou dit jardin les femmes des habitans et leurs bestes communement avortissoient, et toute leur joye estoit convertie en plour et en doulour; les uns estoient yvres et les autres mouroient de fain. Et n'avoit ou dit jardin justice, amour, regle ne policie. Quel merveille, car le fort mangoit le foible, et tirannie y regnoit ou quart degre, par tele maniere que les preudommes du dit jardin desiroient plus la mort [65v] que la vie.

Encores est assavoir que ou milieu du jardin avoit une trouble et obscure fontaine, de laquele xv. ruissiaux partoient et arousoient tout le jardin, et non pas sans fumee et tres mauvaise odour. Les noms des xv. ruisseaux puent estre appelez et nommez par leur effect, c'est assavoir cruaulte, tirannie, simulacion, ypocrisie, rapine, vengence et merencolie, excusacion de pechie, mendace et jactance, traison, suspicion et iniquite, effusion de sanc, et toute inhumanite.

Encores, de la dicte trouble fontaine partoient iiii. ruissiaux / principaux, dont tous les habitans, ou la plus grant partie, communement estoient abuvrez. Par le premier ruissiau les habitans estoient enclins a diverses heresies; par le second a supersticions et villaines sorceries; par le tiers a l'art magique et invocacion des demons; et par le quart as jugemens advenir qui cheent en franc arbitre aus jugemens d'astrologie. Le premier ruissiau estoit appele paour continuelle, le second labour sanz repos, le tiers deffaulte de tous biens, et le quart mescognoissance et ingratitude envers Dieu; corespondant aus inclinaci-[66r]ons sustoucies. Encores, ou milieu du jardin avoit un ancien palais descouvert, ouquel jadis furent figurees les effusions du sanc humain des le commencement du monde, c'est assavoir des premiers jaians, qui se combatirent l'un contre l'autre en espandant sanc humain sans mesure, sicomme la sainte escripture le recite.

Encores y estoit figuree la bataille de Hannibal, roy d'Aufrique, encontre les Rommains, devant la cite de Romme, en laquelle bataille ot tant de sanc espandu des Rommains que Hannibal victorieux fist requellir iii. muys d'aneaux / d'or des chevaliers romains qui moururent en la bataille. Encores y estoit figuree la bataille de Othovien, l'empereur de Romme, encontre Anthone, empereur des royaumes d'orient, et fut la bataille en mer entre le royaume de Chippre et Surie, a laquele, selonc les croniques, avoit m. galees armees, sans les grosses naves et autres navires sans nombre. Et la fut desconfit Anthone, qui s'enfouy en Egypte et se fist mourir par venin. Et Cleopatras sa mie, royne d'Egypte, pour laquelle fu commenciee la guerre, auxi se fist mourir par venin. A laquele bataille ot tant de sanc hu-[66v]main espandu que la mer en devint toute vermeille.

Encores y estoit figuree la grant bataille des iii. filz de Loys le debonnaire, empereur de Romme et roy de France, filz du grant Charlemaine, lesquelz iii. filz, c'est assavoir, Loys roy d'Alemaingne, Lotaire roy d'Italie, et Charles roy de France, iii. freres, par avarice, envie et ambicion, se combatirent ensamble empres de la cite d'Auserre, et y ot tant de sanc espandu qu'il ne se lit pas que du commencement du monde tant de sanc des Francois eust este espandu. Qui pourroit descripre a plain les effusions du sanc humain entre les paiens, / Sarrasins et crestiens, qui a este espandu par les morteles guerres, qui ont este des le commencement du monde? Il seroit impossible. Mais toutesfois il seroit expedient a ceulz qui ont volente de commencier les guerres, et par especial encontre leurs freres crestiens, qu'il eussent en un miroir continuelment devant eulz l'effusion du sanc humain cy dessus recitee, pour refraindre leur perilleuse volente. Et ce souffice du sanc humain espandu paint et figure en la dicte sale descouverte, et tout au desplaisir de Dieu, et encontre la divine bonte, et a la destruction de la [67r] crestiente.

Encores, sur les xv. ruissiaux puans du jardin infortune croissoit une herbe a grant habundance, qui estoit appelee sanguinolence, laquele grant partie des habitans du dit jardin mangoient a grant avidite avec toutes leurs viandes. Et estoit la dicte herbe sanguinolence de telle nature que toute la viande que les dis habitans mangoient estoit convertie en sanc, sans ce que les mangens en eussent aucune abhominacion, qui estoit un grant horreur a veoir aus preudommes habitans ou dit jardin. La dicte herbe sanguinolence faisoit son office, / c'est assavoir par le roy du jardin et par ses chevetaines, qui tout ainsi comme l'omme faims ardaument va a la viande, tout ainsi aloient espandre le sanc de leurs freres crestiens ou dit jardin habitans, par batailles, par murdres, par injustice, et autrement. Pour lequel apetit desordene tout estoit converti en sanc, et selonc leur office crueux, par la sentence du prophete David, il estoient realment appeles hommes de sanc et non digne de edifier a Dieu son temple.

Encores, es dis xv. ruissiaux avoit sensues sans nombre, grandes et petites, qui sussoient le sanc des habi-[67v]tans du jardin partout la ou elles pooient attaindre, et en prenoient tant que les plussieurs crevoient parmy et mouroient, et des habitans les uns en estoient alegie et plus sain pour le mauvais sanc que les sensues avoient sussie, les autres avoient perdu tant de leur sanc par les sansues que il en mouroient de povrete. Parlant moralment, les sensues es dis ruissiaux ce sont les chevetaines et les gens d'armes, qui sussent le sanc des povres hommes, c'est assavoir les biens de quoy ilz doivent vivre, par rensons, par pillages, par gabbelles, par imposicions, et par desordenees opressions. / Et aucunefois avient que ceulz qui sont pillie ou ronsonne avoient trop de biens temporeux et mal acquis, et pour ce, apres la perte, il en deviennent plus sain, vivant plus sobrement et gardant soy d'acquerre injustement. Et toutesfoiz aucunes des sensues en prenoient si gloutement, qu'il en crevoient parmi et en mouroient de male mort et en peril d'estre dampne. Et pour occasion des sansues, les habitans du dit maleureux jardin vivoient en tel paour qu'il ne pooient ne dormir ne reposer.

Encores, ou dit jardin avoit tresgrant quantite de locustes a [68r] grans dens, qui mangoient et rungoient les blez et tous les fruis et toute l'erbe verte du jardin jusques a la racine. On a veu ou royaume de Cypre et ailleurs, de nostre temps, en un champ de fin fourment prest a soier, a un des lez du champ descendre tant de locustes que sans nombre, et a celle heure de l'autre part du champ les soieurs en grant quantite faisant leur office, et toutefoiz les locustes de leur part du champ mengoient plus du fourment, jusques a la racine, que les soieurs ne pooient abatre; et estoient desconfis les soieurs des locustes, par tele maniere que celle journee ne demouroit ou champ ne espy / ne grain de fourment, que tout ne fust mengie des locustes. C'y a male beste et perilleuse. Ce sont, parlant moralment, ou jardin les chevetaines, gens d'armes et pillars, qui sont crueulx et a grans dens ou quart degre, devant lesquelz riens ne demeure, s'il n'est trop chault ou trop pesant. Et dureureux seront les habitans, qui pour leurs pechiez seront mis ou dit jardin, soubz la verge ou aguillon des dictes sansues et locustes.

Encores, autour du dit jardin perilleux, en la closture des espines poingnans, avoit vii. portes, ouvertes et communes, qui estoient entitulees par certains signes, escrip-[68v]tures et banieres des vii. pechiez mortelz, c'est assavoir, d'orgueil, d'envie, de yre, de peresse, d'avarice, de gloutonnie, et de luxure. Et oultre ce y avoit iiii. portes principales, dont la premiere estoit composee du bois qui est appellee saux, qui est verde et ne porte point de fruit; la seconde porte estoit d'un bois qui a nom fou; la tierce porte estoit du bois qui a nom tramble; et la quarte porte estoit d'un bois qui a nom such, dont les fueilles et le fruit sont tous puans. La premiere porte des iiii. principales est appelee presumpcion, sanz fruit avec le saux; la seconde estoit appelee oultrecuidance avec le fou; / la tierce estoit appelee lamentacion, avec le tramble, qui tramble de paour a tous vens; et la quarte porte estoit appelee desesperacion avec le seuch, ouquel arbre de such Judas se pandi, selonc le dit des vieilles.

O que perilleuses portes pour entrer ou dit jardin perilleux! Trop mieulx vauldroit estre povre habitant ou gracieux vergier de paix cy dessus recite, que estre roy couronne ou jardin perilleux, rempli de tant de maulz; duquel jardin, de son roy, et de ses chevetaines, Dieu nous vueille garder et nous vueille hebergier ou gracieux vergier a paradis terrestre fi-[69r]gure.

Tenant donques a la concordance, par le jardin perilleux darrainement propose, puet estre entendu chascun royaume des crestiens qui a les condicions cy dessus recitees du dit jardin. Et par la fontaine trouble et obscure ou milieu du jardin, proprement puet estre entendue la guerre dominant ou dit royaume. Et par les xv. ruissiaux, par l'erbe sanguinolente, par les iiii. ruissiaux principaux, par les sansues et locustes, et par les portes du jardin perilleuses et misterieuses, puent estre entendu generalment et particulierement les maulz et perilz / infinis, qui jour et nuit s'ensuivent de la guerre, et les maledicions qui en viennent.

Cestui jardin perilleux, par l'efect de ses oeuvres merveilleuses, doit estre appele fortune a ii. visages, et la perilleuse garde. Mais le roy du jardin doit estre appele par son droit nom Nemproch, qui edifia la tour Babel, et fu le premier roy tirant en ce monde, qui sousmit a soy et a sa tirannie les pueples de son temps. Et Dieu vausist que en son office le dit Nemproch eust este brehaignes, et qu'il n'eust pas eu tant de successeurs en son cruel office, qui au jour duy, helas, a la lettre gardent [69v] trop bien ses loys.

Encores est assavoir que, tout ainsi par aucune comparacion contraire, que ou gracieux vergier cy dessus tant loe, les belles vierges et pucelles, doulcement esmeues des doulz instrumens qui resonnoient de toutes pars ou vergier, doulcement chantoient les loenges a Dieu et les gracieuses chansonnettes amoureuses, et tout sans vilenie, tout ainsi par contraire ou jardin perilleux les vierges et pucelles ne chantent autre chansons que lamentacions et ve, gittans larmes et soupirs en lieu de gracieuses cantiques. Quel merveille, car elles sont souvent / et habituelment espoantees des trompettes qui souvent sonnent, Alarme, alarme! des campanes auxi qui provoquent les habitans a bataille, et de la lamentacion des mors et des navrez, qui sont souvent mal hostelez. Encores y a une autre chanson qui a donne mainte suspicion, c'est assavoir des povres habitans du jardin qui par force sont mis autour du jardin chascun en sa garde, et sans repos toute la nuit, au vent et a la pluie, chantent, Garde, la garde. Et ce souffice assez prolixement du jardin perilleux.

La concordance des ii. vergiers par le moien des ii. [70r] grans perilz de mer, l'un appele Sillam et l'autre Caripdim

Tres excellent et tres puissant prince et digne roy de la Grant Bretaingne, les ii. vergiers ou jardins cy dessus assez largement proposez par le vieil solitaire, a grant reverance et amour soient presente a vostre royale majeste et a vostre tres ame frere auxi, Charles, le roy de France, aus princes royaux et d'un coste et d'autre, et a la vaillant chevalerie et d'Angleterre et de France, c'est assavoir ii. vergiers, l'un de clarte, l'autre de tenebres, l'un de repos, l'autre de travail, l'un de grant peril et l'autre de grant seurte, l'un de / joye et l'autre de tristesse, l'un bieneure et l'autre maleure, l'un des esleus de Dieu ardaument desire, et l'autre des reprouvez diligaument cultivez, l'un la voye de paradis et l'autre la voie d'enfer le puant.

Tres debonnaire et tres devot roy, il est en vostre franc arbitre, et de vostre frere de France auxi, de prendre ou l'un ou l'autre. Si seroit grant pitie et grant damage a toute la crestiente se vous vous bouties es fumees puans du jardin perilleux, et laississies la doulce odour et les precieux aromas du gracieux vergier a paradis terrestre figure. Tres catholique prince, saint Augustin recite en son livre [70v] de la cite de Dieu que, en certaines contrees de la mer, a ii. roches, ii. vorages, ii. tres grans perilz de mer, entre lesquelz il est expedient que les naves, qui par fortune se treuvent ou dit peril, soient bien avisees de sagement passer entre ii. roches, car les dictes naves ne pourroient si peu forvoier du milieu qu'elles ne fussent peries. Et sont appelez ces ii. perilz par saint Augustin, et par les escriptures des poetes, l'un Sillam et l'autre Caripdin.

Tres debonnaire roy, vous et vostre frere de France, par la vocacion de Dieu et dispensacion divine, estes ii. grans patrons de ii. naves royales, les / plus solempnelles qui soient en la mer occiane, et estes ordenez par la divine bonte de conduire en vostre temps les ii. dictes naves, alans en orient, devers Jherusalem, et toutesfois vous ne pouez eschaper que vous ne passies par entre les ii. perilz cy dessus proposez, c'est asvoir entre Sillam et Caripdim. Si est expedient et de necessite que vous ii. patrons ayes continuelment vostre regart a l'estoille de north, c'est a l'estoille tremontaine, c'est a la Vierge Marie, et que tout avant vous doies faire vos appaux et ensais pour le dit voiage saint ou biau et delitable vergier tant loe, sans [71r] le fruit duquel vous ne pourres emprendre ce que tant avee desire, enfuiant du tout en tout le jardin perilleux et ses fruis amerz et mal savoureux.

Et ce faisant sagement et vaillaument, tres gracieux princes, grans patrons des naves royales, selonc l'oroison du benoit saint Augustin, vous, a mon vouloir, trespasseres entre Sillam et Caripdim, sans regarder a destre ne a senestre, par le milieu, c'est assavoir par la voie royale, et finablement le doulz vent d'orient attraiant a tout vos ii. naves, chargiees et remplies d'une riche marchandise de vertus, / parvendres et arriveres a vray port de salut; laquele chose Dieu vous vueille ottroier, comme vous vouldries et mon cuer le desire.

Tres aimable et tres debonnaire roy, par les ii. grans perilz de mer, Sillam et Caripdim souventesfoiz repetes, entre lesquelz perilz navez royales et autres sans nombre, des le commencement du monde, y ont este peries, pour ce que la mer y est continuelment boulant et courant, sans mesure ne repos, parlant moralment, puent estre entendu les ii. parties de la chevalerie de France et d'Angleterre, c'est assavoir ceulz qui on este nourris ou jar-[71v]din perilleux en esmouvent continuel-ment la tempeste de mer, c'est la guerre maldicte; entre lesquelz, pour parvenir unefoiz au biau vergier desire, et apres conduire vos navez royales a la voie d'orient, il est expedient que, avec le doulz Jhesu qui trespassa par le milieu des Juyfs qui le vouloient mettre a mort, vous doies trespasser vaillaument par le milieu des dessus diz, acoustumes de boire le sanc de leurs freres crestiens, sans regarder a destre ne a senestre.

Et s'il vous diront, tres debonnaires princes, ou proces de l'edificacion du biau vergier, c'est assavoir de la paix, Seigneur, pour ac-/quitter nostre loyaute a vostre royale majeste, gardez l'onnour de la couronne d'Angleterre, et les autres, Gardez l'onnour de la couronne de France, se vous passez cestuy traitie, vous estes deshonnourez. Auxquelz vous pouez tres sagement respondre par le moien du proverbe commun, c'est assavoir, Qui a le proufit de la guerre, il en a le vray honnour; le vray honnour et plaine victoire de la guerre si est la vraie paix, quar l'empereur en sa loy civile, par maniere de sentence dit, Nous faisons guerre pour avoir paix. Et ce respondant, par la bonte de Dieu, quant il [72r] verront vostre constance, grant vaillance, et haulte prouesse, et que, non obstant leurs paroles, vous aures ja passe en esperit Sillam et Caripdim, et cognoistront en vous la vertu divine, lors il vous suivront apres, et par nouvelle grace seront anombres avec les bieneureux du gracieux vergier et de vostre sainte chevalerie. Laquele chose Dieu vous vueille ottroier. Et se souffice assez prolixement des ii. jardins figurez et de leur mistere, voire pour eslire l'un, et l'autre de laissier.

Une briefve excusacion du vieil solitaire de la prolixite de ceste presente epistre

Pour faire fin a / ceste escripture foiblement composee, a ceste epistre prolixe et mal salee, il est assavoir que le vieil solitaire recognoist bien que les materes, diverses et entrelaciees l'une en l'autre, comprises en ceste presente epistre, par un vaillant orateur et solempnel dictateur, par conclusions trop plus briefves eussent este mises et reduites en escript, pour ce que au jour duy les grans seigneurs, pour leurs manificences et afaires temporeulz, se delitent fort en briefves escriptures. A laquele instance ou objection le povre solitaire puet respondre qu'il ne puet issir du sac fors ce qui y estoit, c'est assavoir rudesse et [72v] gros engien, foible dictie prolixe et male desclarie. Saint Pierre l'apostre dist au malade, Je n'ay or ne argent, mais ce que j'ay je te donne, c'est assavoir sante. Dieu scet que le vieil solitaire desire la sente et vraie paix de la royale majeste. Et pour ce, avec saint Pierre, et avec la povre veesve femme qui offri ii. minutes en gasophilacion, il offre ce qu'il a, c'est assavoir sa bonne volente qu'il a de la paix et de la vraie amiste des ii. rois, en ceste epistre souvent repetee et non pas en briefve escripture. Quel merveille, car si haultes materes et pluseurs, touchans a des plus

grans roys de / la crestiente, et au tres grant bien ou au tres grant mal
de leurs personnes, de leurs royaumes, de l'eglise, de Dieu, et de toute
la generacion crestienne, par un vieil ydiote escripvain, qui abaie sa
fosse et au soir et au matin, en briefve escripture ne eussent pas legierement estees ramenees ne desclariees. Si demande le povre escripvain
pardon de la prolixite et de ce qu'il a trop parle, en sousmetant soy a
la correction de la benigne pacience de la royale majeste des iii. lupars
dores, par la bonte de Dieu transmuez de rigour en doulcour, de
cremour en amour, et [73r] de crueuse proie en l'amour de Mont Joye;
laquelle amour Dieu par sa sainte grace vueille adrecier et confermer, a
la loenge de sa divine bonte et consolacion de toute la crestiente.

*La ix^e matere et la darrainne de ceste presente epistre, c'est
assavoir une briefve recapitulacion de la sustance de la dicte
epistre, et confirmacion de la paix et amour des ii. roys par
le moien d'une doulce aliance par mariage gracieux, qui sera
occasion en Dieu de la paix de la crestiente*

Or venons donques a la conclusion de ceste froide epistre, en racapi-
tulant briefment l'effect du merveilleux / songe figure du vieil solitaire,
c'est assavoir du fin baulme transfourme en l'escharboucle, et du fin
aymant transmue en fin dyamant, qui de nouvel ont pris leur naissance
par le commandement de l'aucteur de nature es froides regions de
France et d'Angleterre; laquele chose, se a la lettre et simplement, n'est
pas legiere a croire, maiz toutefoiz, par l'interpretacion morale, le songe
est veritable, comme il appert clerement en la premiere matere de ceste
presente epistre.

Il fu dit que le fin baulme, pris en figure morale pour la tres haulte
personne royale de Charles, par la grace de [73v] Dieu roy de France,
par sa grant vertu treble, de sa part jusques a ores a reclose la grant
plaie perilleuse, largement descripte en ceste presente epistre, c'est assavoir la guerre des ii. royaumes de France et d'Angleterre. Encores fu
dit que selonc l'interpretacion de *Karolus*, c'est assavoir Charles, qui
vault autant a dire comme chiere lumiere, le dit baulme est converti en
une fine escharboucle, rendant une grande lumiere, moult proufitable a
ceulz qui estoient en tenebres, comme il appert plus clerement en son
propre chapitre.

Encores fu dit que le fin aymant, pris en figure morale pour la tres haulte per-/sonne royale de Richart, par la grace de Dieu roy d'Angleterre, par sa grant vertu attraiant, largement a atrait a son amour en Dieu son frere le roy Charles, ses oncles, et frere, et les preudommes du roiaume de Gaule, et quant est a son royaume d'Angleterre, ses oncles auxi, et ses barons, et la vaillant chevalerie de la Grant Bretaingne, par tele maniere que, par la grace de Dieu, quant de sa part et jusques a ores, la perilleuse plaie puet estre dicte reclose, et ne faut pour la finale consolidacion de la dicte plaie que le darrain emplastre de toute garison, c'est assavoir la presence et vision mutuele et charitative des ii. [74r] personnes des roys, pour confirmacion de toute sante, de vraie amour, de paix et de doulce charite.

Encores fu dit que le vray aymant seroit converti et transmue en un fin dyamant, retenant tousjours sa gracieuse vertu actrative, de laquele transmutacion jusques a ores en ceste epistre n'a este faite aucune mencion. Or venons briefment a la dicte transmutacion, pour concordance de l'amour des ii. roys, et declaracion au propos de la vertu des dictes pierres precieuses asses grossement moralisiez. Richart, digne et vaillant roy d'Angleterre, en ceste / epistre pris en figure pour le fin aymant, duquel aymant prenez le premier 'a' et le metes apres 'y', et en lieu du dit 'a' metes 'd', vous trouveres clerement 'dyamant'. O quele gracieuse et briefve transmutacion de pierres precieuses, c'est assavoir de aymant en dyamant. Mais escoustes encores une autre transmutacion du dit nom, plus briefve et trop plus glorieuse, c'est assavoir adjoustes une seule lettre a dyamant, c'est assavoir un 'u' apres 'y', vous trouveres clerement que nostre precieux dyamant sera converti en 'dieu amant'. Ceste interpretacion darraine, par l'effect de sa [74v] grant vertu passe toutes les vertus des autres pierre precieuses.

O que belle convercion morale de la personne de nostre josne roy Richart en fin aymant atraiant; et encores plus gracieuse conversion de l'aymant atraiant en un fin dyamant royal et emperial; mais la tierce convercion est trop plus solempnelle, c'est assavoir du fin dyamant en une pierre precieuse qui par or ne par argent ne se pourroit estimer, c'est assavoir Dieu amant, l'amour de Dieu, l'amour du doulz Jhesu; par le moien de laquele amour le fin baulme, converti en escharboucle rendant / clere lumiere, merveilleusement a este atrait par l'aymant a son amour en Dieu, comme il est dit dessus. Encores, le dyamant a conserve l'amour et transporte par grant charite de l'un en l'autre, par telle maniere que la grant plaie est estanchiee et auxi comme toute sanee et reclose. De rechief, par le moien de la dicte amour, le fin baulme, converti en fin rubis, c'est en la precieuse escharboucle, et l'aymant, converti en fin dyamant, ont este, sont, et seront, a mon voloir, tres doulcement baignie et saintement enyvrez ou precieuse vin des vignes d'Engadi, c'est de l'amour du benoit Saint Esperit.

[75r] Mais que se dira moralissant de l'interpretacion du nom de Richart, nostre tres sage et tres debonnaire roy? L'interpretacion de son nom a la lettre est toute clere, c'est assavoir, riche et art; riche de bonne volente de la paix de la crestiente; riche d'atraire a son amour en Dieu son frere le roy Charles, et les vaillans chevaliers de France, qui souloient estre ses anemis; riche de vertu de justice et de bon gouvernement; riche de compassion du pueple crestien, et de la vertu de misericorde; riche de la sainte foy catholique, de doulce esperance de reparacion de l'eglise et de la crestiente; riche de sainte charite a / Dieu et au proesme; riche des vertus cardinales, et de grant desir de parvenir unefoiz aus viii. beneurtez par le doulz Jhesu proposees en sa sainte evvangile. Et ce souffice de l'interpretacion de la premiere sillable de son nom.

Or venons a la seconde interpretacion de la secunde sillabe de Richart, c'est assavoir 'art'. Il se puet dire qu'il est auxi comme impossible que Dieu li eust faites tant de graces, c'est assavoir de convertir les cuers de ses anemis a son amour en Dieu, sicomme les Francois; de refraindre l'office de l'espee de sa chevalerie encontre les Francois, des sa jonesce en bataille nourrie; [75v] de enter de nouvel paix es cuers de ceulz qui estoient et de fait habitues a la guerre; et, que plus est, de sousmettre nagaires a s.. plaine seignourie, sans sanc espandre, une si grande generacion sauvage et male nourrie comme sont les Hybernois, habitans es montaignes avec les bestes sauvages, et les habitans auxi des illes, nourris sans grant policie avec la fortune de la mer; ces choses cy, si grandes, si merveilleuses, et en grant temps autrefois non veues, en si brief temps par la grace divine si glorieusement acomplies, Dieu ne li eust pas ottroier se, selonc l'interpretacion de la secunde sil-/labe de son nom, il n'eust este ardant en l'amour de Dieu, et, par consequant, en l'amour de son proesme. Les oeuvres approuvans cy dessus et en ceste epistre largement repetees, il se puet dire donques, sans user l'oingnement popilion, qu'il est et sera, a mon voloir, ardant de la paix de ses freres crestiens, ardans de l'union de l'eglise, et finablement ardans de faire le saint passage en la compaignie de son tres ame frere Charles, roy de France; laquele chose Dieu leur vueille ottroier. Et ce souffice de l'interpretacion du nom de Richart, tres excellent roy d'Angleterre.

Saint Augustin [76r] dit que la vertu de perseverance est oeuvre parfaite. Il n'y a autre chose en la matere proposee que de bien perseverer par les ii. roys en l'amour l'un de l'autre. Ce qui est bien commencie, soit bien en Dieu moienne et au fin desire ramene, la fine escharboucle soit souvent transmuee en aymant atraiant, et en fin dyamant et dieu amant; et le dyamant soit auxi souvent transmue en l'escharboucle reluisant, tous ii. enoins du fin baulme, dont l'oudour tres souef, selonc le dit de l'apostre saint Pol, soit espars partout et jusques en Jherusalem. Et pour ce que en toute vraie aliance de grans seigneurs et sainte policie, de-/puis que la pomme par Adam fu mengiee, ne furent absens ceulz qui ont acoustume de semer ou forment la sizanie, pour ce est il expedient que par les ii. roys, a telle gent perilleuse, publiquement et secretement soient sagement exposees les maledicions qui sont escriptes ou livre de Moyses sur ceulz qui semoient la sizanie, qui destourboient la paix et bon estat du pueple d'Israel, et murmuroient contre Dieu, comme il fut dit autrefois. Et s'il ne se vouldront chastier, telle gent soit banie des nobles consaulz royaux, et soient mises et ordenees bonnes gardes, par la grace de Dieu, a telle ge-[76v] neracion murmurant, afin qu'elle ne puisse nuyre, procedant tousjours avant vaillaument, selonc l'inspiracion du benoit Saint Esperit. Et a ceulz qui seront bien disposez, et ardans de la paix et reparacion de la crestiente, par les ii. roys auxi soient devotement exposees les saintes benedictions de Aaron, du tres saint Samuel, et du saint patriarche Jacob, apele Israel, et des sains patriarches et prophetes; et, ou nouveau testament, les benedictions du doulz Jhesu, qu'il donna a sa tres doulce mere, la Vierge Marie, a Marie Magdalene, a ses sains apostres, quant il leur dist, Je vous donne/ma paix, non pas celle que le monde donne; la benediction auxi des sains martirs, confes, et glorieuses vierges, qui suivent l'Aignelet occis partout la ou il va; usans tousjours les ii. roys en leurs consaulz du conseil du tres sage Thusi, le loyal et sage conseillier du tres saint roy David, en reprouvant et fuiant sagement et cautement le conseil de Architofel et de ses adherens; laquele chose Dieu leur vueille ottroier et ma vieillesse eslessier.

Tres debonnaires roys et de France et d'Angleterre, pour conservacion de vostre vraie amour, l'un a l'autre, a mon voloir, le fin dya-[77r] mant par le loien du saint sacrement de mariage deviengne filz de l'escharboucle reluisant, et lors les bouches seront closes de ceulz qui vont querent le quint pie de mouton, c'est assavoir la guerre, voire par le moien du mariage suspicioneux en son propre chapitre assez largement desclarie. Ceste sainte aliance est la plus briefve pour faire taire tout homme. Lors les ii. roys seront comme le pere et le fil, concordans et habitans en un temple de Dieu, en une amour, et en une volente.

Et se aucuns vouldront dire que la fille de l'escharboucle est trop josne d'aage, et qu'il / est expedient au fin dyamant qu'il preingne famme de laquele yl puist avoir des enfans prestement, pour consolacion de luy et de ses loyaux subgies, a ce se puet assez respondre, La volente et grace de Dieu partout avant presupposee; c'est assavoir que, combien que le dyamant par le conseil de ses hommes prenist femme par mariage, c'est assavoir bonne, belle, et en souffisant aage, toutefois d'avoir se prestement lignie comme les creatures le vouldroient, il n'est pas en france volente de l'omme, car cestui don de Dieu avoir lignie, et bonne lignie, est reservee tant seulement a la divine providence, sicomme largement il fu des-[77v]clarie en la quarte matere de ceste presente epistre.

Encores, il est assavoir que qui se veult bien aidier en bataille et ailleurs d'un cheval, il est expedient que le dit cheval en sa jonesse soit bien endoctrine, et obeissant aus regles du frain et des autres doctrines, et par especial celui qui aura endoctrine le cheval, s'en saura trop mieulx aidier que nulle autre personne.

L'oliphant est des plus grans bestes de ce monde et des plus fieres bestes quant on li monstre le vin des meures pour luy aguisier a felonnie, comme il appert ou livre des Machabees en la Bible. Et / toutesfoiz le dit oliphant, portant sur luy un chastel de bois et xxx. hommes armez, par un seul homme tout desarme est gouverne et a luy obeissant. Quel merveille, car le dit oliphant en sa jonesse apris la doctrine d'estre ainsi obedient a un seul homme, en grant merveille de toute gent. N'il n'est pas en puissance d'omme de baillier la doctrine a l'oliphant quant il est parcreux.

Cestui example assez groz soit presente au propos et des hommes et des femmes, qui le ploy et la doctrine qui leur sera bailliee en leur jonesse communement retendront, comme fait le ploy du cha-[78r]melot, en leur vieillesse.

Or venons a la doctrine des femmes, et par especial des josnes femmes de grant lignie. Il se dit en proverbe que les filles en bonnes meurs ou autres suivent volentiers leurs meres. Quele merveille, car le ploy qu'elles auront pris avec leur mere en leur enfance, elles le gardent de commun cours en leur plain aage; et n'est pas legiere chose de muer les condicions auxqueles par longue exercitacion elles sont enclines.

Et se puet dire moralisant qu'il seroit aucunefois plus legiere chose de baillier la garde de grant plente de gelines a / Dant Renart, et qu'il en feist bien son devoir sanz elles atouchier, qu'il ne seroit de transmuer la nature et condicions de certaines josnes femmes, habitues des leur enfance a leur inclinacion et plaine volente. Ce sevent ceulz qui non pas par escript maiz de fait l'ont esprouve. La doctrine de la josne fille, je ne dy pas de toutes maiz de certaines, n'est pas mains forte, qui tout vouldroit conter, que la doctrine de l'oliphant.

Or venons briefment a la concordance des dis examples, pour faire sagement en Dieu, selonc le conseil de l'apostre saint Pol, tout ce qui sera a faire au propos. Le fin [78v] dyamant figure, Richart, nostre tres sage et tres gracieux roy d'Angleterre, qui ja par lonc temps a essaie et souffisaument esprouve les loys et condicions du fort lien de mariage, voire sans avoir lignie de son corps, comme il a pleu a Dieu, se de son secont mariage donques il vouldra en Dieu estre consolez et, par consequent, ses subgies et amis, ne vault il pas mieulx que la dame qu'il prendra pour compaigne et espouse, des son enfance et avant qu'elle ait discrecion d'encorporer en son ymaginacion les choses nuysables, par la prudence et sage ordenance de la roy-/ale majeste du dit fin dyamant figure soit bien nourrie et saintement endoctrinee, premierement en la doubtance et amour de Dieu, comme fu la sainte royne Hester, et apres en bonnes meurs royales, et es condicions et bonnes volentez de son seigneur et mary, que se il presist une autre dame de plus grant aage, qui eust plus plainement la cognoissance des choses nuysasables, et inclinacions aux choses reprouvees? Et de laquele auxi le fin dyamant bonnement et plainement ne peust pas bien estre enformes de sa doctrine en son enfance, ne des secretes meurs de la mere, qui est une cho-[79r]se assez necessaire.

Il se dit en proverbe que l'erbe que on cognoist, on le doit loier sur son doit. Qui veult ploier une josne verge il y a trop pau a faire, mais qui atant tant qu'elle soit endurcie, elle se laisseroit avant brisier qu'elle se daignaist ploier. Grant consolacion est a un roy, et don de Dieu singulier, d'avoir femme et estre doulcement acompaignie de telle espouse qu'il aura faite par doctrine et nourrie par la grace de Dieu toute a sa volente et a confirmacion de ses meurs, et pourra dire, Ceste est m'espouse, ceste est ma fille. Et la dame auxi qui ainsi dili-/gaument aura este nourrie, et n'aura sentu les aguillons des choses foraines nuisables, ne des temptacions volans, aura tousjours en son cuer a son seigneur et mary une reverence paternelle, une obedience filiale, comme la sainte Sarra avoit au saint patriarche Abraham, son seigneur et mary, qui l'avoit nourrie josne et endoctrinee a ses meurs; de laquele il n'ot pas tantost des enfans, mais atendi jusques a sa vieillesse et que Sarra estoit brehaigne. Et toutesfoiz pour sa grant foy, il engendra en sa vieillesse le saint patriarche Ysaac, qui vault autant a dire comme risee, qui fu plus grant joye a sa gener-[79v]acion que s'il eust engendre en sa jonesse xl. filz du commun cours des autres.

Benois sera donques et doulcement consolez en Dieu nostre tres debonnaire roy, a dyamant figure, qui aura a espouse celle qu'il aura nourrie selonc ses meurs et condicions; c'est assavoir la fille du fin baulme, de l'escharboucle reluisant, sa propre niece, selonc le commandement de Dieu fait a sains peres du vieil testament, c'est assavoir la fille de son ainsne frere, et tous ii. filz du benoit saint Loys. Par ceste sainte aliance toute suspicion sera banie, et de l'un royaume et de l'autre, car en vraie amour paternelle et filiale les ii. / royaumes seront comme un royaume et une sainte policie; voire en confirmant par le precieux dyamant, converti en dieu amant, au faire le mariage, les loys royales du royaume de Gaule, c'est assavoir que a la couronne de France femme ne puet heriter, pour obvier sagement en Dieu au cas semblable ou temps advenir, s'il advenoit, que ja n'aviengne, pour lequel cas depuis lx. ans en ensa c. mile ames par aventure sont este portees en enfer. Les ii. filz donques du tres vaillant roy de France, saint Loys, sont tenus en Dieu de remedier et pourveoir a tous cas perilleux advenir, par lesquelz dissencion, [80r] haine, ou guerre puisse sourdre et advenir es ii. royaumes de France et d'Angleterre, conjoins ensamble en grant amours par la sainte aliance de mariage du fin dyamant a la belle blanche pelle transmuee, fille de l'escharboucle reluisant; laquele chose Dieu leur vueille ottroier pour le tres grant bien de la crestiente.

Et se par l'engien de l'archepirate d'enfer, aucune difference sourdra en la lignie royale, entre les barons, le clergie, ou le pueple, nostre belle blanche pelle, nostre tres fine esmeraude, fille de l'escharboucle, par la bonte de Dieu, sans arester, tout apaisera.

Et par sa sainte chaste-/te conjugale la furour de l'unicorne non tant seulement sera apaisie, maiz la dicte unicorne saintement sera prise au lach, qui longuement a este tendu sans riens prendre, c'est assavoir au lach de la vraie paix, des preudommes si longuement desiree; laquele chose Dieu nous vueille ottroier.

Encores, pour respondre au josne aage de nostre josne marguerite, pierre precieuse, la belle blanche pelle, il se puet dire que, a un prince vertueux et constant, ii. ans ou iii. sont tost passez, pour attendre si grant bien que de la reparacion et reformacion de la crestiente. Et vous

souviengne, tres vertueux et tres de-[80v]bonnaire roy, du saint patriarche Jacob, qui attendy vii. ans pour avoir a espouse la belle et sainte
Rachel, dont il ot en la fin ii. nobles et puissans lignies, c'est assavoir
Joseph et Benjamin. Et vous souviengne encore, tres devost roy, de
l'expectacion pour avoir sainte lignie du saint prophete Zacharias, qui
en la fin de son aage engendra le tres benoit saint Jehan Baptiste.

Nulz ne pourroit descripre a plain les graces singulieres que Dieu fera
a vostre royale majeste et a vostre tres ame frere et, a mon voloir, pere,
Charles, roy de France, voire se vous seres constans en la vocacion que
Dieu vous a / appelez au gouvernent de son pueple, et que vous soies
aournez en Dieu de vraye pacience et de la vertu de longanimite; laquele
chose Dieu vous vueille ottroier et tous vos fais adrecier a l'amour de
Dieu et a vraie paix desiree.

Ceste sainte aliance cy dessus proposee, par la bonte de Dieu traitiee,
faite et acomplie, comme faire se pourra pour le josne aage de nostre
tres gracieuse esmeraude, ja mise ou doit du tres excellent roy de la
Grant Bretaigne, et par luy mise en l'escole de la sainte doctrine comme
dit est dessus, et la doulce paix auxi formee et reformee [81r] en Dieu
es ii. royaumes et entre le pere et le fil, il vous souviengne de la doulce
parole du Saint Esperit, escripte par le prophete ou psautier, disant, O,
que bonne chose est et joieuse les freres habiter en un, c'est assavoir nos
ii. roys, non tant seulement par la dessus dicte sainte aliance devenus
filz et pere, mais ii. freres auxi comme germains filz du tres vaillant roy
saint Loys, c'est assavoir habiter ensamble en un propos, en une volente, en une perseverance de vraie amour fraternelle et en Dieu embra-
see, laquele toute l'yaue de la mer et de tous les flumaires du monde
n'ait puissance de l'estaindre; lors l'un de / vous ii. roys par grant vaillance soit David et l'autre soit Jonathas, qui en vraie amour jusques a
la mort s'amerent l'un l'autre, comme la sainte escripture le recorde.

Et quant a doulce compaignie en fait d'armes, voire encontre les
anemis de la foy, l'un de vous ii. soit Rollant le vaillant et l'autre soit
le tres debonnaire Olivier.

Mais quant a magnificence royale et imperiale, l'un de vous ii. soit
par imitacion les tres vaillant et tres preux Charlemaine, et l'autre soit
le tres excellent et tres preux roy Artus, c'est assavoir contre les anemis
de la foy, contre [81v] les scismatiques et hereges. Amez bien donques
l'un l'autre, par le moien d'une doulce reverence fraternelle, paternelle,
et filiale, et ne crees par legierement les mahommes, raporteurs du contraire. Et quant a aucunes differences es traities l'un de l'autre, plaine-

ment non accordees par les royaux conseilliers, armez vous de l'escu de doulce pacience, comme il est dit dessus, par laquele vous possederes vos ames, et du haubert de liberalite, par laquele vous remeteres et quitteres l'un a l'autre ce que vos conseilliers n'oseroient atempter. Quel merveille, car mieulx vauldra ce que vous ten-/dres par acort et en paix, que xii. royaumes en guerre et en haine. Et qui plus sera liberaulz l'un a l'autre, ce sera celuy qui monstrera plus grant signe d'amour, ensuivant la doctrine de saint Gregoire, docteur de l'eglise, qui dit que le signe de dilection est de l'euvre la demonstrance et l'exibicion.

Et que plus est, quant par la grace de Dieu vous aures conqueste Turquie, Egypte et Surie, qui sont remplis de toutes manieres de richesses et de delices, par la bonte du doulz Jhesu et par la vertu de la foy, vous feres pou de compte de vos royaumes d'occident, qui sont et [82r] frois et engelez, et a orgueil et a avarice et a luxure souventefois enclins et dedies.

Tres excellens et tres debonnaires princes catholiques, et dignes rois esleus de Dieu en France et en Angleterre, se ainsi comme dit est dessus grossement et rudement vous vous maintendres ensamble, perseverant l'un avec l'autre, et par vostre sainte conversion enluminant toute la crestiente, et que une toute seule heure ou moment vous ne oublies pas chascun en son doit le fin dyamant, c'est assavoir dieu amant, ensuivant a vostre pooir la sainte vie de vostre grant pere saint Loys, et des sains mar-/tirs et confessours, vos predecesseurs roys, le doulz Jhesu, Roy des roys, par sa grace sera tousjours ou milieu de vous ii., et vous adressera de vertu en vertu, de royaume en royaume, et jusques a la cite de Jherusalem militant; et apres victoires infinies et longue vie meritoire, a mon voloir, vous hebergera glorieusement en la cite de Jherusalem triumphant; laquele chose Dieu vous vueille ottroier. *Amen.*

Tres excellent et tres debonnaire prince et digne roy de la Grant Bretaingne, mon tres singulier et tres ame seigneur en Dieu, se en ceste presente epistre, rude et mal asavouree, par maniere d'un [82v] songe d'un vieillart pensee et ymaginee, et par la benivolence et expres commandement de la royale majeste de vostre tres ame frere, Charles, roy de France, dittee et composee, j'ay use envers vostre royale majeste plus rigoureusement qu'il n'apartenist a un tel vil pecheur et vieil solitaire, non digne d'estre nomme, de l'oingnement des apostres, corrosif et reprehensif et, a la fin, mondificatif, je vous suppli tres humblement qu'il me soit pardonne, et vous plaise a souvenir, tres sage roy, que a la court des grans roys souvent se treuvent aucuns fusiciens qui usent fort de l'oingnement popilion / appele, c'est assavoir d'un emplastre alectif, qui a nom placuerunt.

Et pour ce que cestui abortif solitaire, aucunefois en son temps indigne, a demoure longuement a la court de plussieurs roys et papes, et a bien cogneu par la bonte de Dieu que le dit popilion laisse la plaie ouverte, pour ce est il que, luy confiant du souverain medicin, le doulz Jhesu, de sa tres doulce mere, et de la sainte doctrine de ses tres sains apostres, a present il c'est enhardis d'user plainement de l'oingnement des apostres, combien qu'il soit aucunement mordificatif, c'est assavoir pour parvenir unefoiz a plaine sante [83r] de la plaie en ceste epistre assez largement desclarie.

Si prie au tres doulz Jhesu, doulcement et devotement, et de toute ma sustance, pour finable conclusion et oroison que, non obstant qu'il voult use de l'oingnement, et corrosif et trop mondificatif, en sa propre personne, pour le salut de la plaie universelle, c'est assavoir pour racheter les ames d'enfer, et pour ouvrir a ses esleuz la porte de paradis, en respandant son precieux sanc en l'abre de la vraie croix, que, pour souder a plain et reclorre a tousjours la plaie des ii. royaumes, tant de fois repetee, pour confirmacion de la vraye paix et d'amour / cordiale de nos ii. roys, et de leur tres vaillant chevalererie, il li plaise de sa doulce pitie et grace especiale a mander du ciel a nos ii. roys l'emplastre souverain, qui est appele *gracia dei*, et par sa sainte misericorde il leur vueille inspirer qu'il en sachent bien user.

Tres excellent et tres debonnaire, digne roy d'Angleterre, et mon tres singulier et tresame seigneur ou doulz Jhesu, le Dieu de paix et dilection, par la priere de la tres doulce Vierge Marie, soit avec vous tousjours et vous doint paradis apres tres longue vie. *Amen*.

Cy fine l'epistre introductive a la paix et vraie amour [83v] des ii. roys de France et d'Angleterre, adrecie au roy d'Angleterre.

BIBLIOGRAPHY

MANUSCRIPT SOURCES

Philippe de Mezieres, *Epistre au Roi Richart*, B. L. Royal 20 B VI.
—— *De la Chevallerie de la Passion de Jhesu Crist*, Bib. Arsenal 2251.

PRINTED SOURCES

Albertus Magnus, *Opera Omnia*, vol. v, lib. i, Mineralium (1890).

Arnould, E. J., *Étude sur le Livre de Saintes Médecines du duc Henri de Lancastre* (1948).

—— *Le Livre de Seyntz Medicines*. Anglo-Norman Texts II (Oxford, 1967).

Beazley, C. R., *A Note-Book of Medieval History* (1917).

Brewer, Deryk, *Chaucer in his Time* (1963).

Chaucer, Geoffrey, *The Canterbury Tales*, trans. Nevill Coghill (Penguin Books, 1970).

Clarke, M. V., *Fourteenth Century Studies*, ed. L. S. Sutherland and M. McKisack (1937).

Coopland, G. W., *Le Songe du Vieil Pèlerin of Philippe de Mézières* (1969).

—— *The Tree of Battles of Honoré Bonet* (Liverpool and Cambridge, Mass., 1949).

Daviot, Gordon, 'Richard of Bordeaux', *Famous Plays of 1933* (1933).

De Barante, M., *Histoire des ducs de Bourgogne*, t. i, ii (1835).

De la Bere, Ivan, *The Queen's Orders of Chivalry* (1961).

Douet-d'Arcq, Louis C., *Comptes de l'Hôtel des rois de France aux XIVe et XVe siècles* (1865).

Duples-Agier, H. (ed.), *Registre criminel du Châtelet de Paris du 6 Septembre 1389 au 18 Mai 1392*, t. 1. (1861), t. 2 (1864).

Fedden, Robin, *Syria and Lebanon* (1965).

Fowler, Kenneth, *The King's Lieutenant* (1969).

Frank, Grace, *The Medieval French Drama* (Oxford, 1954).

Hamdy, A. H., 'Philippe de Mézières and the new Order of the Passion', *Bulletin of the Faculty of Arts* (Alexandria University, Egypt), vol. xviii (1964).

Holmes, G. A., *The Estates of the Higher Nobility in Fourteenth Century England* (1957).

Jones, R. H., *The Royal Policy of Richard II* (1968).

Jorga, N., *Philippe de Mézières, 1327–1405, et la croisade au XIVe siècle* (1896).

Kervyn de Lettenhove, *Oeuvres de Froissart: Chroniques*, t. xv (1871), t. xvi (1872).

L'Art de vérifier les dates, vols. 5 and 7 (1818).

Lavisse, Ernest, *Histoire de France illustrée depuis les origines jusqu'à la Revolution*, t. iv, pt. i (A. Colville), *1328–1422*.

Loomis, L. H., 'Secular dramatics in the Royal palace, Paris, 1378, 1389, and Chaucer's tregetoures', *Speculum*, vol. xxxiii (Cambridge, Mass., 1958).

Mathew, Gervase, *The Court of Richard II* (1968).

Myers, A. R., *England in the Late Middle Ages* (Pelican Books, 1952).

Palmer, J. J. N., 'English foreign policy, 1388–99', *The Reign of Richard II; Essays in Honour of May McKisack*, ed. F. R. H. Du Boulay and Caroline M. Barron (1971). (Palmer quotes Philippe de Mézières and Professor Coopland [p. 103]).

—— 'The background to Richard II's marriage to Isabel of France (1396)', *Bulletin of the Institute of Historical Research*, vol. xliv, no. 109 (May 1971).

Puiseux, Léon, 'Robert l'Ermite: étude sur un personnage Normand du XIVe siècle', *Mémoires de la Société des Antiquaires de Normandie*, vol. xxiv (1859).

Roques, Mario (ed.), *L'Estoire de Griseldis*. Textes littéraires françaises (1957).

Steel, Anthony, *Richard II* (1962).

Thubron, Colin, *Mirror to Damascus* (1967).

Vast, Henri, *Histoire de l'Europe, 1270–1610* (1891).

Valois, Noel, *La France et le Grande Schisme d'Occident*, t. 3 (1901).

Young, Karl, *The Drama of the Medieval Church*, vol. ii (Oxford, 1933).

INDEX